Balanced, Sustainable and Competitiveness Enhancement Study for Vietnam:
A Critical Evaluation with Development Potentials

NUS National University of Singapore

Lee Kuan Yew School of Public Policy
ASIA COMPETITIVENESS INSTITUTE

In 2016 and 2017, ACI was ranked 13th globally, 2nd in Asia and 1st in Singapore amongst 90 think tanks worldwide under the "Best University Affiliated Think Tank" category by the Think Tanks and Civil Societies Program at the University of Pennsylvania, USA.

About ACI

The Asia Competitiveness Institute (ACI) was established in August 2006 as a research centre at the Lee Kuan Yew School of Public Policy (LKYSPP), National University of Singapore (NUS). It aims to build the intellectual leadership and network for understanding and developing competitiveness in the Asia region. ACI seeks to contribute to the enhancement of inclusive growth, living standards and institutional governance through competitiveness research on sub-national economies in Asia. It identifies mitigating issues and challenges for potential public policy interventions through close collaboration with regional governments, business corporations, policy think-tanks and academics. ACI's three key research pillars include (i) sub-national economies level competitiveness analysis and city-level liveability analysis, (ii) firm-level competitiveness analysis in 16 Asia economies, and (iii) Singapore's long-term growth strategies and public policy analysis.

ACI's value propositions may be encapsulated in its acronym:
Analytical inputs to initiate policies for policy-makers and business leaders in Asia
Capacity building to enable others through improvement in productivity and efficiency
Intellectual leadership to create pragmatic models of competitiveness and inclusive growth

The institute's core research competencies can also be encapsulated in this acronym describing our evidence-based assessments conducted on public policies for **A**SEAN in the context of the rise of **C**hina and **I**ndia.

Vision and Mission

- ACI's over-arching vision is to build up its research credibility with policy impact, contributing as a professional, world-class think-tank.
- ACI's mission is to establish our niche as a leading policy think-tank by identifying competitiveness trends, opportunities and challenges, as well as promoting competition and synergising complementarities amongst Asian economies and business corporations.
- ACI endeavours to articulate sound recommendations, entice discourse, and shape agenda in the arena of public policy amongst Asian governments.
- ACI undertakes evidence-based analysis of public policy issues and decisions, in order to provide assessment of their effectiveness as well as economic and societal impact.

Research Initiatives and Collaborations

I. Identify trends of competitiveness and policy analysis on trade and investment of ASEAN, within the regional context of competition and complementarities with China and India.
II. Identify competitive strengths and conduct policy analysis on Singapore within the context of regional economies with international benchmarking.
III. We are regularly releasing three indices on liveability ranking including 64 Global Cities, 100 Greater China Cities and 17 Shandong Cities.
IV. We have established an Ease of Doing Business Index on Attractiveness to Investors, Business Friendliness and Competitive Policies for 21 sub-national economies of India and 33 sub-national economies of Indonesia.
V. We have signed Memoranda of Understanding with The World Bank (2015), SPRING Singapore (2014) and European Central Bank (2014). The Memorandum of Understanding between The World Bank and National University of Singapore, coordinated through ACI, was signed in 2016.

VI. We have signed Memoranda of Understanding with various institutions in Greater China economies, including Shanghai Academy of Social Sciences (2016), Shandong Academy of Social Sciences (2015), Chongqing Municipal People's Government (2015), China Institute for Reform and Development, Haikou (2015), Counsellors' Office of the People's Government of Guangdong Province (LOI, 2014) and Chung-Hua Institution for Economic Research, Taiwan (2015).

VII. We have signed Memoranda of Understanding with six Chief Ministers' Offices in Andhra Pradesh (2015 & 2017), Bihar (2015), Chhattisgarh (2015), Madhya Pradesh (2015), Odisha (2015) and Punjab (2015).

VIII. We have signed Memoranda of Understanding with Committee for Acceleration of Priority Infrastructure Delivery at Coordinating Ministry for Economic Affairs, Indonesia (2016), Indonesia Investment Coordinating Board (2014), Indonesian Agency for Agricultural Research and Development at Ministry of Agriculture (2014), Indonesian President's Delivery Unit for Developing Monitoring and Oversight (2013) and Employer's Association of Indonesia (2013).

IX. We have signed Memoranda of Understanding with ASEAN think-tanks and institutions, including Vietnam Chamber of Commerce and Industry (2016), Centre for Strategic and International Studies, Indonesia (2015), Institute of Strategic & International Studies, Malaysia (2015), Philippine Institute for Development Studies (2015), Thailand Development Research Institute (2015) and Central Institute for Economic Management, Vietnam (2015).

About ACI's Research Pillars

ACI has consciously engaged in economic research that has significant relevance to Singapore and the Asian region. Over the years, ACI has focused on our expertise in quantitative competitiveness analysis and simulation, spinning off volumes of research output in the applications of our methodology and regional insight. At this stage, ACI has identified three core research pillars that will guide and define its research efforts moving forward. The three research pillars are as follows:

Pillar I. Sub-national Economies Competitiveness Analysis

ACI engages in systematic and methodical competitiveness analyses of the *sub-national economies* by using an evidence-based, empirical approach involving a comprehensive list of relevant indicators, which are categorised under multiple layers called the 'environments'. A number of our projects, including competitiveness analyses of Greater China, ASEAN-10, India, and Indonesia, as well as other thematic research projects, were conducted by adopting this common methodology, with potential variations in the specific environments and indicators. ACI's competitiveness analysis of Asian economies goes beyond the usual ranking to offer constructive policy recommendations on how individual member states can improve their rankings vis-à-vis their sub-national or regional peers through the application of the 'what-if' simulation, which provides the projected improvements of each state's ranking whereby the bottom one-fifth of its indicators are enhanced.

Pillar II. Micro-based Firm Level Competitiveness Analysis

Micro-based firm level competitiveness analysis is ACI's second research pillar that has been developed in view of the intrinsic importance of firm-level competitiveness in terms of productivity, efficiency, and governance. In the context of globalisation, mobility of economic activities, and blurring of borders, an understanding of the determinants and dynamics of firm-level competitiveness is paramount, in order for policy makers to make adjustments and prepare their industries for an increasingly competitive economic landscape. To this end, ACI has partnered with the European Central Bank to carry out research in this area, possessing a solid foundation in firm-level productivity research in the form of European Competitiveness Network database and methodology. ACI envisaged the expansion of CompNet into Asia, thereby pioneering the Asia CompNet research network encompassing 16 economies in Asia.

Pillar III. Singapore's Long-term Economic Growth Strategies and Public Policies Analysis

The third and imminent research pillar focuses on Singapore's long-term economic growth strategies in the context of changing circumstances, future trends, and emerging opportunities for Singapore in the decades ahead. In particular, ACI will take on the task of critically examining Singapore's public policy strengths and areas of improvement by assessing policy successes of the past, identifying new issues to address and the current policy gaps, through a systematic and evidence-based research inquiry using quantitative methodology and empirical data, leveraging on our network of policy experts.

Founding Patron and International Advisory Panel

Founding Patron

Mr George Yeo
Visiting Scholar, Lee Kuan Yew School of Public Policy, National University of Singapore & Former Minister of Foreign Affairs, Singapore

International Advisory Panel

Co-Chairs:

Professor Michael Porter (2006-2010)
Bishop William Lawrence University Professor

Ms Marjorie Yang (2006-2012)
Chairman, Esquel Group

Members:

Professor Kishore Mahbubani
Dean, Lee Kuan Yew School of Public Policy, National University of Singapore

Dr Kuntoro Mangkusubroto
Head, President's Delivery Unit for Developing Monitoring and Oversight (UKP4), Indonesia

Mr Narayana Murthy
Chairman, Infosys Technologies Limited

Mr Philip Yeo
Chairman, SPRING Singapore

Mr Loh Khum Yean
Permanent Secretary, Ministry of Trade and Industry

Ms Yong Ying-I
Permanent Secretary, Public Service Division

Professor Chan Kam Leung Alan
Dean, College of Humanities, Arts and Social Sciences, Nanyang Technological University

Asia Competitiveness Institute

Co-Directors:

Associate Professor Tan Khee Giap (2011 till now)
Professor Tan Kong Yam (2011 till now)

Asia Competitiveness Institute - World Scientific Series

(ISSN: 2424-9912)

Series Editor: Tan Khee Giap (*Lee Kuan Yew School of Public Policy, NUS, Singapore*)

In the tradition of the Asia Competitiveness Institute (ACI) at the Lee Kuan Yew School of Public Policy, National University of Singapore (NUS), our research publications make a distinctive contribution to the understanding of economic development in Asia. These books, first published in 2013, in the Asia Competitiveness Institute - World Scientific Series evaluate and track competitiveness for the sub-national economies of China, India, Indonesia and ASEAN annually through combining leading-edge methodologies with an extensive dataset. The study covers four environments of competitiveness: (1) Macroeconomic Stability, (2) Government and Institutional Setting, (3) Financial, Businesses and Manpower Conditions, and (4) Quality of Life and Infrastructure Development. It also conducts "what-if" policy simulations to propose policy suggestions.

2017

2017 Annual Competitiveness Analysis and Impact of Exchange Rates on Foreign Direct Investment Inflows to ASEAN Economies
by Tan Khee Giap, Luu Nguyen Trieu Duong, Chuah Hui Yin & Nguyen Duy (Lee Kuan Yew School of Public Policy, NUS, Singapore)

Balanced, Sustainable and Competitiveness Enhancement Study for Vietnam: A Critical Evaluation with Development Potentials
by Vu Tien Loc (Vietnam Chamber of Commerce and Industry, Vietnam), Tan Khee Giap, Luu Nguyen Trieu Duong & Nguyen Duy (Lee Kuan Yew School of Public Policy, NUS, Singapore)

2017 Impact Estimation of Exchange Rate on Foreign Direct Investment Inflows and Annual Update of Competitiveness Analysis for 34 Greater China Economies
by Tan Khee Giap, Zhang Xuyao, Leong Puey Ei & Tan Yang En Isaac (Lee Kuan Yew School of Public Policy, NUS, Singapore)

2017 Annual Competitiveness Analysis and Impact of Exchange Rates on Foreign Direct Investment Inflows to Sub-National Economies of India
by Tan Khee Giap, Sasidaran Gopalan, Jigyasa Sharma & Leong Puey Ei (Lee Kuan Yew School of Public Policy, NUS, Singapore)

2017 Annual Competitiveness Analysis and Impact of Exchange Rates on Foreign Direct Investment Inflows to Sub-National Economies of Indonesia
by Tan Khee Giap, Mulya Amri, Nursyahida Ahmad & Diamanta Vania Lavi (Lee Kuan Yew School of Public Policy, NUS, Singapore)

2016

2016 Annual Competitiveness Analysis and Growth Slowdown Analysis for ASEAN-10
by Tan Khee Giap, Nguyen Le Phuong Anh & Luu Nguyen Trieu Duong (Lee Kuan Yew School of Public Policy, NUS, Singapore)

*More information on this series can also be found at http://www.worldscientific.com/series/aciwss

(Continued at end of book)

Balanced, Sustainable and Competitiveness Enhancement Study for Vietnam:

A Critical Evaluation with Development Potentials

Vu Tien Loc

Chairman and President, Vietnam Chamber of Commerce and Industry

Tan Khee Giap

Co-Director, Asia Competitiveness Institute
Lee Kuan Yew School of Public Policy, National University of Singapore

Luu Nguyen Trieu Duong

Research Associate, Asia Competitiveness Institute
Lee Kuan Yew School of Public Policy, National University of Singapore

Nguyen Duy

Research Assistant, Asia Competitiveness Institute
Lee Kuan Yew School of Public Policy, National University of Singapore

Reviewer

Nguyen Dinh Cung

President, Central Institute for Economic Management (CIEM), Vietnam

Lee Kuan Yew School of Public Policy
Asia Competitiveness Institute

NUS National University of Singapore

World Scientific

Published by

World Scientific Publishing Co. Pte. Ltd.
5 Toh Tuck Link, Singapore 596224
USA office: 27 Warren Street, Suite 401-402, Hackensack, NJ 07601
UK office: 57 Shelton Street, Covent Garden, London WC2H 9HE

British Library Cataloguing-in-Publication Data
A catalogue record for this book is available from the British Library.

Asia Competitiveness Institute – World Scientific Series
BALANCED, SUSTAINABLE AND COMPETITIVENESS ENHANCEMENT STUDY FOR VIETNAM
A Critical Evaluation with Development Potentials

ISBN 978-981-3273-02-3

Desk Editor: Jiang Yulin

Typeset by Stallion Press
Email: enquiries@stallionpress.com

Contents

Foreword

With a population of nearly 100 million people, over 60 percent of whom are under the age of 35, Vietnam is well-positioned to supply a young, abundant and quality workforce at competitive cost. Characterised by political, social and macroeconomic stability, Vietnam has continuously improved its institutional framework and transparency to gradually align with international commitments and standards. The Government of Vietnam has committed to creating favourable conditions for all investors and businesses, as they execute their long-term investment plan and actively participate in the global supply and value chain.

Vietnam continues to drive the global economic integration agenda and expects to maintain an annual average GDP growth rate of 6.5 percent to 7 percent over the period of 2016–2020. Its priority is on green growth and sustainable development, with three main engines: Promotion of exports, domestic market growth and investment expansion. Vietnam is currently focusing on improving the business environment and increasing the competitiveness, supported by the Government's commitments to integrity, innovation and action to serve businesses and citizens. Vietnam expects to become a dynamic country and an attractive investment destination in ASEAN and strives to integrate into the regional and global value chains.

The Vietnamese Government commits to support and create the most favourable conditions for foreign businesses investing and operating in Vietnam.

Nguyen Xuan Phuc
Prime Minister of Vietnam

Preface

Vietnam today stands at one of the most promising moments since the reunification of the country. Since its inception in 1976, the *Doi Moi* (Renovation) reform has enabled Vietnam to rapidly transform from a low-income to a dynamic middle-income economy with millions lifted out of poverty. With a large, young, educated and low-cost workforce, Vietnam is well-positioned to benefit from the outward shift of foreign direct investment from China and become the next manufacturing hub in Asia.

Nevertheless, future development is not guaranteed. It is contingent on the successful implementation of good policies which help to realise the country's economic potentials while addressing outstanding structural weaknesses. In this context, the publication of this book entitled *Balanced, Sustainable and Competitiveness Enhancement Study for Vietnam: A Critical Evaluation with Development Potentials* comes in a very timely way. The fruit of the research collaboration between National Research Project on Improving Vietnam's Competitiveness and the Asia Competitiveness Institute (ACI) at Lee Kuan Yew School of Public Policy (LKYSPP), National University of Singapore (NUS), the book has the potential to make significant contributions to the policy discourse in Vietnam.

Drawing on a copious amount of good research works, particularly ACI's annual ranking and simulation studies on member economies of the Association of Southeast Asian Nations (ASEAN), this book assesses Vietnam's economic competitiveness *vis-à-vis* its ASEAN neighbours and identifies potential impediments to the country's development. Furthermore, it outlines a clear policy roadmap with specific recommendations for Vietnam to embark on a dynamic growth path which would allow it to catch up to the ASEAN-5 countries by 2040.

At the same time, this work helps to complement the growing ties between Singapore and Vietnam. Singapore has consistently been one of Vietnam's most important trading partners and top investors with registered cumulative investments of over US$ 30 billion in more than 1,300 projects. More importantly, experiences and lessons from Singapore's journey from the third world to the first can be shared with Vietnam to help the latter with its development. For instance, among its many insights, this book has proposed the extension of the study on the productivity and efficiency of Singapore's small and medium enterprises to Vietnam as well as the adaptation of Singapore's policy initiatives on human development and digital economy to the Vietnamese context. These are meaningful recommendations which will help Vietnam achieve balanced, sustainable and equitable development in the age of the Fourth Industrial Revolution.

The mission of the LKYSPP is to be the leading global public policy school in Asia, developing thought leadership, improving standards of governance and transforming lives for a more sustainable world. ACI's research on Vietnam and its collaborations with leading Vietnamese institutions are helping our School to fulfil its broader mission. I am therefore proud to present this excellent book to all policy-makers and public intellectuals who are passionate about the economic future of Vietnam.

Ramkishen Sundara Rajan, PhD
Vice Dean (Research) and Professor
Lee Kuan Yew School of Public Policy
National University of Singapore

Acknowledgements

The Asia Competitiveness Institute (ACI) at the Lee Kuan Yew School of Public Policy (LKYSPP), National University of Singapore (NUS) has combined leading-edge research methodologies with extensive data collection efforts to evaluate and track economic competitiveness since 2000 at both national and sub-national levels for over 100 Asian economies including Greater China, India and the 10 member states of the Association of Southeast Asian Nations (ASEAN). Furthermore, ACI has developed extensive expertise in conducting evidence-based, policy-oriented research on a variety of topics including growth slowdown analysis by income thresholds; productivity tracking and efficiency monitoring for small and medium enterprises; and ease of doing business index, among others.

Drawing on these studies, this book entitled *Balanced, Sustainable and Competitiveness Enhancement Study for Vietnam: A Critical Evaluation with Development Potentials*, which is a joint research collaboration between the National Research Project on Improving Vietnam's Competitiveness and ACI-LKYSPP-NUS, provides a detailed assessment of the Vietnamese economy. We contend that Vietnam is at a critical juncture in its development whereby a new wave of far-reaching reforms is required to address persistent structural weaknesses and unleash the country's economic potentials. In addition, Vietnam's new growth model must tackle widening regional disparities, which puts Vietnam at risk of becoming one country with two economies where the southern region of Vietnam pulls too far ahead of its northern and central counterparts. Based on our analysis, we propose a comprehensive policy roadmap for Vietnam to achieve balanced and sustainable development for enhanced competitiveness. The successful completion of this reform agenda will set Vietnam firmly on a dynamic growth path which will allow Vietnam to catch up with the more advanced ASEAN countries by 2040.

We wish to thank the following reviewer who gave his constructive comments and insights on the findings outlined in this book:

Dr Nguyen Dinh Cung
President, Central Institute for Economic Management

At the same time, this book would not have been possible without the dedicated effort of all our colleagues at ACI. Thus, we note with tremendous appreciation the high team spirit of all

ACI staff especially Dr Mulya Amri, Chow Wen Kang, Diamanta Danila Lavi, Jeremy Ho, Linda Ji, Yap Xin Yi, Tracy Cai Jiao, Nurliyana Binte Yusoff and Dewi Jelina Ayu Johari.

Vu Tien Loc, PhD
National Research Project on Improving Vietnam's Competitiveness

Tan Khee Giap, PhD
Luu Nguyen Trieu Duong
Nguyen Duy
Asia Competitiveness Institute
Lee Kuan Yew School of Public Policy
National University of Singapore

About the Authors

Vu Tien Loc

Dr Vu Tien Loc has been the Chairman and President of Vietnam Chamber of Commerce and Industry since 2003. He is a member of the 11th, 12th, 13th and 14th Vietnam National Assembly (2001–2016) and a member of the Economic Committee of the National Assembly. Dr Loc is also Chairman of Central Council of Vietnam Business Association; Vice Chairman of the Prime Minister's Advisory Council for Administrative Procedure Reform; Co-chair of Vietnam Business Forum (VBF) as well as Chairman of ASEAN Chamber of Commerce. Furthermore, Dr Loc was the Chairman of APEC CEO Summit 2017. He has recently been appointed ABAC Vietnam Chair, ABAC Co Chair 2018.

As a politician and the head of the national organisation of Vietnam business community, he has contributed greatly to Vietnam's economic reform and improving national competitiveness. Dr Loc directly presides over and directs the implementation of programmes to promote and improve business environment in Vietnam, to develop small and medium enterprises, as well as to build the business association systems in Vietnam, and other trade-investment promotion programmes between Vietnam and other countries in the world.

Tan Khee Giap

Tan Khee Giap is a Co-Director of the Asia Competitiveness Institute (ACI) and Associate Professor at the Lee Kuan Yew School of Public Policy, National University of Singapore. He is also the Chairman of the Singapore National Committee for Pacific Economic Cooperation. Upon graduating with a PhD from University of East Anglia, England, in 1987 under the Overseas Research Scheme awarded by the Committee of Vice-Chancellors and Principals of the Universities of the United Kingdom, he joined the banking sector as a treasury manager and served as secretary to the Assets and Liabilities Committee for three years, thereafter he taught at the Department of Economics and Statistics, National University of Singapore, 1990–1993. Dr Tan joined Nanyang Technological University in 1993 and was Associate Dean, Graduate Studies Office, 2007–2009.

Dr Tan has consulted extensively with the various government ministries, statutory boards and government-linked companies of Singapore government including Ministry of Finance, Ministry of Trade & Industry, Ministry of Manpower, Housing & Development Board, Civil Aviation Authority of Singapore, Singapore Tourism Board, Trade Development Board, Maritime Port Authority, Ministry of Information, Culture & Arts, Economic Development Board, Ministry of National Development, Media Development Authority, Ministry of Environment and Water Resources, Singapore Design Council, Ministry of Community Development, Youth & Sports,

Singapore Press Holdings, Yayasan Mendaki, StarHub, CapitaLand and Great Eastern Life. He has also served as a consultant to international agencies such as the Asian Development Bank, Asian Development Bank Institute, United Nations Industrial Development Group, World Bank Group, World Gold Council, ASEAN Secretariat, Central Policy Unit of Hong Kong, Kerzner International, Las Vegas Sands and Marina Bay Sands.

Dr Tan is the lead author for more than 20 books, serving as journals editor and published widely in international refereed journals. He is the associate editor of the journal *Review of Pacific Basin Financial Markets and Policies* (US) and is on the editorial advisory board of the journal *Competitiveness Review* (UK). His current research interests include Cost of Living and Purchasing Power Index for World's 105 Cities, Global Liveable Cities Index, Ease of Doing Business Index and competitiveness analysis on sub-national economies of China, India, Indonesia and Association of South East Asian Nations.

Dr Tan was Deputy President of the Singapore Economic Society, 2004. He served in the 2002 Economic Review Committee (ERC), served as Chairman of the Task Force on Portable Medical Benefits (PMB), served as the Deputy Chairman of the IPS Forum for Economic Restructuring (IFER) in 2003 and served as a member of the Resource Panel of the Government Parliamentary Committee for Transport, Government Parliamentary Committee for Finance and Trade & Industry and Government Parliamentary Committee for Defence and Foreign Affairs since 2007. Dr Tan is currently an Independent Director of the publicly listed BreadTalk Group, Boustead Projects, TEE Land and Chengdu Rural Commercial Bank.

Luu Nguyen Trieu Duong

Luu Nguyen Trieu Duong is a Research Associate at the Asia Competitiveness Institute (ACI), Lee Kuan Yew School of Public Policy (LKYSPP), National University of Singapore (NUS). Luu graduated from NUS with a Second Upper Class Honours Bachelor of Social Sciences in Economics. A recipient of the ASEAN Undergraduate Scholarship, Luu was placed on the Dean's List and Dean's Scholar List on multiple occasions during his course of study. Luu's research interests include international economics, growth and development, applied econometrics and public economics. At ACI, Luu is the coordinator of research projects on econometric modelling of domestic and external engines of growth; the effects of exchange rate movements and volatility on exports as well as growth slowdown analysis by income thresholds for ASEAN economies. Furthermore, he coordinates ACI's research on city-level cost of living, wages and purchasing power for expatriates and ordinary residents. He also helps to oversee the ASEAN research cluster. Throughout the course of his work at ACI, he has co-authored journal articles, books and editorial-opinions on growth dynamics, cost of living and ASEAN economic development.

Nguyen Duy

Nguyen Duy is a Research Assistant at the Asia Competitiveness Institute (ACI), Lee Kuan Yew School of Public Policy (LKYSPP), National University of Singapore (NUS). Duy received his

Bachelor (Honours) degree in Biology with first class honours from NUS and was also a recipient of the ASEAN Undergraduate Scholarship. His most recent publications are: "How Do Exchange Rates Affect Foreign Direct Investment Inflows?" and "Impact of Real Effective Exchange Rate Movements and Volatility on Foreign Direct Investment Inflows into Indonesia: An Empirical Assessment". His research interests and current research tasks being assigned in ACI are quantitative estimations such as Vector Error Correction Model and competitiveness ranking and Simulation Studies for ASEAN-10. He is also being involved in building and computing survey data for small and medium enterprises in Singapore and maintaining the data matrix for Cost of Living, Wages and Purchasing Power Index for expatriates and ordinary residents in 105 cities across the world.

List of Abbreviations

ACI	Asia Competitiveness Institute
ACV	Airports Corporation of Vietnam
ADB	Asian Development Bank
AEC	ASEAN Economic Community
AIIB	Asian Infrastructure Investment Bank
ASEAN	Association of Southeast Asian Nations
ASW	ASEAN Single Window
BRI	Belt & Road Initiative
CLMV	Cambodia–Laos–Myanmar–Vietnam
CPTPP	Comprehensive and Progressive Agreement for Trans-Pacific Partnership
DDT	Dividend Distribution Tax
DEA	Malmquist Index Data Envelopment Analysis
Depocen	Development and Policies Research Centre
EDB	Ease of Doing Business
EF	Education First
EFIV	Enterprise Future Initiative for Vietnam
EIU	Economist Intelligence Unit
EPZ	Export Processing Zones
ERIA	Economic Research Institute for ASEAN and East Asia
FBMC	Financial, Businesses and Manpower Conditions
FDI	Foreign Direct Investment
FTA	Free Trade Agreement
FTAAP	Free Trade Area of the Asia-Pacific
GCI	Global Competitiveness Index
GDP	Gross Domestic Product
GIS	Government and Institutional Setting
GLCI	Global Liveable Cities Index
GSO	Vietnam's General Statistics Office
GVC	Global Value Chains
HDI	Human Development Index

ICT	Information and Communication Technologies
IIM	Industrial Internship Model
IIPEC	Industrial Internship Productivity Enhancement Council
IMF	International Monetary Fund
IoT	Internet of Things
IPO	Initial Public Offering
ISEAS	Institute of Southeast Asian Studies
LKYSPP	Lee Kuan Yew School of Public Policy
MA	Moving Averages
MAT	Minimum Alternate Tax
MNCs	Multinational Corporations
MOET	Ministry of Education and Training
MOF	Ministry of Finance
MOIT	Ministry of Industry and Trade
MOLISA	Ministry of Labour, Invalids and Social Affairs
MPI	Ministry of Planning and Investment
MS	Macroeconomic Stability
N.A.	Not Applicable
NS	National Service
NUS	National University of Singapore
OECD	Organisation for Economic Co-operation and Development
p.a.	per annum
PA	People's Association
PCI	Provincial Competitiveness Index
PetroVietnam	Vietnam Oil and Gas Group
PMETs	Professionals, Managers, Executives and Technicians
PPP	Purchasing Power Parity
PTE	Placed-Trained-Employed
PTEM	Productivity Tracking and Efficiency Monitoring
QLID	Quality of Life and Infrastructure Development
R&D	Research and Development
RCEP	Regional Comprehensive Economic Partnership
SAEZ	Special Administrative-Economic Zone
SEZ	Special Economic Zone
SME	Small and Medium Enterprise

SOEs	State-Owned Enterprises
SSC	State Securities Commission
TC	Technological Change
TEC	Technical Efficiency Change
TFP	Total Factor Productivity
TPP	Trans-Pacific Partnership
UK	United Kingdom
UNCTAD	United Nations Conference on Trade and Development
UN DESA	United Nations Department of Economic and Social Affairs
UNFPA	United Nations Population Fund
UNIDO	United Nations Industrial Development Organisation
US	United States
USAID	United States Agency for International Development
VCCI	Vietnam Chamber of Commerce and Industry
VCP	Vietnam Communist Party
Vinacomin	Vietnam National Coal–Mineral Industries Holding Corporation Limited
VNTP	Vietnam Posts and Telecommunications Group
WEF	World Economic Forum

List of Boxes, Figures and Tables

Boxes

Chapter 3

Figures

Chapter 1

Chapter 2

Chapter 3

Tables

Chapter 1

Chapter 2

Chapter 3

Executive Summary

Vietnam has been a rising star among the 10 member economies of the Association of the Southeast Asian Nations (ASEAN). Its transformation from a war-torn, backward, low-income economy to a peaceful, dynamic, middle-income country is among the world's great development success stories. Over the past two to three decades, Vietnam has achieved one of the fastest growth rates in Gross Domestic Product (GDP) and GDP per capita in ASEAN and more broadly in Asia. It has become a darling among investors with exponential increase in foreign direct investment (FDI) inflows while also showing remarkable improvements in basic social development outcomes especially in terms of education, healthcare and poverty reduction.

Vietnam's rapid development over the past 30 years has been underpinned by the transition from a centrally-planned to a more market-oriented system with structural shifts of factors of production from subsistence agriculture to industrial and service sectors. Moreover, Vietnam's success is also attributable to its export-led industrialisation strategy which has been driven by the availability of a large, young, literate and relatively low-cost workforce.

Going forward, natural endowments in terms of vast fertile lands, abundance in natural resources and scenic landscapes bless Vietnam with tremendous potentials for upgraded development of its agriculture, industrial and service sectors. Moreover, the country's pursuit of a deepened and comprehensive international integration strategy synergises well with its export-led industrialisation strategy, creating many opportunities for Vietnam to benefit from trade, investment and people-to-people exchanges. Furthermore, Vietnam stands to gain from the southward shifts of FDI from China due to rising labour costs in the latter. If harnessed well, this will prove to be the golden chance for Vietnam to establish itself as Asia's next manufacturing hub with modern industries in high value-added sectors.

However, further development is not guaranteed as there are fundamental challenges facing the Vietnamese economy. First, while the country is still enjoying a "golden population structure" with twice the number of working persons as compared to the number of dependents, rapid shifts in demographic forces including declining fertility rate and lengthening life expectancy may force Vietnam into an ageing population structure sooner rather than later. At the same time, like many other countries, Vietnam will experience technological disruptions as the world embarks on the Fourth Industrial Revolution. These two megatrends will erode Vietnam's labour cost advantage in due course.

Against this backdrop, it does not bode well for the Vietnamese economy that it suffers from sluggish labour productivity growth, especially in the agriculture sector, rampant inefficiencies in a bloated state sector which is propped up by market distortions in favour of state-owned enterprises (SOEs) and lack of synergies, particularly in terms of technological transfers, between multinational corporations (MNCs) and local firms. In addition, institutional reforms have not caught up with economic reforms. As a result, gaps in institutional quality represent the fundamental challenge to future development. Lack of coordination among government agencies at both the national and local levels as well as weak governance have hampered the implementation of policy measures aimed at addressing Vietnam's economic malaises.

Analysis on economic competitiveness among the ASEAN-10 by ACI shows that Vietnam has only managed to outperform Cambodia, Laos and Myanmar. However, it still lags far behind the ASEAN-6 in many aspects, especially in terms of productivity performance, human capital development, quality of physical infrastructure, as well as market mechanism and regulatory framework. Moreover, through a comprehensive examination of socio-economic indicators at the sub-national level and detailed comparison of Hanoi and Ho Chi Minh City in terms of their economic development, liveability, cost of living and purchasing power, we observe that Vietnam is beset with widening regional imbalances which put it at risk of becoming one country with two economies — the more developed Southern Vietnam *vis-à-vis* provinces in Northern and Central Vietnam. If left unresolved, this situation of "One Country-Two Economies" will impede Vietnam's development, worsen inequality and weaken national cohesion.

Thus, Vietnam is at a critical juncture in its development. Rather than "renovation" as it has been doing for the past 30 years, the Vietnamese government must look to "revitalise" the economy through sweeping, wide-ranging reforms. The successful completion of a new reform agenda will be make-or-break for Vietnam as it will either become overwhelmed by structural weaknesses and unable to adapt to the challenges of technological disruptions and ageing population, or it will achieve growth breakthroughs which allow it to catch up to the more developed economies in ASEAN and across Asia.

Based on our assessment of the Vietnamese economy, we propose a comprehensive policy roadmap to unleash Vietnam's economic potentials so that the country can achieve balanced and sustainable development for enhanced competitiveness. Our vision is for Vietnam to grow its GDP per capita by at least seven percent in real terms so that it may surpass Philippines and be on par with Indonesia and Thailand by 2040. This is totally feasible provided that the government ensures the following:

(i) **Facilitates private sector development** by strengthening market mechanism and pushing forward with SOE reforms for a level playing field;
(ii) **Enhances interregional connectivity and pursues the upgraded development of Hanoi to ignite the broader development of Northern Vietnam** so as to mitigate regional disparities and prevent the emergence of "One Country-Two Economies";
(iii) **Nurtures small and medium enterprises (SMEs),** which are the backbone of the economy, by alleviating information asymmetries; fostering synergies between SMEs and MNCs; building research capacity to track and monitor SMEs' productivity, efficiency and internationalisation potentials; improving ease of doing business and building digital capacity for SMEs to help them thrive in the Fourth Industrial Revolution;
(iv) Implements the Skills Future Initiative, the Tripartite and Targeted Industrial Internship Model with Placed–Trained–Employed Scheme as well as policies to foster data literacy, soft skills and English proficiency to **ensure the holistic development of the workforce and promote constant skill upgrading and deepening**;

(v) Through proactive national economic planning, **transforms Vietnam into a vibrant, diversified economy** whereby Vietnam shall become a leading manufacturing hub and excellent centre for service-based industries with a productive and climate-resilient agriculture sector;

(vi) **Fosters special economic zones as engines of growth and test-beds for administrative and economic reform measures** through a comprehensive strategy with clear targets and tracking of policy objectives.

Instrumental to achieving these objectives is a strong political leadership which is committed to the reform agenda, capable of marshalling popular support for reforms and supported by a modern and effective public administration system. As a result, far-reaching institutional reforms to improve the capacity of public officials and enhance political communication with the people will be essential. Additionally, synergies between domestic reforms and international integration must be leveraged on to overcome internal inertia and reinvigorate the reform momentum when necessary. The road ahead is challenging, but Vietnam will traverse it successfully if the government can mobilise the Vietnamese people's diligence, dogged determination and resourcefulness towards the goals of economic development.

Chapter 1

Vietnam's Economic Landscape: Past, Present and Future

1.1 Economic Vision and Mission after the Unification of Vietnam

After the Unification of Vietnam in 1975, the Fourth Party Congress in December 1976 resolved to "turn Vietnam into a socialist country with modern agriculture and industry within 20 years".[1] The Vietnam Communist Party (VCP) adopted the Second Five-Year Plan (1976–1980) which prioritised agriculture development and investment in heavy industry. Meanwhile, a grand socialist transformation programme was implemented throughout Southern Vietnam where the state collectivised agriculture and nationalised industry and commerce.

Due to economic hardships, the early 1980s saw the implementation of some early measures of reforms driven by bottom-up pressures from the ground.[2] The VCP acknowledged that at least for a definitive period of time, private ownerships had to be tolerated, either in the form of private enterprises or state-private joint enterprises. The household economy was also encouraged to develop, though households' economic activities had to be consistent with the plans of the cooperatives.[3]

In agriculture, Directive No. 100 CT/TU of 1981 (Directive 100 for short) stipulated the widespread adoption of the end-product contract system (*khoan san pham*) which had been experimented with in some localities. Under this system, peasants were contracted to farm lands owned by the cooperatives. If output surpassed the pre-set quotas, peasants were allowed to keep the surplus to consume and sell on the private domestic market or sell to the government at negotiated prices. Changes in the incentive system resulted in improvement in agricultural production. Nevertheless, the results were limited. From 1983, peasants who returned parts of the lands operated under the end-product contact system after meeting all their obligations to the cooperatives tended to receive only 16–17 percent of the contract outputs which was not sufficient to cover production expenses.[4]

The reform era of the Vietnamese economy officially began in 1986. The Sixth Party Congress announced the *Doi Moi* (Renovation) Policy which ushered in the transformation of the centrally planned economy to a "socialist-oriented market economy": a type of market-based mixed economy where state planning through five-year plans is still executed and state-owned enterprises (SOEs) play a major role. Rationing and price controls were abolished for many

[1] See Pham *et al.* (2007).

[2] See Riedel and Turley (1999) and Pham *et al.* (2007).

[3] See Vo (1990).

[4] *Ibid.*

commodities. In 1987, the Law on Foreign Investment was promulgated, sanctioning foreign investment in the country.

In April 1988, the Politburo's Resolution No. 10/NQTU on the "Renovation of economic management in agriculture" (Resolution 10 for short) took the end-product contract system a long way forward by recognising the household as the basic production unit in agriculture. It leased out farm lands to households for longer duration of 15 years as compared to three years under Directive 100 and gave the households total autonomy in their farming activities. Coupled with the 1988 Land Law, Resolution 10 marked the start of the decollectivisation of agriculture. As a result, it helped to liberalise resources in the rural economy, and Vietnam became a rice exporter in 1989.[5] Throughout 1988 and 1989, more measures were implemented to encourage the development of the private sector. Additionally, SOEs were accorded more autonomy in setting their business plans.

Since 1990, Vietnam has intensified its efforts to integrate into the global economy, especially after the collapse of the Soviet Union in 1991. An export-oriented industrialisation strategy was adopted. The withdrawal of troops from Cambodia paved the way for the restoration of relations with countries in the Association of the Southeast Asian Nations (ASEAN), culminating in Vietnam becoming the seventh member of ASEAN in 1995. The trade embargo with the US was also lifted in 1995, and in 2007 Vietnam became a member of the World Trade Organisation. Since then, Vietnam has continued to pursue deeper international integration through bilateral free trade agreements and multilateral initiatives such as the ASEAN Economic Community, the Regional Comprehensive Economic Partnership, the Comprehensive and Progressive Agreement for Trans-Pacific Partnership, the Free Trade Area of the Asia-Pacific and the Belt & Road Initiative. In 2017, Vietnam successfully hosted the Asia-Pacific Economic Cooperation summit for the second time.

1.2 A Report Card on the *Doi Moi* Reform

After 30 years of economic reforms, Vietnam has made tremendous progress. Figure 1.1 tracks the real Gross Domestic Product (GDP) growth rate and real GDP per capita growth rate of the country from 1986 to 2016. Over the period, real GDP has grown at about 6.5 percent per annum (p.a.) on average, while GDP per capita has averaged an annual growth rate of almost 5 percent. Furthermore, as Figure 1.1 demonstrates, the Vietnamese economy has exhibited resiliency during the Global Financial Crisis as it still maintained positive growth in both real GDP and GDP per capita in 2008 and 2009 and the decline in growth rates was relatively modest as compared with that during the Asian Financial Crisis.

In fact, Vietnam has consistently been one of the fastest growing economies in ASEAN over the past two decades. Its average real GDP growth rate between 2000 and 2016 was 6.4 percent p.a., faster than the ASEAN's average of 5.2 percent p.a. (see Figure 1.2).

Furthermore, the Vietnamese economy has a high savings rate. As shown in Figure 1.3, the share of gross domestic savings in GDP has risen over the years, from 4.4 percent in 1986

[5] See Pham *et al.* (2007).

Figure 1.1: Real GDP and Real GDP per Capita Growth Rates in Vietnam, 1986–2016

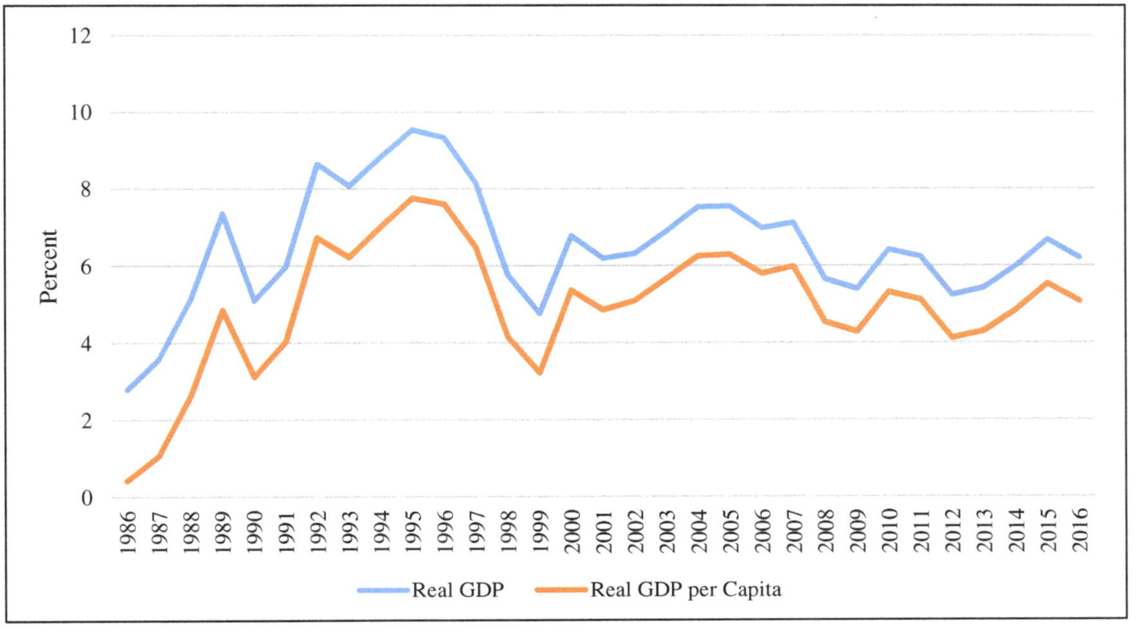

Source: World Bank, World Development Indicators

Figure 1.2: Real GDP Growth Rates of Vietnam *vis-à-vis* Selected Economies, 2000–2016

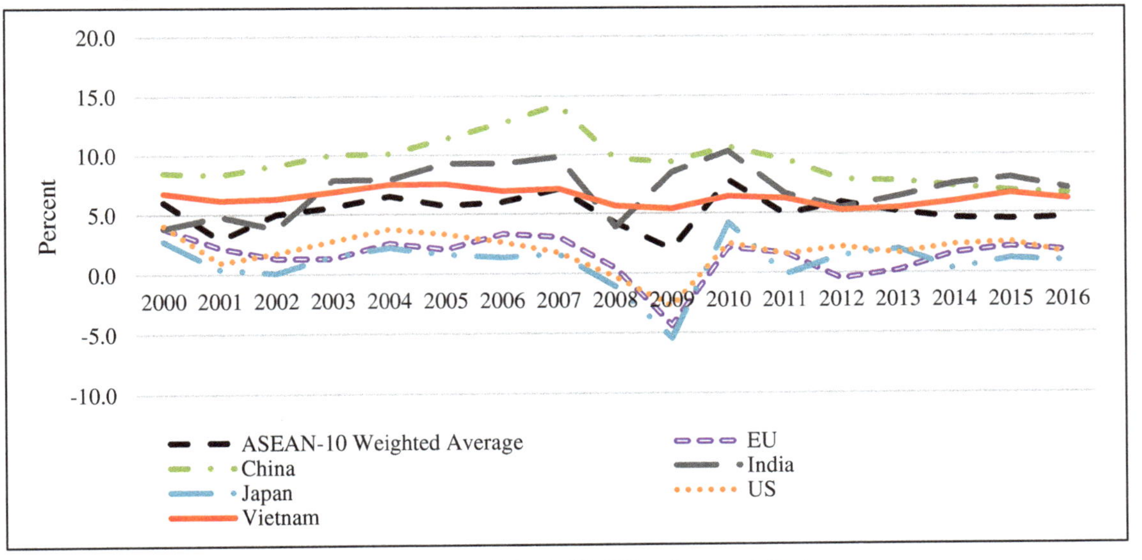

Source: Authors' calculation based on data from the World Bank, World Development Indicators

Figure 1.3: Share of Gross Domestic Savings, 1986–2015 and Share of Gross Fixed Capital Formation in Vietnam's GDP, 1994–2016

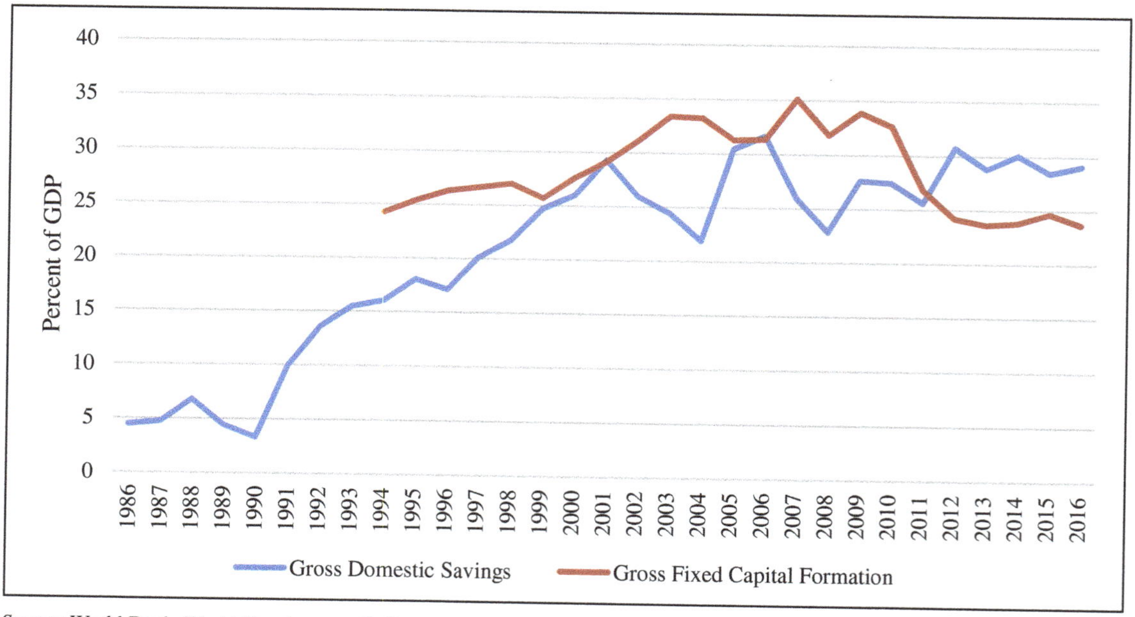

Source: World Bank, World Development Indicators

to 29.1 percent in 2016, though there were considerable fluctuations between 2001 and 2009. Meanwhile, gross fixed capital formation has consistently increased in absolute terms but its share in GDP has declined since 2010. The fact that domestic savings are now higher than gross fixed capital formation indicates that there are ample resources to meet Vietnam's future investment needs. However, this is provided that savings can be channelled to productive investment through an efficient financial system.

Moreover, as a result of *Doi Moi*, Vietnam has undergone three fundamental structural transformations, from an agrarian economy to an industrial and service-based economy, from a predominantly state-owned economy to a multi-actor economy and from a closed economy to an open one. These features of *Doi Moi* shall be explored in more detail in Chapter 2 when we discuss Vietnam's growth model.

Figure 1.4 displays Vietnam's annual inflation rate between 1980 and 2016. Prior to the implementation of *Doi Moi*, Vietnam was gripped in an economic crisis with inflation hovering around 100 percent a year. With the removal of price controls, inflation skyrocketed, worsened by the fact that the huge budget deficits during this period were financed by money printing. The annual inflation rate shot above 300 percent p.a. between 1986 and 1988, peaking at 453.1 percent in 1986. It was not until 1989 and the early 1990s that inflation was back under control, dropping to single digit in 1993. In more recent years, the economy experienced high inflation volatility between 2008 and 2011 with annual inflation rate reaching 23.1 percent and 18.7 percent, respectively, in these two years. However, the government has managed to keep inflation under control as it has been on a declining trend since 2012. According to data

Figure 1.4: Vietnam's Annual Inflation Rate, 1980–2016

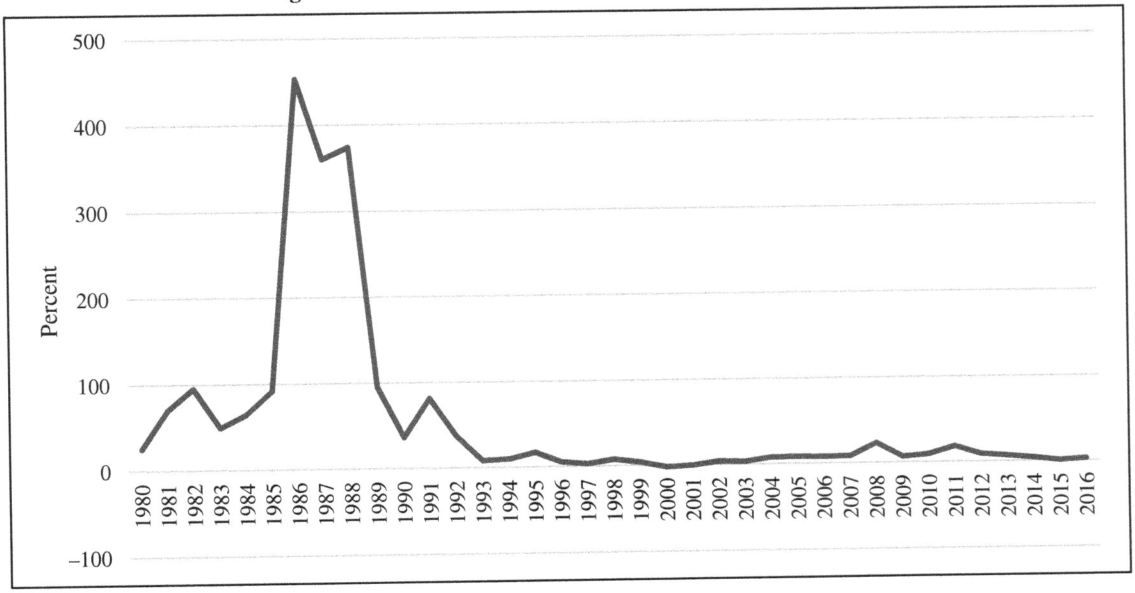

Source: IMF, World Economic Outlook

published by the International Monetary Fund (IMF), Vietnam's annual inflation rate was 2.7 percent in 2016, and it is projected to be around four percent in the long run.[6]

The country has also made great strides in terms of poverty reduction with tens of millions lifted out of poverty over the past two decades. Figure 1.5 shows Vietnam's poverty headcount ratios based on international poverty lines in 1992 and 2014. In 1992, 49.2 percent of the population lived below US$1.90 a day at constant 2011 prices adjusted for purchasing power parity (PPP), while 77.1 percent lived below US$3.10 adjusted for PPP. By 2014, these figures have been reduced to 3.1 percent and 12.0 percent, respectively.

Throughout its reforms, Vietnam has retained a strong emphasis on social development. The government's approach to education changed with the launch of *Doi Moi* with education being viewed as a necessary investment for development.[7] By 2015, the country's adult literacy rate reached 97.1 percent, the highest among the Cambodia–Laos–Myanmar–Vietnam (CLMV) subgrouping (see Table 1.1). In terms of healthcare, Vietnam performs exceptionally well in basic care. Its infant mortality rate dropped steadily from 37.7 per 1,000 live births in 1990 to 17.2 per 1,000 live births in 2015. Life expectancy rose from 70.1 years in 1990 to 75.8 years in 2015, the third-highest in ASEAN after Brunei and Singapore. Moreover, Vietnam's ratio of physicians per 10,000 population almost tripled from 4.0 in 1990 to 11.9 in 2013. Reflecting improvements in education and healthcare, Vietnam's human development index (HDI) had risen from 0.477 to 0.683 between 1990 and 2015.

[6] See IMF, World Economic Outlook database, October 2017 version.

[7] See World Bank and Ministry of Planning and Investment of Vietnam (2016, 85).

Figure 1.5: Vietnam's Poverty Headcount Ratios Based on International Poverty Lines, 1992 and 2014

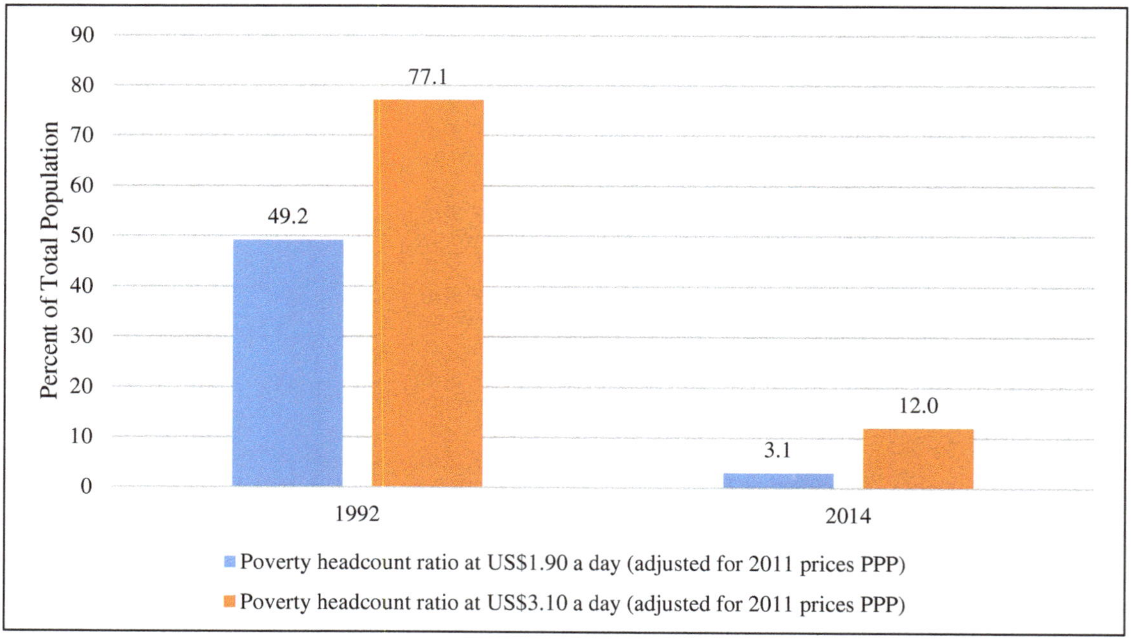

Source: World Bank, World Development Indicators

Table 1.1: Vietnam's Performance in Basic Social Development Indicators, 1990 and 2015

Indicators	1990	2015
HDI (index value)	0.477	0.683
Infant Mortality Rate (per 1,000 live births)	37.7	17.2
Life Expectancy at Birth (years)	70.1	75.8
Ratio of Physicians per 10,000 People	4.0	N.A. (11.9 in 2013)
Adult Literacy Rate (percent of population aged 15 and above)	N.A. (87.6 in 1989)	97.1

Source: World Bank, World Development Indicators

Nonetheless, there are still major social issues to be resolved. Overcrowding, outdated facilities and the prevalence of "out-of-pocket payments" are perennial problems plaguing Vietnam's public healthcare system.[8] Furthermore, there is a lack of access to quality care in the provincial-level public hospitals as patients tend to flock to national-level hospitals in the major metropolises for treatment. In addition, though it has been relatively contained in the past, inequality is on the rise. Studies by Oxfam and the World Bank have pointed to the rise in the number of superrich individuals (those with more than US$30 million) and the disproportionate lack of

[8] See *The Economist* (2014).

opportunities for women, ethnic minorities and the impoverished are the two of the more worrisome trends with regard to inequality in Vietnam.[9]

1.3 Future Economic Potentials of Vietnam

The *Doi Moi* reform has mobilised factors of production from agriculture to manufacturing and services, enabling economic activities to flourish. Going forward, Vietnam stands to benefit from greater foreign direct investment as MNCs relocate their production facilities southward from China due to the latter's rising labour costs. This will serve to deepen Vietnam's participation in the global value chain and facilitate its rise as a key manufacturing hub in Asia. Moreover, the country's abundance in scenic landscapes and fertile lands provides a natural advantage for the development of Vietnam's agriculture and tourism sectors.

The Vietnamese people have always set a high bar for success. The preambles to the Vietnamese Constitution articulate the national aspiration to achieve "prosperity for the people, a strong country, and an equitable, democratic and civilised society".[10] In the recent Socio-economic Development Plan for the 2016–2020 Period, the Vietnamese government aims to "maintain macro-economic stability while striving for higher economic growth than previous years".[11] The several economic objectives under the latest Five-Year Plan are hoped to promote sustainable, equitable and inclusive economic development across Vietnam, bringing about higher standards of living for all Vietnamese nationals.

Indeed, if Vietnam can build on the accomplishments of the past three decades to achieve breakthroughs in development, it will be able to catch up with the more developed ASEAN economies. Figure 1.6 displays projections of Vietnam's real GDP per capita up to 2040 *vis-à-vis* the ASEAN-5 countries (Indonesia, Malaysia, Philippines, Singapore and Thailand). We consider three growth scenarios for Vietnam, while future GDP per capita of the ASEAN-5 are projected based on three-year moving averages (MA) as follows:

- Under a "business-as-usual scenario" with three-year MA projection where Vietnam's real GDP per capita grows at 5.2 percent p.a. in the long run, it will reach US$6,600 (constant 2011 prices) by 2040 or around 71 percent of Philippines' real GDP per capita level in the same year.
- However, under a "moderate" growth path of 6 percent p.a., which necessitates an average annual real GDP growth rate of 6.8 percent, Vietnam's real GDP per capita by 2040 will reach US$7,900 (constant 2011 prices), which would be more than 85 percent of Philippines' real GDP per capita.
- Under a "dynamic" growth path of 7 percent p.a., which requires an average 7.8 percent p.a. GDP's growth rate in real terms, Vietnam's real GDP per capita by 2040 will surpass that of

---

[9] See Lefur (2017).
[10] See Government of the Socialist Republic of Vietnam (2013).
[11] See ADB (2016).

Figure 1.6: Vietnam's Real GDP per Capita and Projections *vis-à-vis* ASEAN-5, 2000–2040

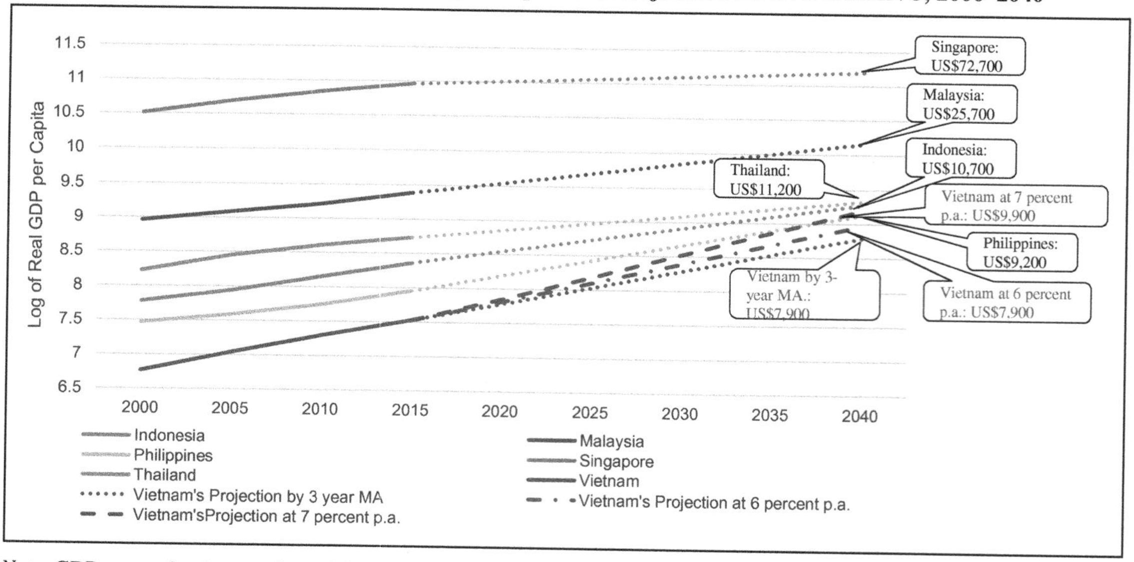

Note: GDP per capita data are logged for better illustration purposes. Projections for ASEAN-5, which are represented by their respective lines, are computed through three-year MA. Figures in the bubbles show the projected GDP per capita in US$ (constant 2011 prices) of ASEAN-5 and Vietnam under different scenarios by 2040.

Source: Authors' calculation based on data from the World Bank, World Development Indicators and the United Nations, World Population Prospects 2017 Revision

Philippines and at US$9,900 (constant 2011 prices), as well as more than 92 percent and 88 percent of the real GDP per capita levels of Indonesia and Thailand respectively.

However, success is contingent on the implementation of appropriate policies to address structural impediments to growth that are prevalent in the Vietnamese economy. As the analysis in Chapter 2 shall demonstrate, these include, but are not limited to, low economic competitiveness, inefficiency of SOEs, persistent infrastructure bottlenecks, poor human capital development and declining productivity growth. The most fundamental challenge, however, is weak institutional quality.

Furthermore, policy-makers must also guard against the emergence of "One Country-Two Economies", where imbalanced regional development may lead to a wide divergence in prosperity level, living standards and quality of life between Southern Vietnam and the other two regions — Northern and Central Vietnam. For instance, as illustrated in Figure 1.7, industrial parks are mainly concentrated in Southern Vietnam. Differences in development level and availability of economic opportunities have engendered persistent disparities in living standards between the different regions. Such gaps need to be narrowed as they may hinder Vietnam's development progress, contribute to rising inequalities and undermine national cohesion.

Figure 1.7: Distribution of Industrial Parks and Economic Zones in Vietnam

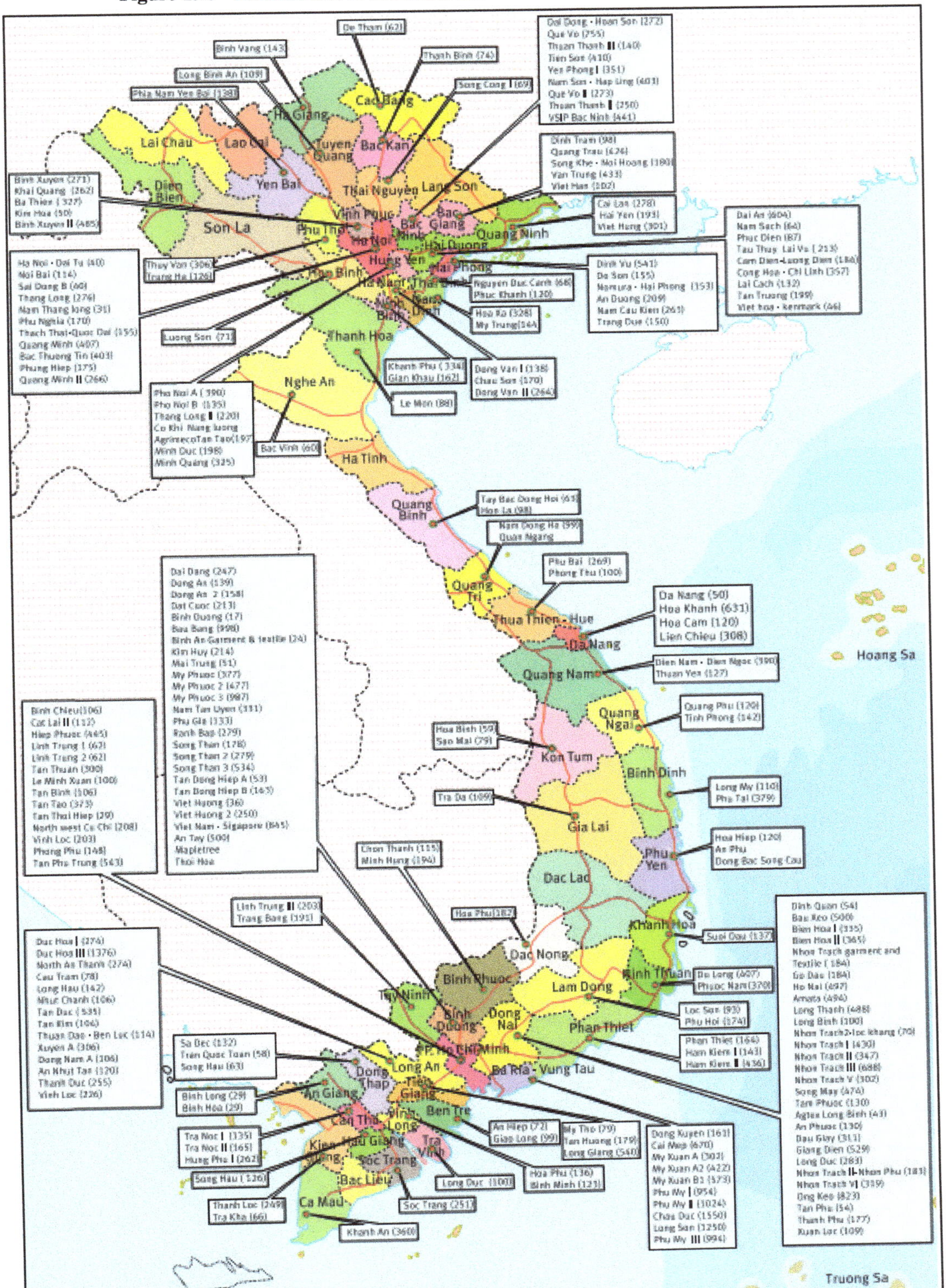

Source: Ministry of Planning and Investment, as appeared in UNIDO (2015)

1.4 Expected Contributions and Roadmap of the Book

Drawing mainly on empirical research works by the Asia Competitiveness Institute (ACI), Lee Kuan Yew School of Public Policy, National University of Singapore, this book comprehensively assesses the prospects of the Vietnamese economy. Based on our analysis, the study will formulate important policy recommendations for Vietnam in its quest to enhance its economic competitiveness and achieve balanced and sustainable development.

Specifically, Chapter 2 shall discuss opportunities and challenges facing Vietnam in the next phase of its development. The chapter shall dwell on the structural transformations which have taken place since the beginning of *Doi Moi* and shed light on outstanding challenges which call for a re-thinking of the current growth model. Next, we will present the findings of ACI's competitiveness analysis for ASEAN-10 and benchmark Vietnam against its fellow ASEAN members in terms of economic competitiveness. Furthermore, we will conduct a deep-dive into the various dimensions of competitiveness in ACI's competitiveness framework, identifying key relative strengths and weaknesses of Vietnam. To be sure, Vietnam's current growth model must be enhanced to address macroeconomic challenges plaguing the Vietnamese economy as well as the widening development gaps between Northern, Central and Southern Vietnam. Such gaps are explored both through socio-economic indicators and a detailed case study on liveability, cost of living and purchasing power of ordinary residents in Hanoi and Ho Chi Minh City. Finally, the chapter shall also consider Vietnam's future development in the international context.

Policy recommendations are laid out in Chapter 3. We identify ways to facilitate private sector development through revitalising SOE reforms and strengthening market institutions as the immediate priority for Vietnamese policy-makers as the economic future of Vietnam has to be underpinned by private sector dynamism. Next, policies to mitigate regional disparities to prevent the emergence of "One Country-Two Economies" will be discussed. The highlight of this set of policies is the proposal to leverage Hanoi's advantage as the national capital to bring about the development of the city, thus catalysing the broader development of Northern Vietnam.

The chapter shall then present recommendations to foster growth in small and medium enterprises (SMEs) as well as to develop human capital to ensure Vietnam is well-positioned to achieve sustained and inclusive growth given challenges arising from future disruptions including an aging population and the Fourth Industrial Revolution. In addition, we shall describe our vision for Vietnam to become a manufacturing and service hub, supported by a highly productive and climate-resilient agriculture sector. This is then followed by a discussion on the role of special economic zones (SEZs), especially the three newly-proposed special administrative-economic zones (SAEZs) in Van Don, Bac Van Phong and Phu Quoc, as engines of growth and laboratories for new policy initiatives. The chapter also contains a section on the People's Association (PA) model in Singapore (see Section 3.8). A description of the PA model shall hopefully provide relevant policy lessons on bridging the gap between the people and the government, facilitating the communication of government's policies to citizens and building support for Vietnam's next wave of economic reforms.

Finally, Chapter 4 shall conclude with a summary of the major findings and policy initiatives proposed in the book, followed by a discussion about the synergies between international integration and domestic reform.

References

ADB. 2016. *Viet Nam, 2016–2020 Fostering More Inclusive and Environmentally Sustainable Growth.* Manila: Asian Development Bank (ADB).

Government of the Socialist Republic of Vietnam. 2013. *The Constitution of the Socialist Republic of Vietnam (2013).*

Lefur, Babeth. 2017. "Vietnam inequality challenges — next generation of Doi Moi?" *Tuoi Tre News*, 12th January, available at http://tuoitrenews.vn/society/38983/vietnam-inequality-challenges-next-generation-of-doi-moi (accessed on 23 March 2017).

Pham, Quang Ngoc, Trinh Bui, and Duc Nguyen Thanh. 2007. "Economic performance of Vietnam, 1976–2000: New evidence from input–output model". Depocen Working Paper No. 2007/13, Development and Policies Research Centre (Depocen), Hanoi.

Riedel, James, and William S. Turley. 1999. "The Politics and Economics of Transition to an Open Market Economy in Viet Nam". OECD Development Centre Working Paper No. 152, OECD Development Centre, Paris.

The Economist. 2014. "Healthcare in Vietnam: Limping Along." 20th December, available at http://www.economist.com/news/asia/21618894-ordinary-folk-are-sick-and-tired-their-public-hospitals-limping-along (accessed 23 March 2017).

UNIDO. 2015. *Economic Zones in the ASEAN: Industrial Parks, Special Economic Zones, Eco Industrial Parks, Innovation Districts as Strategies for Industrial Competitiveness*. Vienna: United Nations Industrial Development Organisation (UNIDO).

Vo, Nhan Tri. 1990. *Vietnam's Economic Policy Since 1975*. Singapore: Institute of Southeast Asian Studies (ISEAS).

World Bank and Ministry of Planning and Investment. 2016. *Vietnam 2035: Toward Prosperity, Creativity, Equity, and Democracy*. Washington DC: World Bank.

Chapter 2

Assessing Vietnam's Economic Competitiveness: Meeting Challenges and Seizing Opportunities

2.1 Introductory Notes

After 30 years since the launch of *Doi Moi,* Vietnam has transformed from a backward low-income economy to a dynamic middle-income economy. However, Vietnam still lags behind its fellow members in the Association of Southeast Asian Nations (ASEAN) in many aspects. As seen in Table 2.1, Vietnam's real Gross Domestic Product (GDP) per capita was US$1,770 (constant 2010 prices) in 2016, 64 percent that of Philippines and 44 percent that of Indonesia. In terms of the Human Development Index (HDI), Vietnam ranked seventh out of 10 ASEAN countries as of 2016.

As stated in Chapter 1, Vietnam has the potential to become the rising star among the ASEAN-10 countries and catch up to its more developed counterparts. However, this can only be realised if suitable policies are implemented to address the short- and long-term impediments to growth. In this regard, the Asia Competitiveness Institute (ACI) has crafted a comprehensive and rigorous methodological framework not only to produce annual rankings of competitiveness for ASEAN but also to provide policy roadmap for individual member states to identify gaps that need to be addressed to achieve greater competitiveness on their respective pathways to sustainable and inclusive economic development.

Leveraging on ACI's research, this chapter conducts a holistic assessment of Vietnam's current growth model and its economic competitiveness *vis-à-vis* other ASEAN countries to

Table 2.1: ASEAN-10 in a Snapshot, 2016

Country	Total Land Area (thousand km²)	Population (millions)	GDP (million constant 2010 US$)	GDP per Capita (constant 2010 US$)	HDI
Brunei	5.3	0.4	13,302	31,431	0.864
Cambodia	176.5	15.8	17,009	1,079	0.558
Indonesia	1,811.6	261.1	1,037,688	3,974	0.686
Laos	230.8	6.8	11,102	1,643	0.582
Malaysia	328.6	31.2	344,052	11,032	0.787
Myanmar	653.1	52.9	74,470	1,408	0.552
Philippines	298.2	103.3	284,477	2,753	0.679
Singapore	0.7	5.6	294,947	52,601	0.924
Thailand	510.9	68.9	406,425	5,902	0.738
Vietnam	310.1	92.7	164,105	1,770	0.678

Source: World Bank, World Development Indicators

shed light on the opportunities and challenges facing Vietnam. In particular, Section 2.2 describes the economic transformations that resulted from the *Doi Moi* reform and highlights the limitations of the current growth model. This is followed by Section 2.3 which reports the latest findings of ACI's competitiveness analysis for the 2000–2014 period. These macroanalyses are then supplemented by a closer look at the sub-national level which focuses on regional disparities between Northern, Central and Southern Vietnam. We contend that if the current development gaps between the Southern provinces and their Northern and Central counterparts are allowed to widen, Vietnam stands to suffer from a situation of "One Country-Two Economies". Next, Section 2.5 examines Vietnam's challenges and opportunities in the international context. Finally, Section 2.6 concludes.

2.2 Evaluating Vietnam's Growth Model

2.2.1 Structural Transformations after 30 Years of *Doi Moi*

Since the transition from a centrally planned economy to a more market-based system was launched in 1986, Vietnam has experienced three major structural adjustments. First, it has transformed from an agrarian to an industrial and service-based economy. Figure 2.1 plots the evolution of the sectoral shares in Vietnam's GDP based on data from the United Nations Conference on Trade and Development (UNCTAD). We observe that the GDP share of agriculture started to decline since the late 1980s; its percentage share has more than halved from 42.8 in 1988 to 18.9 in 2015. The share of the industrial sector, on the other hand, has almost doubled from 18.6 percent to 37.0 percent over the same period. In addition, the share of

Figure 2.1: Share of Vietnam's GDP by Sectors, 1976–2015

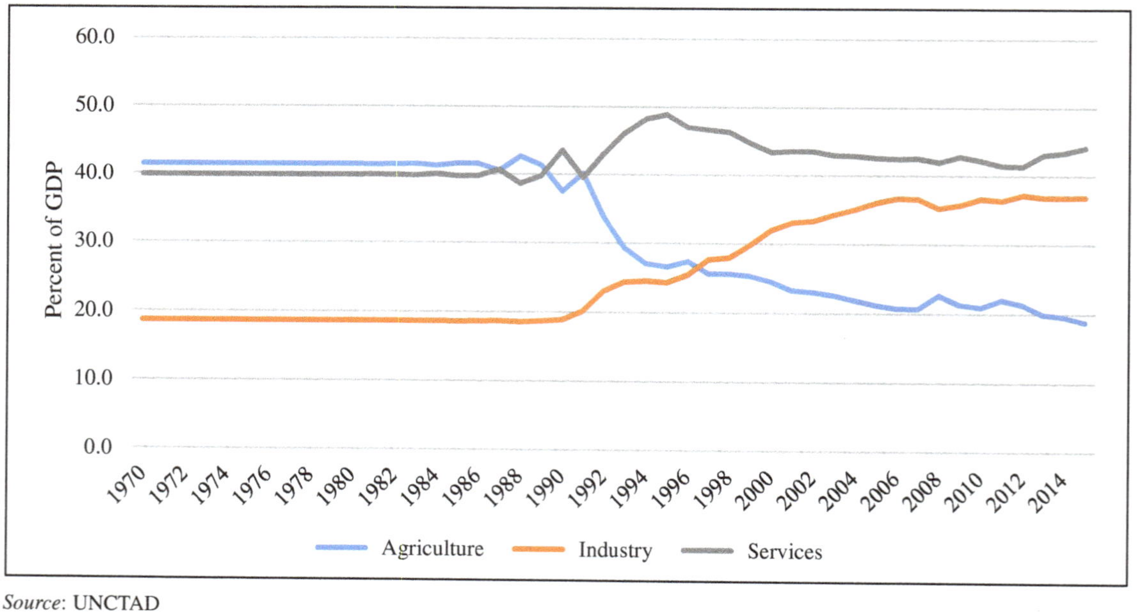

Source: UNCTAD

Figure 2.2: Investment in the Vietnamese Economy by Types of Ownership, Period Averages for 1995–2005 and 2006–2016

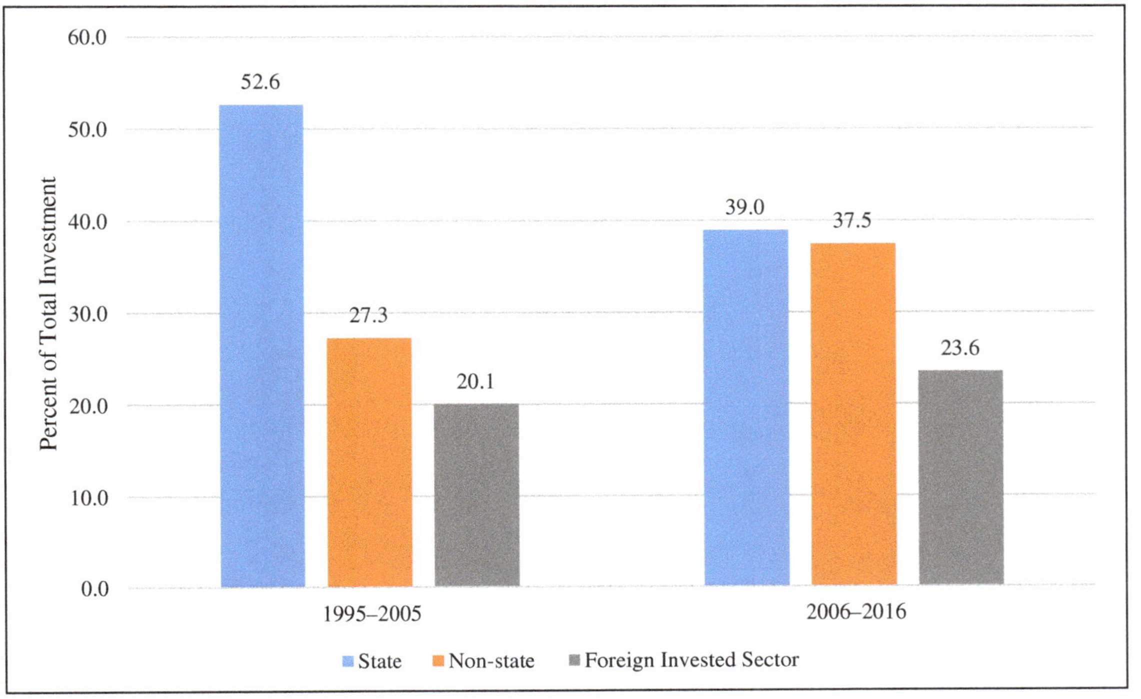

Note: 2016 data are preliminary.

Source: Authors' calculation based on data from Vietnam's GSO

services in Vietnam's GDP has also risen from 38.7 percent to 44.2 percent between 1988 and 2015. In fact, since the early 1990s, the service sector has contributed the most to Vietnam's GDP.

Second, Vietnam has moved from a predominantly state-owned economy to a multi-actor economy. According to data published by Vietnam's General Statistics Office (GSO), investment in the state sector used to constitute more than half of total investment over the period 1995–2005 (see Figure 2.2). However, the share has declined to 39.0 percent for the next 11-year period (2006–2016). In comparison, the investment share of the private sector has increased from 27.3 percent to 37.5 percent between these two periods. Meanwhile, the corresponding share of the foreign-invested sector has risen moderately from 20.1 percent to 23.6 percent.

Third, Vietnam has transformed from a closed economy into an open, globally-integrated economy that actively engages in international trade. As mentioned in Chapter 1, Vietnam has been a member of the World Trade Organisation since 2007 and has avidly supported bilateral and multilateral free trade agreements (FTAs). As of 2016, trade constituted 199.3 percent of Vietnam's GDP, more than eight times higher than the corresponding share in 1986 at 23.2 percent. In fact, as Figure 2.3 demonstrates, Vietnam is the second-most trade-dependent economy in ASEAN after Singapore.

Figure 2.3: Trade in Goods and Services as Percentage of GDP for ASEAN-10, 2016

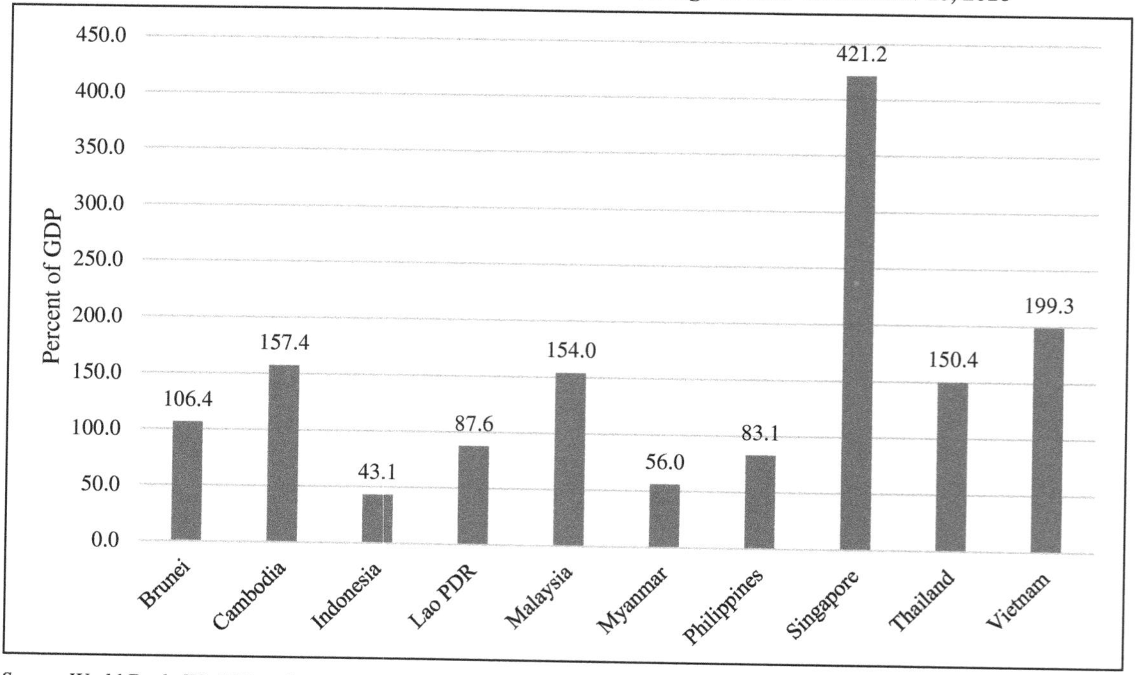

Source: World Bank, World Development Indicators

More encouraging is the fact that as the country pursues economic integration, the technological content of its exports has improved over time. Figure 2.4 illustrates that the share of high-technology exports in total manufactured exports in Vietnam has picked up since 2008. Overall, the share has jumped from a mere 0.1 percent in 1997 to 26.9 percent in 2014.

Vietnam's advancement in high-technology exports is closely linked to the presence of multinational corporations (MNCs), such as Samsung and Intel, in the country. Leveraging on the so-called "China-Plus-One" strategy practiced by MNCs where these firms seek to be active in both China and one other ASEAN country to hold down cost or reduce over-dependence on China,[1] Vietnam has successfully attracted much foreign direct investment (FDI). As shown in Figure 2.5, FDI inflows exponentially increased from –US$0.34 million in 1976, which indicates divestment out of the country, to US$12.6 billion in 2016. FDI has contributed tremendously to the creation of thousands of manufacturing and assembly jobs, especially in the smartphone, footwear and apparel industries. As manufacturing in China matures and labour costs rise, it is expected that more MNCs will shift southward to Vietnam, facilitating its rise as the next manufacturing powerhouse.[2]

In summary, the major thrusts of the *Doi Moi* reform were economic liberalisation and export-led industrialisation fuelled by resource mobilisation from agriculture to the industrial

[1] See *The Economist* (2010).

[2] See Nakamura (2016).

Figure 2.4: Share of High-technology Exports in Total Manufactured Exports in Vietnam, 1997–2014

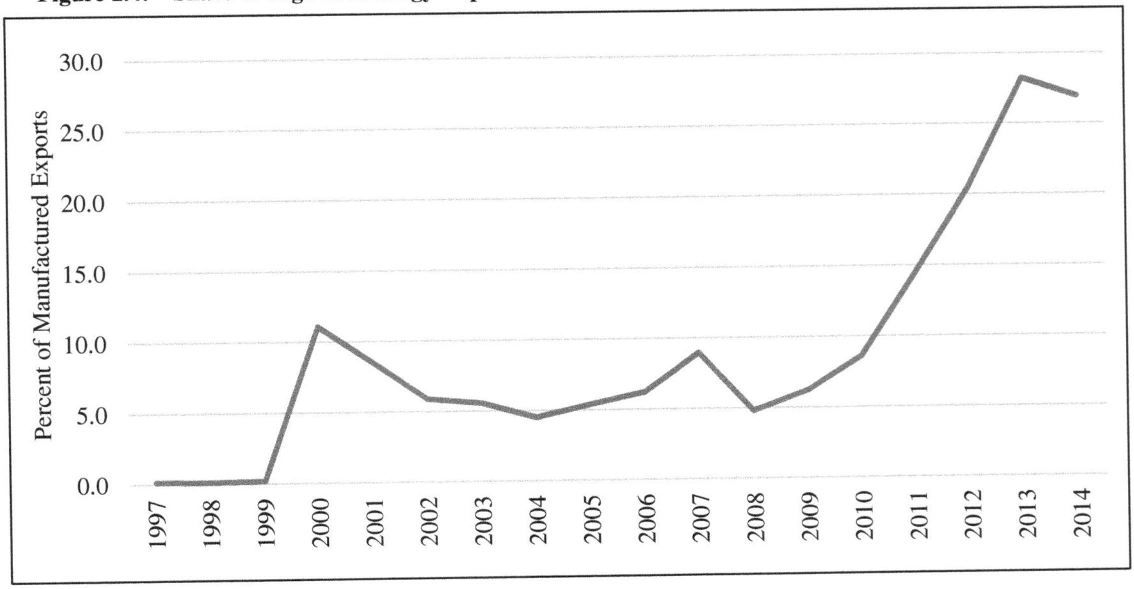

Source: World Bank, World Development Indicators

Figure 2.5: FDI Inflows to Vietnam at Current Prices Million US$, 1976–2016

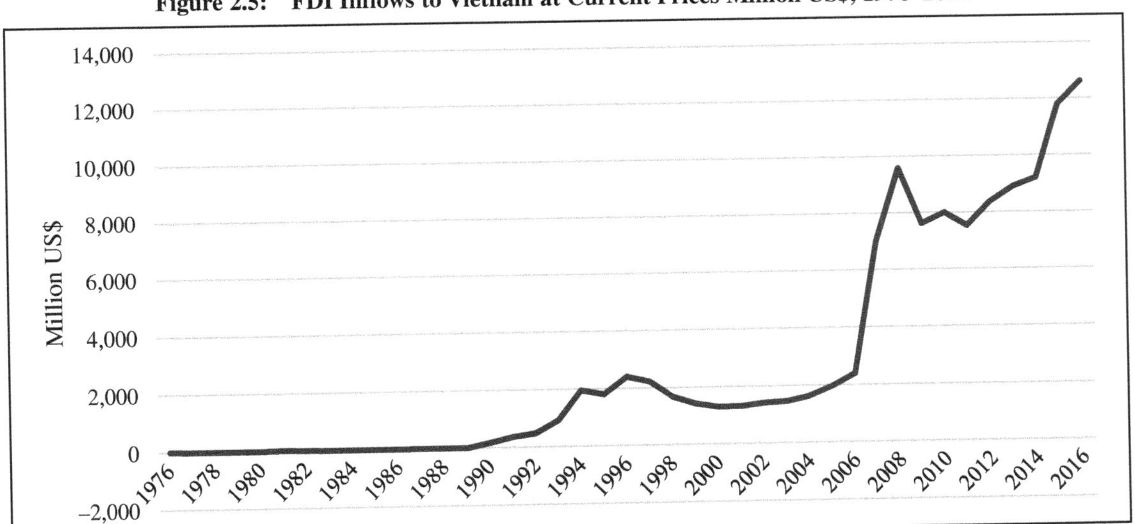

Source: UNCTAD

and service sectors with a large, young and relatively low-cost workforce. While the current growth model has indeed allowed Vietnam to prosper during the past three decades, further reforms are necessary to sustain the momentum of growth. The next section will outline some of the major challenges to Vietnam's current growth model that must be addressed.

2.2.2 Outstanding Challenges in Vietnam's Next Phase of Development

We posit that there are seven major structural weaknesses that Vietnam must overcome in order to maintain its current growth trajectory. These include (i) diminishing demographic dividends due to ageing population; (ii) potential disruptions through rapid technological innovations; (iii) slowdown in labour productivity growth, which is worsened by (iv) the prevalence of market distortions in favour of inefficient state-owned enterprises (SOEs); (v) an agriculture sector which lacks labour productivity; as well as (vi) the lack of synergies between MNCs and local businesses, particularly small and medium enterprises (SMEs). The most important challenge, however, is (vii) gaps in institutional quality.

Ageing population

Although Vietnam is still enjoying a "golden population structure" with the number of working-aged people outnumbering dependents by a ratio of 2:1,[3] the country is undergoing fundamental demographic shifts. On the one hand, Vietnam's average life expectancy has been steadily increasing, reaching 75.8 years in 2015 (see Chapter 1). On the other hand, its fertility rate has been below the replacement level since 2007, making Vietnam one of the largest low-fertility countries in the world.[4]

As a result, there is a risk that Vietnam will grow old before it grows rich. Using population projections by the GSO, the United Nations Population Fund (UNFPA) pointed out that the share of people aged 60 and above in total population has exceeded 10 percent in 2017, signifying Vietnam's formal entry into the ageing phase. In addition, UNFPA has estimated that the proportion of the elderly population aged 60 and above to the child population under 15 years old will exceed 100 percent by 2032.[5] Meanwhile, the Population Division of the United Nations Department of Economic and Social Affairs (UN DESA) has projected that the old age dependency ratio in Vietnam, which stood at 9.6 percent in 2015, will more than triple by 2050 (see Figure 2.6).[6]

A high old dependency ratio means that the labour force has to support a higher number of elderlies. This creates strains on the state budget under the burden of higher public spending on healthcare and pension. Furthermore, an ageing population also indicates slower growth of the labour force, which may contribute to rising labour costs and erode Vietnam's competitiveness in low-cost manufacturing. At the same time, a smaller working-age population also means less domestic resources for productive investments as this group tends to save, while the older population tends to dissave to meet retirement needs. In a recent empirical study on the growth dynamics of ASEAN countries, Greater China economies and sub-national economies in India

---

[3] See Hong (2016).

[4] See UN DESA (2017b).

[5] See UNFPA (2011).

[6] The old dependency ratio reflects the population aged 65 years and above as a percentage of the working-age population between 15 and 64 years old.

Figure 2.6: Vietnam's Old Dependency Ratio and Projections, 1970–2050

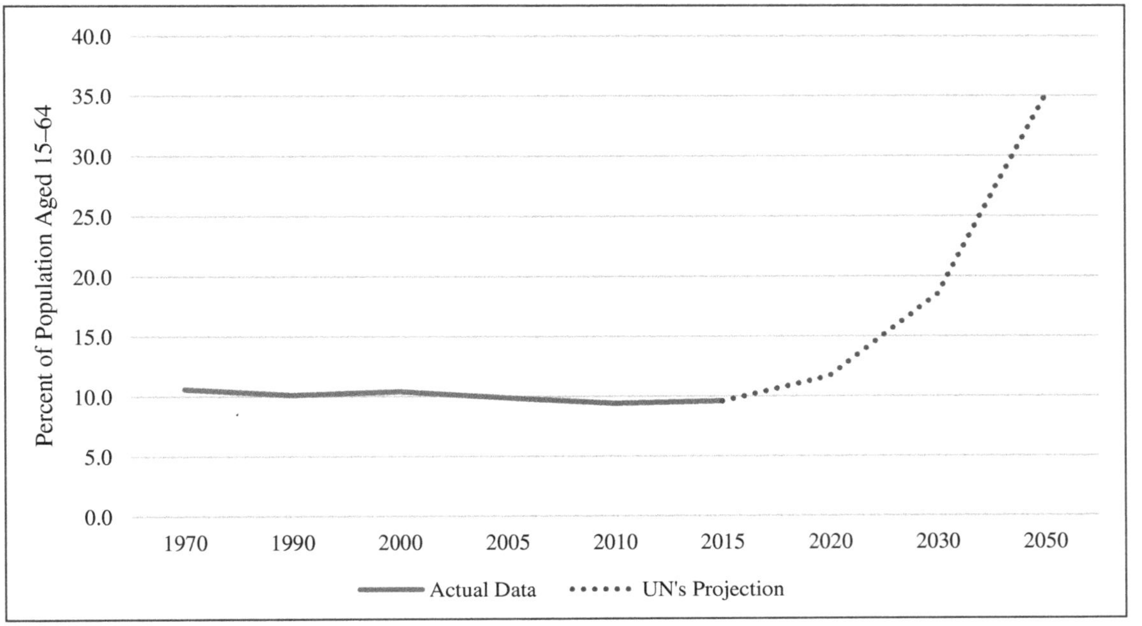

Source: UN DESA (2017a)

and Indonesia by ACI, it was found that lower-middle-income economies with high old dependency ratio are more prone to experiencing growth slowdown.[7]

Technological disruptions

The loss of cost competitiveness due to ageing population may be worsened by potential disruptions arising from rapid advancements in technology which have historically played a great role in altering production processes. The First Industrial Revolution (Industry 1.0) in the late 18th century, which was sparked by the introduction of steam power and mechanisation, significantly reduced the cost and duration of transportation. Meanwhile, the Second Industrial Revolution (Industry 2.0), which came after the introduction of mass production, assembly line and electrical energy in the late 19th century, and greatly altered global patterns of specialisation. In the late 20th century, information and communication technologies (ICT) enabled the production process to be fragmented globally, giving rise to the Third Industrial Revolution (Industry 3.0). Now, the production process is poised to be disrupted once again through the Fourth Industrial Revolution (see Figure 2.7). Widely termed as Industry 4.0, new technologies such as system integration through the Internet of Things, advanced robotics, 3-D printing and data analytics have been touted as innovations that will drive automation and transform industries in the future.

[7] See Tan *et al.* (2017a).

Figure 2.7: Waves of Industrial Revolutions

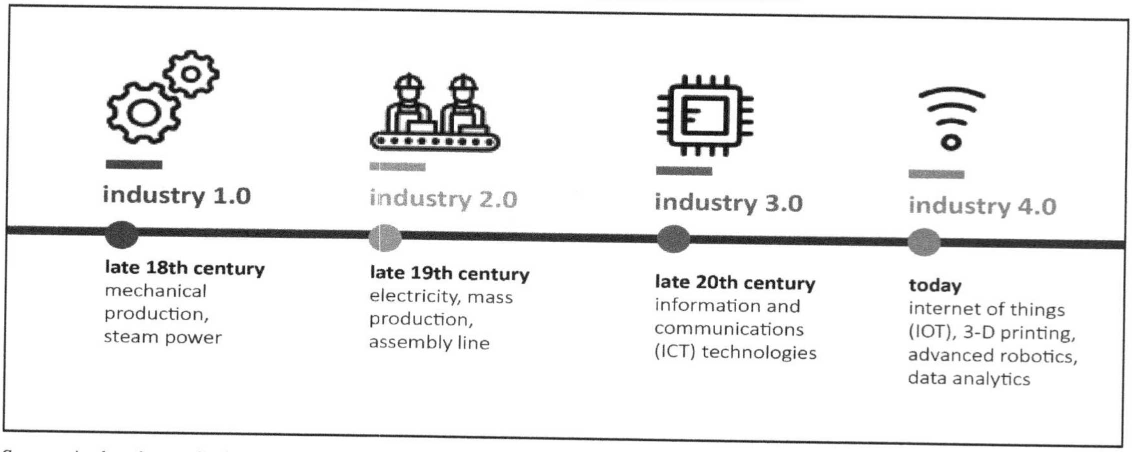

Source: Authors' compilation based on Hallward-Driemeier and Nayyar (2017)

This new wave of technological disruptions may render Vietnam's advantage in low labour cost moot, as additive manufacturing technologies such as 3-D printing are able to replace unskilled, labour-intensive tasks at a much cheaper cost and faster rate. A recent report by the World Bank revealed that 3-D printing has enabled the athletic footwear company Adidas to replace 1,000 low-skilled workers in Vietnam with 160 technicians in Germany and the United States (US).[8] However, if successfully harnessed, technological disruptions, especially in terms of digitalisation, will create new opportunities for Vietnamese firms to find their niche areas, internationalise and scale up quickly. Thus, it is critical that Vietnam engages in constant industrial rejuvenation in which new capacities are developed and new, future-proof growth areas are explored. Whether Industry 4.0 will make or break Vietnam's economic future rests largely on the ability of the economy to achieve industrial upgrading, develop digital capacity for its firms, especially SMEs, and galvanise the workforce for skill upgrading and productivity enhancement.

Sluggish productivity growth

Against this backdrop of the rapidly ageing population and potential disruptions brought about by the Fourth Industrial Revolution, it is worrisome that productivity growth in Vietnam has slowed. As seen in Figure 2.8, real annual growth rate of productivity has generally been on a declining trend over the past 20 years. Despite a slight improvement from 2013 to 2015 following the slowdown that took place between 2005 and 2012, real productivity growth dropped again to 5.0 percent in 2016. According to estimates by the McKinsey Global Institute, Vietnam needs to achieve a breakthrough in raising its productivity growth to at least 6.4 percent annually

[8] See Hallward-Driemeier and Nayyar (2017).

Figure 2.8: Real Annual Growth Rate of Vietnam's Labour Productivity,[9] 1992–2016

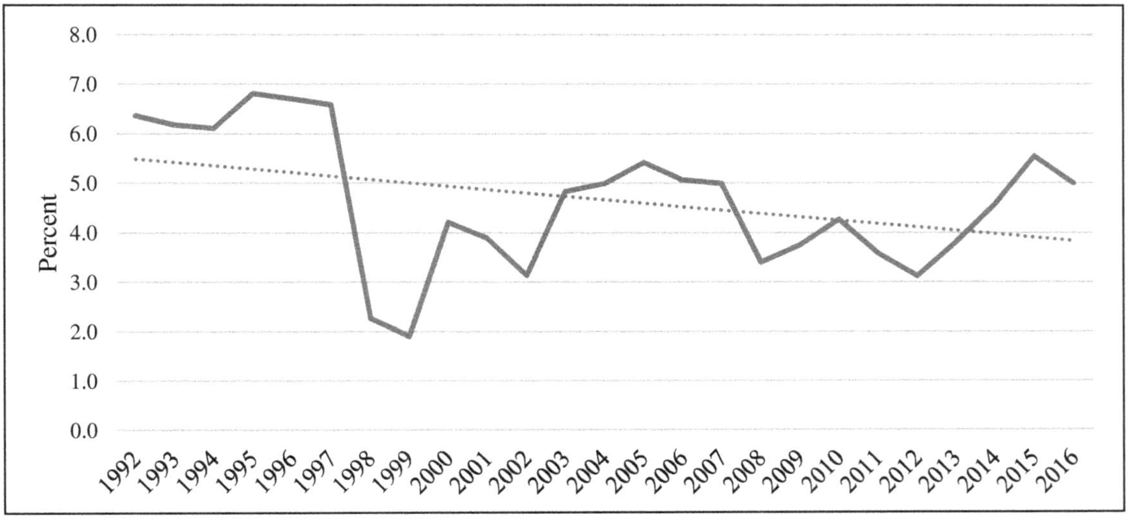

Source: Authors' calculation based on data from World Bank, World Development Indicators

in order to meet the government's target of achieving annual growth of 7–8 percent by 2020.[10] If left unattended, lagging labour growth may put Vietnam at a risk of being caught in a so-called "middle income trap".[11]

Inefficient SOEs

Market distortions which favour large, inefficient SOEs remain widespread. SOEs are historical legacies from the pre-*Doi Moi* era that have come to play a decisive role in the Vietnamese economy even post-reformation despite the gradual transition from a state-dominant to a multi-actor economy.[12] SOEs tend to occupy the majority of land allocated for business activity and are often granted a considerable portion of the new land provided by the government for business rental. Private firms applying for new industrial land are required to go through complex procedures which typically take two to three years and are alleged to involve corruption. Another area where favouritism is salient is access to credit. SOEs are still able to obtain bank loans even when their asset size or profitability do not meet the banks' lending criteria. In terms of market access, while the government usually offers important market opportunities for firms to grow and become competitive through state contracts, eligibility criteria for bidding such contracts are clearly biased towards SOEs. Consequently, the majority of public contracts have been awarded to SOEs.[13]

[9] Labour productivity is calculated as total real values added divided by the total number of workers.

[10] See McKinsey Global Institute (2012).

[11] See Tan *et al.* (2017a).

[12] See Le *et al.* (2014).

[13] See Nguyen and Freeman (2009).

Despite all these advantages, SOEs are incredibly inefficient. Even though they captured 44.5 percent of Vietnam's total investment between 2010 and 2011, they only contributed 36.7 percent to real GDP and 10.4 percent to total employment over the same time period.[14] The ease at which they obtain access to business resources has diminished the SOEs' incentive to improve productivity and engage in industrial upgrading.[15] Moreover, there is a severe lack of transparency and accountability among SOEs.[16] SOE managers tend to invest in non-core, low-hanging fruit business activities which are speculative in nature, since they are more likely to be bailed out by the government in case of failure. Such investment more often than not results in losses, which has led to the eventual failures of some SOEs.[17]

Since 1989, the government has attempted to reduce its stake in SOEs via equitisation and divestment. Equitisation was completed for the first few SOEs in 1992, and the programme halved the number of wholly-state-owned enterprises in Vietnam within the span of 30 years. By 2015, there were only 652 SOEs which remained fully owned by the government.[18]

The equitisation process, however, has been sluggish and cumbersome. The rate at which SOEs are equitised is usually slower than official targets. Most recently in 2017, less than half of the SOEs slated for equitisation completed the process.[19] More importantly, equitisation and divestment have not achieved the primary objective of reducing the government's stake in SOEs. For instance, between 2011 and 2015, 508 SOEs were equitised with the aim of increasing the average shares of ownership by the private sector and strategic investors to 16.7 percent and 15.8 percent, respectively. However, the government's stake in these SOEs still stood at 81 percent, while the private sector and strategic investors ended up holding only 9.5 percent and 7.3 percent, respectively.[20] Moreover, according to a recent study by the Central Institute for Economic Management, the government also faces major challenges in terms of attracting strategic investors in addition to the long, inflexible, complicated equitisation process. Regarding SOEs, restrictive upper limits on stakes held by foreign investors, unreasonable valuation of SOEs and stock pricing, SOEs' general unattractiveness as an investment, lack of transparency, are the most salient problems.[21]

Low agricultural productivity

Vietnam's productivity growth slowdown can also be attributed in part to weak labour productivity growth in the agriculture sector. Although agriculture is no longer the biggest contributor to Vietnam's GDP, the sector still employs the most number of workers. Figure 2.9 plots the sectoral shares in total employment between 1996 and 2017. Despite the overall declining trend, agricultural share of employment still stood at around 44 percent, higher than both employment in the industrial (22.3 percent) and service (33.7 percent) sectors.

---

[14] See Le *et al.* (2014).

[15] See Taussig *et al.* (2016).

[16] See Le (2017).

[17] See Beresford and Tran (2004) and Taussig *et al.* (2016).

[18] See Government of Vietnam (2016, 4).

[19] See *VTV News* (2017).

[20] See Thời Báo Tài Chính (2017).

[21] *Ibid.*

Figure 2.9: Vietnam's Share of Employment by Sector, 1996–2015

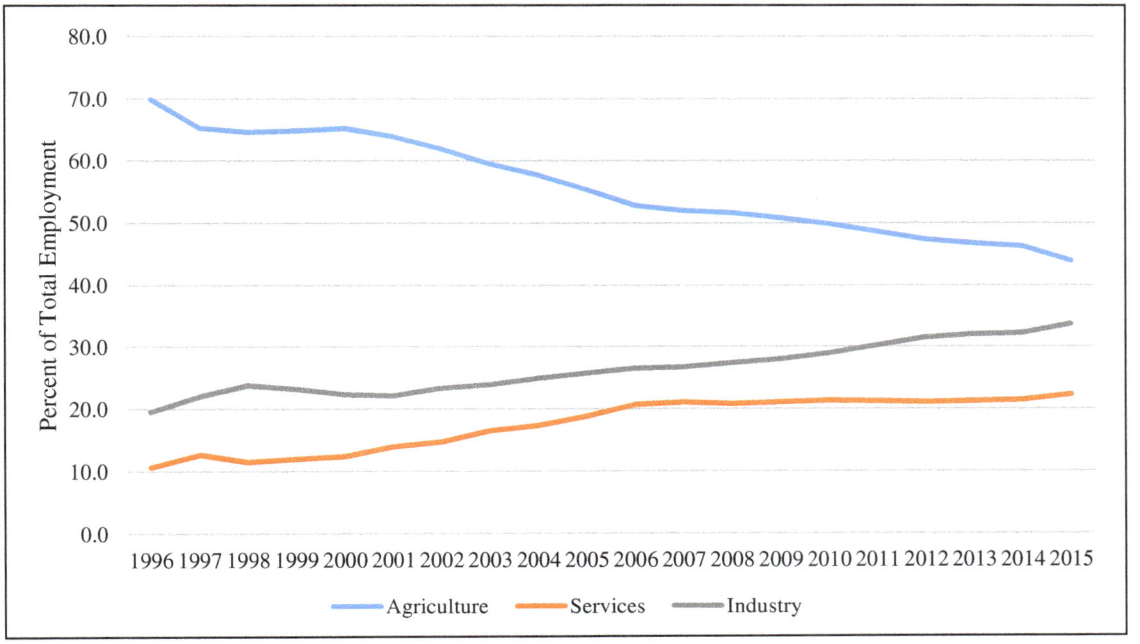

Source: World Bank, World Development Indicators

Vietnam's agricultural growth, which has largely been based on expansion of irrigation and physical inputs, has seen signs of slowdown, falling from over four percent annually in the late 1990s to below four percent in 2006–2007.[22] Land fragmentation, outdated technology, weak supply chains and unregulated quality have eroded the sector's competitiveness. While liberalisation of the sector has taken place, SOEs remain the dominant actor in both agricultural input and output markets, imposing barriers to growth as well as breeding mismanagement. According to ACI's estimates, Total Factor Productivity in the agriculture sector has grown by only 0.5 percent p.a. between 2000 and 2011, as compared to the ASEAN's average of 1.4 percent p.a.[23]

Lack of synergies between FDI firms and local enterprises for moving up the value chain

Since opening up the economy, Vietnam has been actively participating in regional and global value chains (GVCs). The GVC is a phenomenon in which the production of goods and services is no longer contained within a single economy. Rather, production processes are now fragmented across different geographical boundaries. A typical economy in the GVC would use imported content as intermediate inputs to produce its own goods and services, which may in turn be re-exported to other economies. Depending on the extent of its participation and the task

[22] See Coxhead *et al.* (2010).

[23] See Section 3.6.3 in Chapter 3 for more details.

Figure 2.10: Positions in the GVC

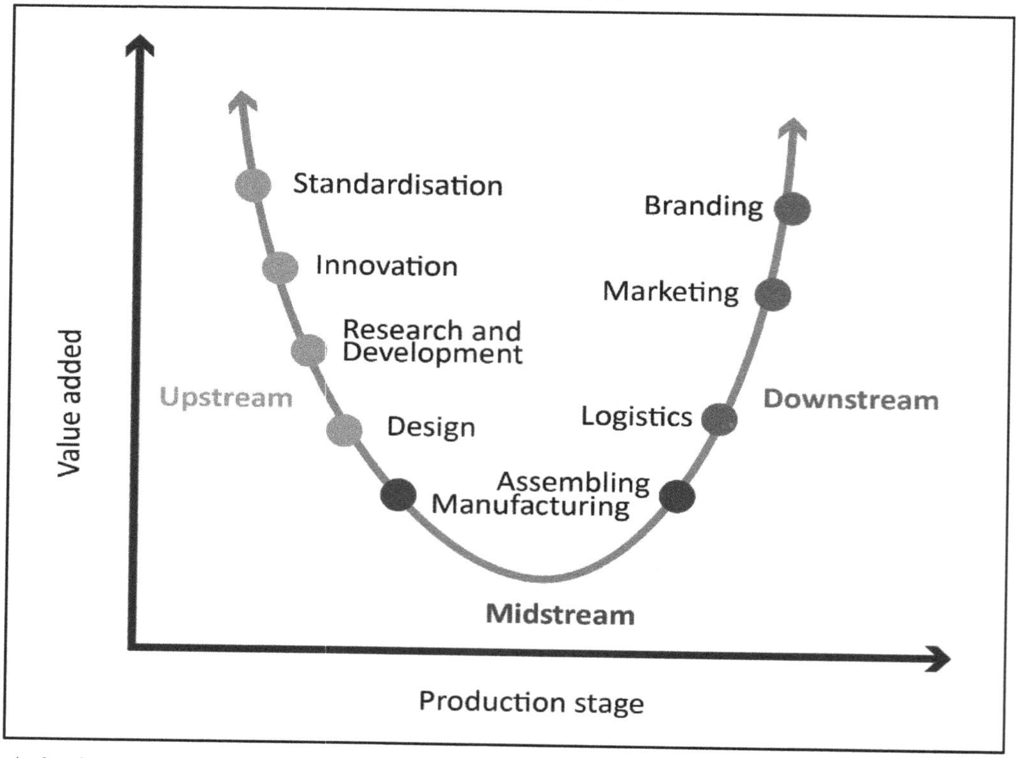

Source: Authors' compilation based on World Economic Forum (2012)

it specialises in, an economy may be thought of as being located upstream, midstream or downstream in the GVC (see Figure 2.10).

Vietnam's role in the supply chain is primarily focused on assembling, placing it in a midstream position in the GVC. The country imports the most important parts of the necessary inputs, such as engines and gearboxes, instead of producing them on its own. As a result, local content makes up a small proportion of Vietnam's exports. A recent report by the World Bank revealed that Vietnam's use of domestic supply currently only stands at around 10–20 percent. Furthermore, they are limited to simple, labour-intensive products such as manufacturing car seats. This number is very low when set against its fellow ASEAN members. For instance, the local content used in Thailand is more than double that of Vietnam at 45 percent.[24] In other words, Vietnam has not developed the necessary support industries to complete more sophisticated tasks. This will hinder its ability to move up the value chains and capture a higher share of value-added content.

The problem is caused in part by a lack of synergies between the FDI sector and the local sector. Vietnam has one of the lowest rates of technology transfer from FDI firms in the world. According to the 2017–2018 World Economic Forum (WEF) Global Competitiveness Index (GCI), Vietnam ranked 89th out of 137 economies for the indicator for FDI and technology

[24] See World Bank (2017).

transfer.[25] In comparison, Singapore topped the ranking among ASEAN countries in this indicator at 2nd, followed by Malaysia (13th), Thailand (40th), and Indonesia (44th). Even Cambodia and Laos, which are less competitive than Vietnam, ranked above Vietnam at 54th and 88th, respectively. In fact, Brunei was the only ASEAN economy that ranked lower than Vietnam at 103rd.[26] Even in previous years, Vietnam has performed poorly in this indicator, with the worst ever performance at 103rd in 2013. These observations signal the country's chronically weak linkages between FDI businesses and local firms.

Gaps in institutional quality as the fundamental challenge to development

Ideally, a high-quality institution's role is to provide public security, balance the needs of the society and the private sector through appropriate regulations, enforce the rule of law, and foster public support for government's policies. These are the prerequisites for successful development. Furthermore, state effectiveness, or the ability of the government to achieve its policy objectives, is crucial for implementing the necessary reforms to address economic weaknesses and resolve adminstrative bottlenecks to growth.

Vietnam's existing institutional structure has facilitated three decades of growth and development. However, it has grown increasingly unable to cope with the demands for further reform as Vietnam progresses. In a sense, the current economic malaises, especially the perpetuation of a bloated, inefficient state sector in the economy, can be traced to weak institutional quality. The overreach of the state in commercial activities through SOEs has created powerful incentives for public officials to exploit their roles as market regulators, law enforcers and allocators of property rights to gain benefits for themselves and members of their networks at the expense of economic efficiency. Indeed, corruption has been identified by the Vietnamese Communist Party as a fundamental problem which needs to be addressed. At the same time, the state also suffers from lack of coordination between ministries, government agencies and especially between the central and local governments. This has created gridlocks and hampered efforts at deeper socio-economic reforms.

As pointed out by the World Bank, the aforementioned problems can be gleaned from the application of the law.[27] Despite Vietnam's effort to establish a sound legal framework for the market economy, particularly in strengthening property rights, major issues persist. The allocation and enforcement of land-use rights is a particularly problematic area. Since local governments mostly depend on land sale proceeds as a major source of revenue, they tend to exploit their power to expropriate land and control prices. As a result, disagreements and complaints over compensation amounts for expropriated lands are prevalent.

Having evaluated Vietnam's current growth model according to its seven most pertinent challenges, we shall turn to benchmarking Vietnam's competitiveness against its ASEAN peers

---

[25] See http://reports.weforum.org/global-competitiveness-index-2017-2018/competitiveness-rankings/#series=EOSQ070 (accessed on 16 January 2017).

[26] The WEF did not cover Myanmar under this indicator. The Philippines' ranking for this indicator in the 2017–2018 GCI was 63rd out of 137 economies.

[27] World Bank and Ministry of Planning and Investment (2016).

in the next section. This exercise serves to make the issues discussed more salient, while also helping to shed light on additional insights.

2.3 Vietnam's Economic Competitiveness *vis-à-vis* Other ASEAN Countries

The notion of regional or *in situ* competitiveness has been explored in various ways. Initially, in the 1980s, "competitiveness" was considered as part of the private sector domain, especially in relation to firm performance.[28] Over time, the discourse expanded onto the domain of macroeconomics, as shown by the establishment of "Council on Competitiveness" or similar institutions in various advanced industrialised countries. Some scholars acknowledge that it is primarily firms that compete, not nations, regions, or places.[29] However, the performance of those firms depends on various factors that are embedded in the firm's location. These include quality of labour and infrastructure, governance, costs of doing business, as well as the performance of competing and complementary firms around the area.[30]

A commonly cited cross-country competitiveness study is the WEF's GCI. The 2017–2018 edition of the GCI has ranked Vietnam 55th out of 137 economies in terms of overall competitiveness. Unlike other existing global competitiveness rankings, ACI's framework centres upon ASEAN with its own distinct characteristics. Our methodology thus represents a customised approach to evaluating and improving national competitiveness — rather than a one-size-fits-all solution — for a region as diverse as ASEAN.

2.3.1 ACI's Competitiveness Framework and Methodology

ACI adopts a holistic and comprehensive approach to defining competitiveness, taking into account various factors deemed to have an effect on an economy's ability to achieve high and inclusive economic development over a sustained period of time.[31] As seen in Figure 2.11, this is achieved through the creation of an index comprising four environments that together define economic competitiveness: (i) Macroeconomic Stability (MS), (ii) Government and Institutional Setting (GIS), (iii) Financial, Businesses and Manpower Conditions (FBMC) and (iv) Quality of Life and Infrastructure Development (QLID). The first two environments largely pertain to economic performance, while the last two environments capture the institutional and social conditions of the country.

In calculating the overall competitiveness score, each of the environments carries an equal weightage of 25 percent. Each environment can be further disaggregated into three sub-environments in a nested approach, each with the same equal weightage of 33.3 percent (see Figure 2.11). The allocation of equal weightage to the environments and sub-environments

---

[28] See Porter (1980).

[29] See Krugman (1994).

[30] See Camagni (2002), Kitson *et al.* (2004) and Bristow (2010).

[31] See Tan *et al.* (2017b).

Figure 2.11: ACI's Competitiveness Framework

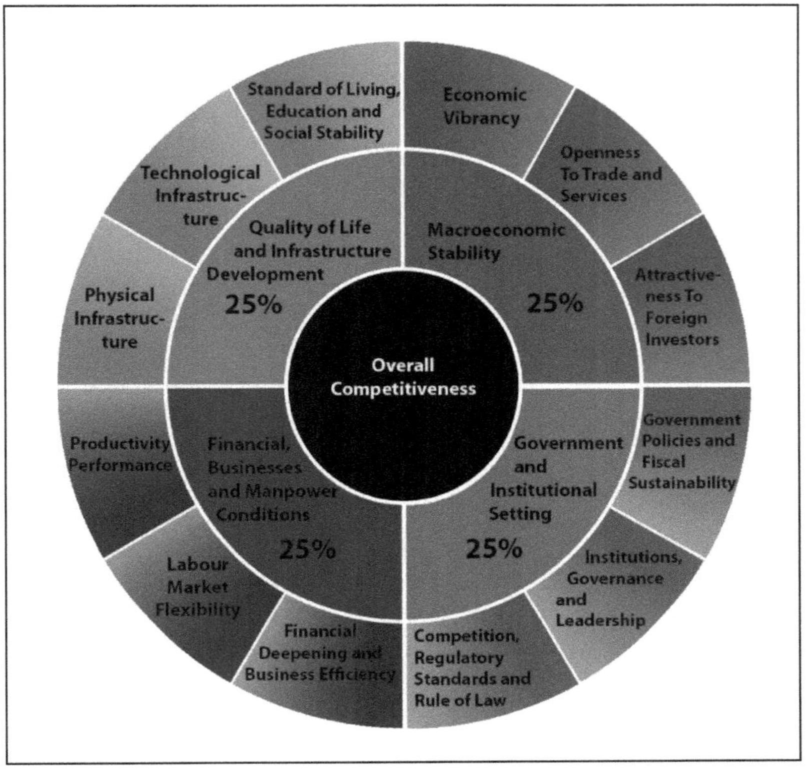

Source: Tan *et al.* (2017b)

of competitiveness reflects our view that unequal weightage allocation is often done arbitrarily. As such, we adopt an equal weightage method in order to achieve a more balanced competitiveness framework.

As a robustness check to this equal weightage approach, we have come up with the Shapley methodology: a mathematical bottom-up approach in which the weight of each indicator, sub-environment and environment is automatically determined by the distribution of these values instead of being predetermined arbitrarily. In the Shapley method, the more unequal the distribution of values, the higher the weightage automatically assigned to that particular factor, as that it would have more impact on an economy's competitiveness. When we compare the weightage distribution of the four environments using the latest data, we can observe that the weightage distribution from the Shapley method is highly similar to that of the ACI equal weightage method, implying that our current ACI framework is robust (see Figure 2.12). Moreover, results generated under the Shapley method are qualitatively similar to the results presented in the subsequent Sections 2.3.1 and 2.3.2. Details on the Shapley weightage methodology are reported in Appendix 3.

121 indicators are used in the study of competitiveness of ASEAN-10 economies. These indicators come from a myriad of sources, ranging from the Asian Development Bank (ADB) to

Figure 2.12: Comparisons between the Equal Weightage Methodology and the Shapley Weightage Methodology

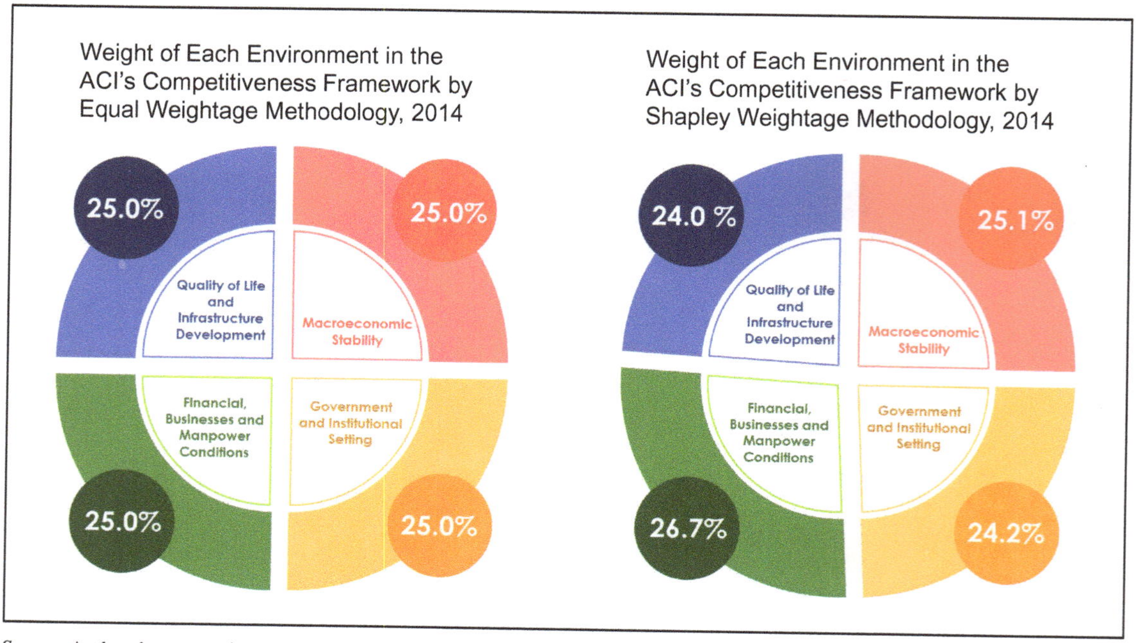

Source: Authors' computation

the Cingranelli–Richards Human Rights Database. The extensiveness of the indicators used in ACI's framework ensures that we have a holistic and vigorous interpretation of each sub-environment and environment of competitiveness. A full list of the indicators can be found in Appendix 1.

We aggregate all the indicators to their respective sub-environments and environments through the statistical approach of 'standardised score'. This method is adopted because of the heterogeneity of the indicators used in our framework, with units of measurement that are wide-ranging in scale and magnitude. The standardised score allows us to make a relative comparison of the performance of a certain economy *vis-à-vis* the sample average. Because this approach measures the relative performance of economies, it renders the units of measurement irrelevant.

In statistical terms, the standardised scores measure how many standard deviations away each economy is from the sample average. If the standardised score for an indicator is zero, it can be interpreted that the economy is an average performer of that particular indicator. On the other hand, a positive standardised score suggests an above-average performance, while a negative score suggests a performance that is below the average. The further away the score is from zero, the further away is the performance of said economy from the ASEAN-10 average.

The standardised scores of each of the indicators are aggregated into their respective sub-environments, which in turn are further aggregated to the four environments following the framework in Figure 2.11. The performance of each ASEAN economy can thus be evaluated across various levels, from overall competitiveness down to each indicator. Details of the algorithm to compute the overall competitiveness index are reported in Appendix 2.

Moreover, another notable feature of ACI's methodology is the *What-if* simulation. A competitiveness ranking in itself is like a beauty contest; it merely identifies who are doing well and who are facing challenges but stops short of giving more constructive advice on improving the rankings. The ACI index goes one step further by tackling the 'so what?' question. What is the policy implication of a competitiveness ranking result for a particular economy? The data used in the ACI index allows us to do an in-depth analysis of the performance of each economy according to the different indicators, sub-environments, and environments. By analysing said data, we are able to identify not just the Overall Competitiveness ranking, but also specific indicators for which the economy is doing well or struggling.

Thus, the ACI conducts a *What-if* competitiveness simulation that is based on an improvement of each economy's top 20 percent weakest indicators,[32] and a recalculation of the standardised score based on such improvements. To do this, we first looked at each economy and sorted the different indicators for each economy from the highest to the lowest score. This allows us to identify the weakest indicators for each economy. Next, we raise the scores of these weakest indicators moderately to match the average score. This means their average score is raised to zero if it has been negative previously. For the dimensions which were already competitive, we leave them unchanged. Once these scores are raised, we recalculate the ranking, assuming that other economies stay constant. Each economy would then have a new, improved standardised score. This allows us to answer the question: if a particular economy improves on its set of weakest indicators while also assuming that other economies remain constant, how will that economy's competitiveness ranking improve?

2.3.2 The 2017 Annual Competitiveness Ranking of ASEAN-10 Countries

In this section, we present the results of the annual ASEAN-10 competitiveness ranking conducted in 2017, focusing on Vietnam. The data used for this exercise spans the period of 2000 until 2014.

For overall competitiveness, the top two-ranked economies have remained consistent for 14 years, with Singapore coming first followed by Malaysia (see Figure 2.13). Thailand's and Brunei's positions used to be stable at third and fourth, respectively, until the latter overtook the former and their rankings in 2014. Meanwhile, Indonesia, has also remained at the fifth position, although its standardised score saw an improvement from –0.1154 in 2000 to 0.0412 in 2014. This means over the study period, Indonesia managed to raise its economic competitiveness to above the regional average.

Vietnam, however, has generally not caught up with these economies. Although it briefly took over Philippines to rank sixth in 2008, 2009 and 2010, it has slipped to the seventh position again thereafter. Moreover, Vietnam's standardised score has consistently remained negative

---

[32] In a list of 121 indicators, the weakest are listed at the bottom and the top 20 percent strongest are listed at the top.

Figure 2.13: Competitiveness Scores and Rankings of ASEAN-10 by Equal Weightage Methodology, 2000–2014

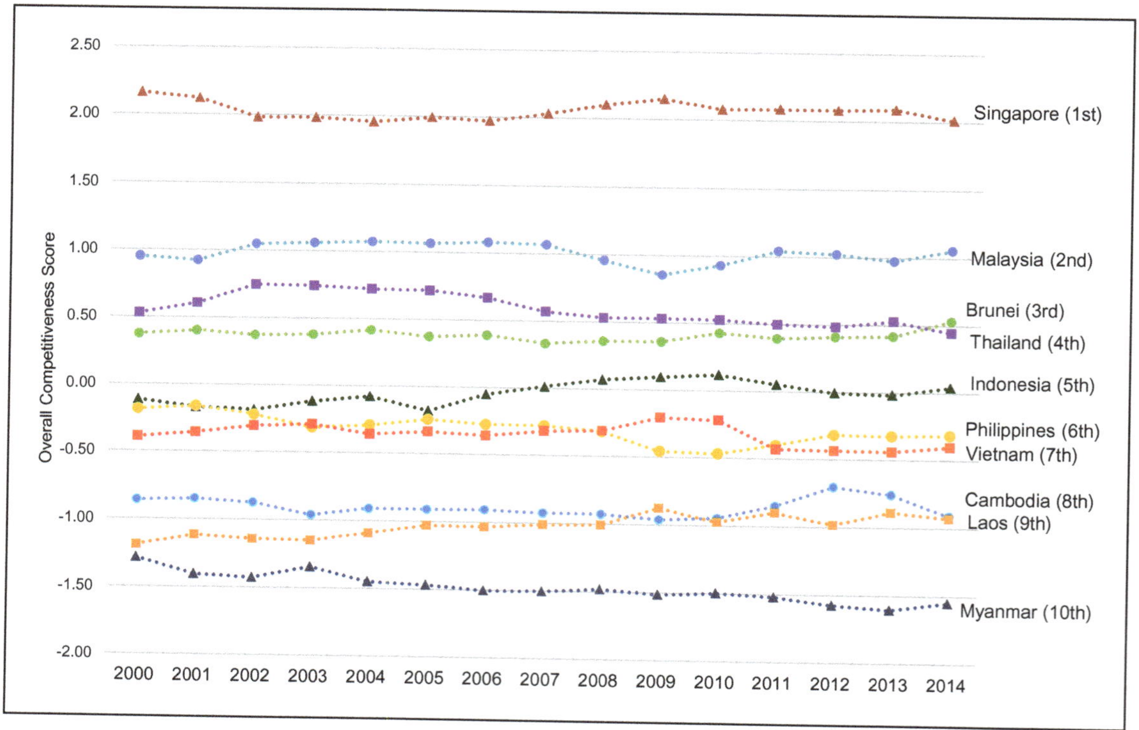

Source: Tan *et al.* (2017b)

throughout the study period, with little improvements since 2011 despite a slight pick-up in 2014. This suggests that Vietnam has always performed below the regional average and is finding it difficult to catch up with the ASEAN-6 economies.

Meanwhile, Cambodia and Laos have been engaging in a neck-to-neck competition for the eighth and ninth positions. Myanmar has consistently been rooted to the bottom of the ranking throughout the 2000–2014 period with deteriorating standardised score. This signifies the magnitude of the challenges faced by the fledging democratic government in achieving development and lifting the people's living standards.

Tables 2.2–2.5 display the ASEAN-10's performances in terms of each environment in ACI's competitiveness framework over the study period. In terms of the four environments, Vietnam has also largely occupied either the sixth or seventh position. Interestingly, the Financial, Businesses and Manpower Conditions used to be one of the more promising environments for Vietnam; it broke into the top-half of the ranking on multiple occasions between 2003 and 2010 with a standardised score above zero. However, Vietnam's competitiveness in this environment had also deteriorated since 2011, with a standardised score of –0.4763 in 2014.

Table 2.2: Macroeconomic Stability Rankings and Standardised Scores, 2000–2014

MACROECONOMIC STABILITY										
	1		2		3		4		5	
Rank	**Economy**	**Score**	**Economy**	**Score**	**Economy**	**Score**	**Economy**	**Score**	**Economy**	**Score**
2000	Singapore	2.1846	Malaysia	0.8498	Thailand	0.6423	Indonesia	0.3645	Brunei	−0.1940
2001	Singapore	2.0775	Malaysia	0.8187	Thailand	0.6765	Indonesia	0.3119	Brunei	0.0289
2002	Singapore	1.9981	Malaysia	0.8583	Thailand	0.7194	Indonesia	0.4046	Brunei	−0.0088
2003	Singapore	2.1469	Malaysia	0.8096	Thailand	0.6324	Indonesia	0.5578	Brunei	−0.1227
2004	Singapore	2.1565	Malaysia	0.8119	Thailand	0.7392	Indonesia	0.4439	Brunei	−0.1678
2005	Singapore	2.1525	Malaysia	0.8500	Thailand	0.7088	Indonesia	0.3852	Brunei	−0.1144
2006	Singapore	2.1087	Malaysia	0.8244	Thailand	0.7035	Indonesia	0.5099	Brunei	−0.1137
2007	Singapore	2.1002	Malaysia	0.8765	Thailand	0.6963	Indonesia	0.5527	Philippines	−0.2618
2008	Singapore	2.0978	Malaysia	0.7631	Indonesia	0.7401	Thailand	0.6948	Brunei	−0.1861
2009	Singapore	2.1904	Indonesia	0.7242	Thailand	0.7021	Malaysia	0.6173	Brunei	−0.1518
2010	Singapore	2.2118	Malaysia	0.6677	Indonesia	0.6528	Thailand	0.5624	Brunei	0.0404
2011	Singapore	2.2279	Malaysia	0.7262	Indonesia	0.6879	Thailand	0.4381	Brunei	0.0618
2012	Singapore	2.1837	Malaysia	0.6854	Thailand	0.6128	Indonesia	0.5869	Brunei	0.0683
2013	Singapore	2.2628	Thailand	0.6861	Malaysia	0.6019	Indonesia	0.4328	Brunei	0.0164
2014	Singapore	2.1709	Thailand	0.7317	Malaysia	0.6255	Indonesia	0.3968	Brunei	0.2478
	6		7		8		9		10	
Rank	**Economy**	**Score**	**Economy**	**Score**	**Economy**	**Score**	**Economy**	**Score**	**Economy**	**Score**
2000	Philippines	−0.3168	Vietnam	−0.4087	Cambodia	−0.5220	Myanmar	−1.2605	Laos	−1.3393
2001	Vietnam	−0.2531	Philippines	−0.3782	Cambodia	−0.5041	Laos	−1.1269	Myanmar	−1.6513
2002	Vietnam	−0.2814	Philippines	−0.2855	Cambodia	−0.6154	Laos	−1.1121	Myanmar	−1.6773
2003	Vietnam	−0.3652	Philippines	−0.4320	Cambodia	−0.6946	Laos	−1.2426	Myanmar	−1.2896
2004	Philippines	−0.3913	Vietnam	−0.5231	Cambodia	−0.5870	Laos	−1.0586	Myanmar	−1.4236
2005	Philippines	−0.4555	Vietnam	−0.4861	Cambodia	−0.5934	Laos	−0.9150	Myanmar	−1.5321
2006	Philippines	−0.3636	Vietnam	−0.5327	Cambodia	−0.6962	Laos	−0.8826	Myanmar	−1.5577
2007	Brunei	−0.2887	Vietnam	−0.5234	Cambodia	−0.7982	Laos	−0.8623	Myanmar	−1.4913
2008	Philippines	−0.4392	Vietnam	−0.5435	Cambodia	−0.7938	Laos	−0.9309	Myanmar	−1.4024
2009	Vietnam	−0.4429	Philippines	−0.6829	Laos	−0.7673	Cambodia	−0.8363	Myanmar	−1.3528
2010	Vietnam	−0.4667	Philippines	−0.5249	Cambodia	−0.8153	Laos	−1.0066	Myanmar	−1.3217
2011	Philippines	−0.4943	Vietnam	−0.6635	Cambodia	−0.7458	Laos	−0.9025	Myanmar	−1.3359
2012	Philippines	−0.3842	Vietnam	−0.5851	Cambodia	−0.7721	Laos	−0.9963	Myanmar	−1.3994
2013	Vietnam	−0.4568	Philippines	−0.5647	Cambodia	−0.6464	Laos	−0.8541	Myanmar	−1.4780
2014	Vietnam	−0.4130	Philippines	−0.5150	Cambodia	−0.8807	Laos	−0.9205	Myanmar	−1.4433

Source: Tan *et al*. (2017b)

Table 2.3: Government and Institutional Setting Rankings and Standardised Scores, 2000–2014

GOVERNMENT AND INSTITUTIONAL SETTING										
	1		2		3		4		5	
Rank	Economy	Score	Economy	Score	Economy	Score	Economy	Score	Economy	Score
2000	Singapore	2.2937	Malaysia	0.7786	Thailand	0.5409	Brunei	0.4489	Philippines	−0.0852
2001	Singapore	2.2819	Malaysia	0.7781	Thailand	0.5476	Brunei	0.3870	Philippines	−0.0453
2002	Singapore	2.1754	Malaysia	0.9528	Thailand	0.6567	Brunei	0.2602	Philippines	−0.1370
2003	Singapore	2.1470	Malaysia	0.9180	Thailand	0.8302	Brunei	0.2487	Vietnam	−0.1745
2004	Singapore	2.0646	Malaysia	1.0267	Thailand	0.7027	Brunei	0.4226	Philippines	−0.2498
2005	Singapore	2.0475	Malaysia	1.0893	Thailand	0.6890	Brunei	0.4037	Philippines	−0.1794
2006	Singapore	2.1149	Malaysia	0.9818	Thailand	0.6208	Brunei	0.4364	Philippines	−0.2331
2007	Singapore	2.1935	Malaysia	0.9685	Thailand	0.5390	Brunei	0.4345	Philippines	−0.2245
2008	Singapore	2.3680	Malaysia	0.7715	Thailand	0.4567	Brunei	0.4400	Vietnam	−0.2976
2009	Singapore	2.4651	Malaysia	0.5640	Thailand	0.4444	Brunei	0.4057	Indonesia	−0.2248
2010	Singapore	2.3205	Malaysia	0.7618	Brunei	0.5035	Thailand	0.4125	Indonesia	−0.1437
2011	Singapore	2.2518	Malaysia	0.9586	Brunei	0.5349	Thailand	0.3902	Indonesia	−0.3295
2012	Singapore	2.2843	Malaysia	0.9430	Brunei	0.4711	Thailand	0.2583	Philippines	−0.1923
2013	Singapore	2.2463	Malaysia	0.9417	Brunei	0.5178	Thailand	0.3499	Philippines	−0.1692
2014	Singapore	2.2851	Malaysia	1.0322	Brunei	0.4421	Thailand	0.1916	Philippines	−0.1345
	6		7		8		9		10	
Rank	Economy	Score	Economy	Score	Economy	Score	Economy	Score	Economy	Score
2000	Vietnam	−0.3486	Indonesia	−0.5787	Cambodia	−0.7935	Laos	−1.1262	Myanmar	−1.1300
2001	Vietnam	−0.2904	Indonesia	−0.5197	Cambodia	−0.8326	Laos	−1.0360	Myanmar	−1.2707
2002	Vietnam	−0.2176	Indonesia	−0.4675	Cambodia	−0.8424	Laos	−1.0618	Myanmar	−1.3188
2003	Philippines	−0.3251	Indonesia	−0.4147	Laos	−0.9875	Myanmar	−1.1182	Cambodia	−1.1238
2004	Vietnam	−0.2644	Indonesia	−0.4217	Laos	−0.9308	Cambodia	−0.9839	Myanmar	−1.3661
2005	Vietnam	−0.2849	Indonesia	−0.5316	Cambodia	−0.9385	Laos	−0.9565	Myanmar	−1.3386
2006	Indonesia	−0.2519	Vietnam	−0.3892	Laos	−0.9224	Cambodia	−0.9674	Myanmar	−1.3899
2007	Indonesia	−0.3602	Vietnam	−0.3925	Laos	−0.8848	Cambodia	−0.9496	Myanmar	−1.3239
2008	Philippines	−0.3246	Indonesia	−0.4261	Laos	−0.8640	Cambodia	−0.9674	Myanmar	−1.1564
2009	Vietnam	−0.2798	Philippines	−0.4877	Laos	−0.7624	Cambodia	−0.9228	Myanmar	−1.2016
2010	Vietnam	−0.3166	Philippines	−0.4025	Laos	−0.9295	Cambodia	−0.9779	Myanmar	−1.2282
2011	Philippines	−0.3429	Vietnam	−0.4744	Cambodia	−0.8101	Laos	−0.8756	Myanmar	−1.3031
2012	Vietnam	−0.3756	Indonesia	−0.4119	Cambodia	−0.7466	Laos	−0.7899	Myanmar	−1.4405
2013	Indonesia	−0.4125	Vietnam	−0.4429	Laos	−0.7919	Cambodia	−0.8484	Myanmar	−1.3909
2014	Indonesia	−0.3317	Vietnam	−0.4344	Laos	−0.8673	Cambodia	−0.9715	Myanmar	−1.2116

Source: Tan *et al.* (2017b)

Table 2.4: Financial, Businesses and Manpower Conditions Rankings and Standardised Scores, 2000–2014

FINANCIAL, BUSINESSES AND MANPOWER CONDITIONS										
	1		2		3		4		5	
Rank	**Economy**	**Score**	**Economy**	**Score**	**Economy**	**Score**	**Economy**	**Score**	**Economy**	**Score**
2000	Singapore	1.8846	Malaysia	1.2700	Thailand	0.5267	Brunei	0.2646	Indonesia	−0.0210
2001	Singapore	1.9099	Malaysia	1.1592	Thailand	0.6945	Brunei	0.2699	Philippines	−0.0701
2002	Singapore	1.5633	Malaysia	1.4114	Thailand	0.9515	Brunei	0.3136	Vietnam	−0.1486
2003	Singapore	1.4880	Malaysia	1.4645	Thailand	0.8605	Brunei	0.4510	Vietnam	−0.0372
2004	Singapore	1.4765	Malaysia	1.4563	Thailand	0.8159	Brunei	0.4308	Indonesia	−0.0538
2005	Singapore	1.6562	Malaysia	1.2916	Thailand	0.8575	Brunei	0.2729	Vietnam	−0.0121
2006	Singapore	1.6281	Malaysia	1.4368	Thailand	0.7533	Brunei	0.3487	Vietnam	−0.1020
2007	Singapore	1.6275	Malaysia	1.4856	Thailand	0.5231	Brunei	0.3527	Indonesia	0.0364
2008	Singapore	1.7300	Malaysia	1.3656	Thailand	0.5240	Brunei	0.2364	Indonesia	0.1160
2009	Singapore	1.6908	Malaysia	1.3606	Thailand	0.5571	Brunei	0.2543	Vietnam	0.0946
2010	Singapore	1.5765	Malaysia	1.4394	Thailand	0.6897	Brunei	0.2934	Vietnam	0.0670
2011	Singapore	1.6336	Malaysia	1.5208	Thailand	0.7637	Brunei	0.1008	Indonesia	0.0579
2012	Singapore	1.6487	Malaysia	1.5194	Thailand	0.7009	Brunei	0.2392	Indonesia	0.0153
2013	Singapore	1.5693	Malaysia	1.4985	Thailand	0.7453	Brunei	0.2932	Indonesia	0.1363
2014	Malaysia	1.6723	Singapore	1.3232	Thailand	0.5671	Brunei	0.5261	Indonesia	0.2875

	6		7		8		9		10	
Rank	**Economy**	**Score**	**Economy**	**Score**	**Economy**	**Score**	**Economy**	**Score**	**Economy**	**Score**
2000	Vietnam	−0.1256	Philippines	−0.1602	Laos	−1.0766	Cambodia	−1.2395	Myanmar	−1.3232
2001	Indonesia	−0.1332	Vietnam	−0.2082	Laos	−1.1108	Cambodia	−1.2396	Myanmar	−1.2716
2002	Philippines	−0.2044	Indonesia	−0.2393	Laos	−1.1822	Cambodia	−1.1956	Myanmar	−1.2698
2003	Indonesia	−0.2712	Philippines	−0.2946	Cambodia	−1.1097	Laos	−1.1184	Myanmar	−1.4329
2004	Vietnam	−0.0710	Philippines	−0.3023	Cambodia	−1.1210	Laos	−1.1943	Myanmar	−1.4371
2005	Philippines	−0.0593	Indonesia	−0.2808	Laos	−1.1101	Cambodia	−1.1611	Myanmar	−1.4548
2006	Indonesia	−0.2168	Philippines	−0.2258	Cambodia	−0.9822	Laos	−1.1822	Myanmar	−1.4578
2007	Vietnam	−0.0207	Philippines	−0.3451	Cambodia	−0.9695	Laos	−1.1612	Myanmar	−1.5287
2008	Vietnam	−0.0560	Philippines	−0.2601	Cambodia	−0.9273	Laos	−1.0946	Myanmar	−1.6339
2009	Indonesia	0.0647	Philippines	−0.3845	Laos	−0.9285	Cambodia	−1.0215	Myanmar	−1.6877
2010	Indonesia	0.0625	Philippines	−0.5980	Laos	−0.9006	Cambodia	−0.9646	Myanmar	−1.6654
2011	Vietnam	−0.2562	Philippines	−0.3687	Cambodia	−0.9359	Laos	−0.9584	Myanmar	−1.5575
2012	Philippines	−0.4246	Vietnam	−0.4260	Cambodia	−0.6165	Laos	−1.0506	Myanmar	−1.6059
2013	Philippines	−0.3491	Vietnam	−0.5127	Cambodia	−0.7198	Laos	−1.0235	Myanmar	−1.6376
2014	Philippines	−0.4753	Vietnam	−0.4763	Cambodia	−0.8090	Laos	−0.9586	Myanmar	−1.6569

Source: Tan *et al.* (2017b)

Table 2.5: Quality of Life and Infrastructure Development Rankings and Standardised Scores, 2000–2014

QUALITY OF LIFE AND INFRASTRUCTURE DEVELOPMENT										
	1		2		3		4		5	
Rank	Economy	Score	Economy	Score	Economy	Score	Economy	Score	Economy	Score
2000	Singapore	2.0777	Brunei	0.9353	Malaysia	0.8222	Thailand	0.3637	Philippines	–0.1579
2001	Singapore	2.0516	Brunei	0.8877	Malaysia	0.8693	Thailand	0.4612	Philippines	–0.1399
2002	Singapore	2.0129	Brunei	0.8840	Malaysia	0.8788	Thailand	0.5955	Philippines	–0.2349
2003	Singapore	1.9430	Malaysia	0.9324	Brunei	0.8956	Thailand	0.5664	Philippines	–0.1647
2004	Singapore	1.9374	Brunei	0.9364	Malaysia	0.8955	Thailand	0.5618	Philippines	–0.1949
2005	Singapore	1.9547	Malaysia	0.9385	Brunei	0.8949	Thailand	0.5528	Philippines	–0.2539
2006	Singapore	1.8983	Malaysia	0.9941	Brunei	0.8552	Thailand	0.5481	Indonesia	–0.2375
2007	Singapore	2.0227	Malaysia	0.8425	Brunei	0.8062	Thailand	0.4781	Indonesia	–0.1765
2008	Singapore	1.9860	Brunei	0.9001	Malaysia	0.8286	Thailand	0.3966	Indonesia	–0.1505
2009	Singapore	2.0038	Brunei	0.8836	Malaysia	0.7853	Thailand	0.3654	Vietnam	–0.1658
2010	Singapore	2.0169	Brunei	0.8351	Malaysia	0.7702	Thailand	0.3984	Indonesia	–0.1090
2011	Singapore	2.0175	Malaysia	0.8602	Brunei	0.8374	Thailand	0.3571	Indonesia	–0.2133
2012	Singapore	2.0236	Malaysia	0.8503	Brunei	0.8231	Thailand	0.3252	Indonesia	–0.2135
2013	Singapore	2.0835	Brunei	0.7987	Malaysia	0.7662	Thailand	0.2863	Philippines	–0.1707
2014	Singapore	2.0429	Brunei	0.8499	Malaysia	0.7720	Thailand	0.2476	Philippines	–0.0913
	6		7		8		9		10	
Rank	Economy	Score	Economy	Score	Economy	Score	Economy	Score	Economy	Score
2000	Indonesia	–0.2155	Vietnam	–0.6377	Cambodia	–0.7859	Laos	–1.1010	Myanmar	–1.3010
2001	Indonesia	–0.3280	Vietnam	–0.6469	Cambodia	–0.7388	Laos	–1.0975	Myanmar	–1.3186
2002	Indonesia	–0.4215	Vietnam	–0.5463	Cambodia	–0.7501	Laos	–1.1048	Myanmar	–1.3135
2003	Indonesia	–0.3325	Vietnam	–0.5440	Cambodia	–0.7934	Laos	–1.1140	Myanmar	–1.3887
2004	Indonesia	–0.2742	Vietnam	–0.5407	Cambodia	–0.8411	Laos	–1.0619	Myanmar	–1.4183
2005	Indonesia	–0.2709	Vietnam	–0.5219	Cambodia	–0.8530	Laos	–1.0278	Myanmar	–1.4134
2006	Philippines	–0.2503	Vietnam	–0.3743	Cambodia	–0.8966	Laos	–1.0508	Myanmar	–1.4862
2007	Philippines	–0.2474	Vietnam	–0.3018	Cambodia	–0.8766	Laos	–1.0240	Myanmar	–1.5231
2008	Philippines	–0.1994	Vietnam	–0.2979	Cambodia	–0.8959	Laos	–1.0083	Myanmar	–1.5592
2009	Indonesia	–0.1929	Philippines	–0.2063	Laos	–0.9199	Cambodia	–0.9297	Myanmar	–1.6236
2010	Vietnam	–0.1350	Philippines	–0.2947	Cambodia	–0.9109	Laos	–0.9458	Myanmar	–1.6252
2011	Vietnam	–0.2667	Philippines	–0.3367	Laos	–0.7445	Cambodia	–0.7948	Myanmar	–1.7161
2012	Philippines	–0.2343	Vietnam	–0.3000	Cambodia	–0.5929	Laos	–0.9796	Myanmar	–1.7020
2013	Indonesia	–0.2269	Vietnam	–0.2902	Cambodia	–0.7224	Laos	–0.7729	Myanmar	–1.7516
2014	Indonesia	–0.1925	Vietnam	–0.2237	Laos	–0.8404	Cambodia	–0.8597	Myanmar	–1.7047

Source: Tan *et al*. (2017b)

2.3.3 Analysis of Vietnam's Relative Strengths and Weaknesses

Competitiveness may also be analysed at the sub-environment and indicator levels. Tables 2.6 and 2.7 showcase Vietnam's top 20 percent strongest and the weakest 20 percent indicators, respectively, in 2014. As shown in Table 2.6, Vietnam, has demonstrated its strengths in the provision of public services and infrastructure such as healthcare (#1), education (#2), access to water (#14), and ICT (#24). Moreover, the availability of a large pool of low-cost workforce (#10, #15, and #16) is a key factor in attracting investors. However, as subsequent analysis in this section shall demonstrate, Vietnam's cost advantage has actually diminished as compared to a decade ago.

Turning to Table 2.7, though Vietnam remains uncompetitive in a wide array of areas, the most salient, and recurring, in the country's top weaknesses are: (i) prevalence of market

Table 2.6: Top 20 Percent Strongest Indicators for Vietnam

Rank	20 Percent Strongest Indicators	Score	Environment
1	Health Expenditure	1.6156	QLID
2	Primary Schooling	1.5993	QLID
3	Money Supply (M2)	1.1607	GIS
4	Cellular Mobile Telephone Subscribers	0.9361	QLID
5	Real GDP Growth	0.8601	MS
6	Tax Revenue/Government Revenue	0.8177	GIS
7	Deposit Interest Rate	0.8090	GIS
8	Exchange Rate Appreciation	0.7879	GIS
9	Domestic Credit to Private Sector	0.7857	FBMC
10	Cost of Management Staff	0.7806	FBMC
11	Interest Rate Spread	0.7531	GIS
12	Domestic Credit Provided by the Financial Sector	0.7004	FBMC
13	Regional Competitiveness	0.6824	GIS
14	Access to Water	0.6506	QLID
15	Cost of Production Labour	0.6240	FBMC
16	Labour Force	0.6195	FBMC
17	Traffic Congestion	0.5773	QLID
18	Urban Population Growth	0.5764	QLID
19	Openness to Trade	0.5282	MS
20	Social Unrest	0.5142	QLID
21	International Monetary Fund Credit	0.4142	GIS
22	Population	0.3916	QLID
23	Internet Subscribers	0.3856	QLID
24	ICT Expenditure	0.3795	QLID

Source: Tan *et al.* (2017b)

Table 2.7: Top 20 Percent Weakest Indicators for Vietnam

Rank	20 Percent Weakest Indicators	Score	Environment
98	Daily Organic Water Pollutant Emissions	–0.7709	QLID
99	Quality of Stock Market Regulatory Authority	–0.7866	FBMC
100	Intellectual Property Rights Protection	–0.7922	GIS
101	Levelness of Playing Field	–0.7961	MS
102	Government Responsiveness	–0.8051	GIS
103	Air Quality	–0.8216	QLID
104	Urban Population	–0.8307	QLID
105	Labour Activism	–0.8466	QLID
106	High-Quality Management Staff	–0.8530	FBMC
107	Government Consumption Expenditure	–0.8893	GIS
108	Local Road System	–0.8978	QLID
109	Labour Market Rating	–0.9218	FBMC
110	Budget Balance	–0.9233	GIS
111	Government Environmental Protection Policies	–0.9248	GIS
112	Sovereign Debt Risk	–0.9390	FBMC
113	Lack of Market Distortion due to State-Ownership	–0.9571	GIS
114	Labour Unrest	–0.9984	QLID
115	Strength of Auditing and Reporting Standards	–1.0177	GIS
116	Bureaucracy/Red Tape	–1.0452	GIS
117	Corporate Income Tax	–1.2661	MS
118	Secondary Schooling	–1.2691	QLID
119	Tax Burden	–1.5056	GIS
120	Freedom of Press	–1.5414	QLID
121	Corporate Governance	–1.5996	GIS

Source: Tan *et al.* (2017b)

distortion (#101, #113), (ii) corporate governance and transparency (#115, #121), and (iii) quality of human capital (#106, #109 and #118). Besides, economic development in Vietnam seems to rule at the expense of the environment (#111) and has led to environmental degradation in Vietnam (#98 and #103).

The above analysis can be supplemented by an examination of how Vietnam's performance in specific sub-environments has changed over the study period. Figure 2.14 shows a web-chart of Vietnam's performance in the 12 sub-environments used by ACI to define competitiveness. The green line indicates Vietnam's score in 2000, while the red indicates the score in 2014. Taken together, Figure 2.14 and Tables 2.6 and 2.7 provide detailed insights into Vietnam's strengths and weaknesses relative to other ASEAN countries.

Figure 2.14: Vietnam's Competitiveness Scores by Sub-environment (by Equal Weightage Methodology), 2000 and 2014

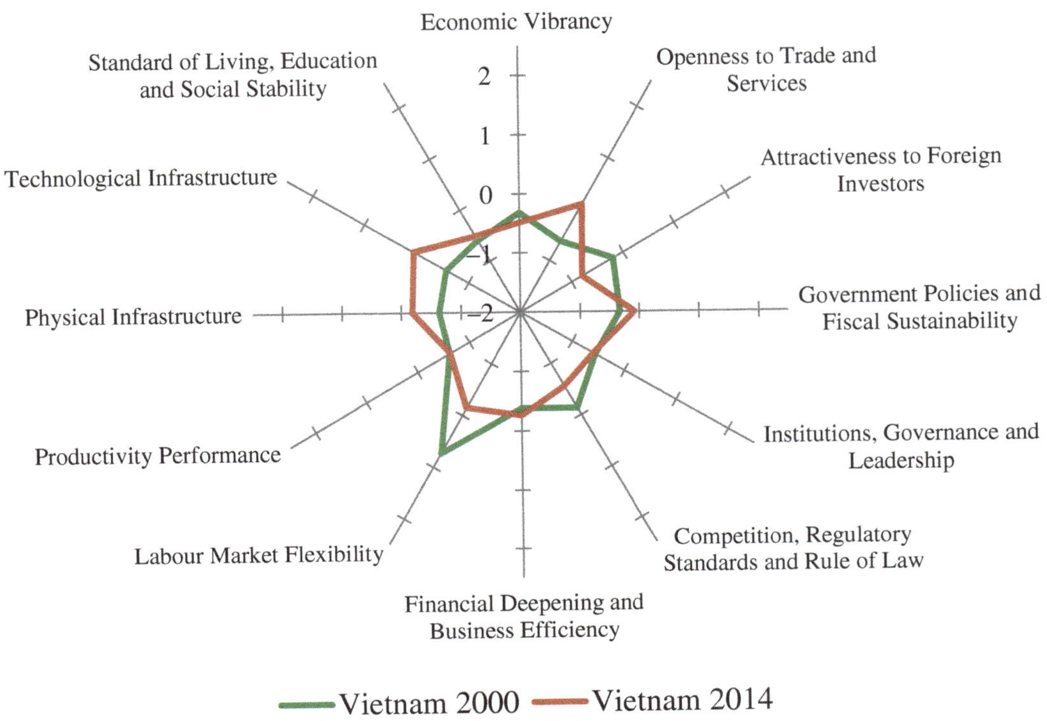

Source: A computation

Due to the productivity growth slowdown described in Section 2.2.2, Vietnam showed no discernible improvement in its "Productivity Performance" relative to other ASEAN-10 economies between 2000 and 2014. Its standardised score for this sub-environment has hovered between –0.6195 in 2000 and –0.6346 in 2014, indicating that it has always performed well below the regional average in terms of labour productivity (see Figure 2.14).

Aside from low labour productivity, skill mismatch and skill shortage are significant challenges to human capital development in Vietnam. As seen in Table 2.7, high-quality management staff is in fact one of Vietnam's weakest indicators. According to a survey conducted by the World Bank (2013), employers in Vietnam find it difficult to hire workers despite the large demand for labour because of two reasons. First, there exists a large skill gap — a situation in which the applicants' skills are insufficient to meet job requirements — especially for managerial, professional and technical positions. Second, there is a shortage in the pool of applicants in more elementary occupations. The workforce also lacks the necessary soft skills and proficiency in conversational English. Moreover, the country ranked 63rd out of 75 for digital literacy in the Economist Intelligence Unit (EIU)'s Inclusive Internet Index in 2017.[33] This further indicates the workforce's low level of preparedness in harnessing the full potential of Internet and data analytics to adapt to the Fourth Industrial Revolution.

At the same time, Vietnam is gradually losing its competitive edge in low labour cost. As demonstrated in Figure 2.14, Vietnam's score in the "Labour Market Flexibility" sub-environment dropped significantly from a high of 0.7270 in 2000 to –0.1505 in 2014. The switch from a positive to a negative score highlights the great extent of the deterioration in Vietnam's relative strength in labour conditions *vis-à-vis* its ASEAN neighbours.

Stagnant productivity growth, coupled with rising labour cost which will only worsen with its ageing population, put Vietnam at risk of losing its attractiveness to foreign investors. This will happen sooner rather than later in the absence of appropriate policy responses. Figure 2.14 shows that Vietnam's score for the "Attractiveness to Foreign Investor" sub-environment has declined from –0.1938 in 2000 to –0.7908 in 2014. The threat is compounded by the emergence of low-cost competitors in ASEAN, namely Cambodia and Myanmar, as well as those in other regions. In fact, Cambodia and Bangladesh now offer cheaper labour cost than Vietnam, even after exchange rate adjustments.[34]

In addition, more should be done to improve the private sector's competitiveness and business environment. As illustrated in Figure 2.14, Vietnam has lagged behind its regional peers in the "Competition, Regulatory Standards and Rule of Law" sub-environment, where its standardised score dropped from –0.1315 in 2000 to –0.5505 in 2014. This is a manifestation of market distortions favouring SOEs and weak institutional capacity as analysed in Section 2.2.2.

Furthermore, despite the rapid infrastructure development that has taken place over the past three decades, physical infrastructure bottlenecks still represent a particularly pressing challenge to Vietnam's economic development. Figure 2.14 shows that Vietnam's standardised score in "Physical Infrastructure" in 2014 was still negative at –0.1850, indicating below-average performance in infrastructure quality. Indeed, according to an assessment by the Economic Research Institute for ASEAN and East Asia (ERIA) in 2015, 37 percent of the country road network was in average condition, while 20 percent was rated as "poor to very poor".[35] According to the same ERIA survey, rapid urbanisation has strained the transport systems in the countries' largest metropolises. Additionally, despite significant investment in energy generation capacity, blackouts and insufficient supply during peak load periods are still expected to increase as energy demand is projected to continue to outstrip supply.

Having examined Vietnam's relative strengths and weaknesses, we conduct the *What-if* simulation analysis as outlined in Section 2.3.1. Table 2.8 displays the simulation results for 10 ASEAN countries in terms of their Overall Competitiveness scores and rankings. We observe that post-simulation, Vietnam has risen one position to sixth, with a significant increase in overall standardised score from –0.3987 to –0.1059. Such results serve to emphasise that improved competitiveness is totally feasible given the right policy adjustments.

---

[33] See https://theinclusiveinternet.eiu.com/explore/countries/VN/performance/indicators/readiness (accessed on 12 October 2017).

[34] See McKinsey Global Institute (2012).

[35] See Duong (2015).

Table 2.8: *What-if* Competitiveness Simulation Analysis on Overall Competitiveness, 2014

	Rank		Score	
Economy	Before	After	Before	After
Brunei	3	2	0.5322	0.9710
Cambodia	8	8	−0.9071	−0.5236
Indonesia	5	4	0.0412	0.4102
Laos	9	8	−0.9241	−0.5018
Malaysia	2	2	1.0568	1.1760
Myanmar	10	8	−1.5501	−1.0245
Philippines	6	6	−0.3133	−0.0266
Singapore	1	1	2.0152	2.1945
Thailand	4	3	0.4477	0.6443
Vietnam	7	6	−0.3987	−0.1059

Source: Tan *et al*. (2017)

2.4 One Country-Two Economies: Regional Imbalances in Vietnam

The analysis in Sections 2.2 and 2.3 shows that Vietnam's current growth model needs to be reformed. Aside from the macroeconomic challenges highlighted in the previous sections, the new wave of reforms must also aim to address persistent regional imbalances among its sub-national economies. If left unsolved, this problem may lead to the emergence of "One Country-Two Economies" with adverse consequences for socio-economic development and national cohesion. This section is devoted to discussing regional disparities between Northern, Central and Southern Vietnam in various development aspects. It shall analyse the development gap between Hanoi and Ho Chi Minh City, which are the two largest cities in terms of population in the North and the South, respectively.

2.4.1 The Persistent Gaps between Northern, Central and Southern Vietnam

Northern Vietnam consists of the Red River Delta, where Hanoi is located and the Northern Midlands and Mountainous Region. Central Vietnam is comprised of the Northern Central and Central Coast as well as the Central Highland. Meanwhile, Southern Vietnam is made up of the Southeast region, which contains Ho Chi Minh City, and the Mekong River Delta. Table 2.9 provides some basic geographic and demographic facts about these regions. As of 2015, the Red River Delta was most densely populated with a population density of 994 people per square kilometre. It was followed by the Southeast and the Mekong River Delta regions, whose densities were 684 people per square kilometre and 434 people per square kilometre, respectively. In terms of population shares, Northern, Central and Southern Vietnam constituted 32.7 percent, 25.3 percent and 33.7 percent of the total population, respectively.

Table 2.9: Land Area, Population and Population Density by Region, 2015

Region	Land Area (thousand km²)	Population (million people)	Population Density (people per km²)
Northern Vietnam			
Red River Delta	21.1	20.9	994
Northern Midlands and Mountainous Region	95.3	11.8	124
Total	**116.3**	**32.7**	**281**
Central Vietnam			
Northern Central and Central Coast	95.8	19.7	205
Central Highland	54.6	5.6	103
Total	**150.5**	**25.3**	**168**
Southern Vietnam			
Southeast	23.6	16.1	684
Mekong River Delta	40.6	17.6	434
Total	**64.2**	**33.7**	**525**

Source: Vietnam's GSO

Economic development has not been evenly distributed among the regions. As mentioned in Chapter 1, industrial parks are largely concentrated in the South. In fact, the Southern provinces have always received more FDI than those in the Northern and Central regions. As seen in Figure 2.15, Southern Vietnam captured the lion's share of registered capital of licensed FDI in 2015 (60.7 percent), while the shares of Northern and Central Vietnam were 34.2 percent and 4.7 percent, respectively. Furthermore, four of the top-five provinces in terms of FDI registered capital were Southern provinces/municipalities, namely Ho Chi Minh City, Binh Duong, Tra Vinh and Dong Nai.

Greater economic opportunities have brought about higher living standards in Southern Vietnam. Table 2.10 displays the average individual's monthly income and poverty headcount ratio in each region. As of 2015, the Southeast region had the highest average individual's monthly income at 4.7 million Dong per month, more than 20 percent greater than that for the Red River Delta region which was the next highest (3.8 million Dong per month). Among the other regions, the average individual's monthly income in the Mekong River Delta was the highest. A similar pattern can also be observed for poverty headcount ratio. The Southeast's ratio had the lowest percentage of its population living in poverty by national poverty lines, followed by the Red River Delta and the Mekong River Delta regions.

The South has also outperformed the North and Central in terms of basic healthcare outcomes. Figures 2.16 and 2.17 show the average infant mortality rates and life expectancies of the Northern, Central and Southern provinces between 2005 and 2016. Throughout this period, Southern Vietnam has had the lowest average infant mortality rate and the highest life expectancy at birth. Furthermore, the gaps between the three regions have arguably widened over the years. In 2005, the average infant mortality rate in Northern Vietnam was 1.5 times higher than the South. This has increased to 1.7 times by 2016. Meanwhile, the probability of an infant dying in Central Vietnam in 2016 was two times higher than that in Southern Vietnam.

Figure 2.15: Total Registered Capital of Licensed FDI Projects by Region, 2015

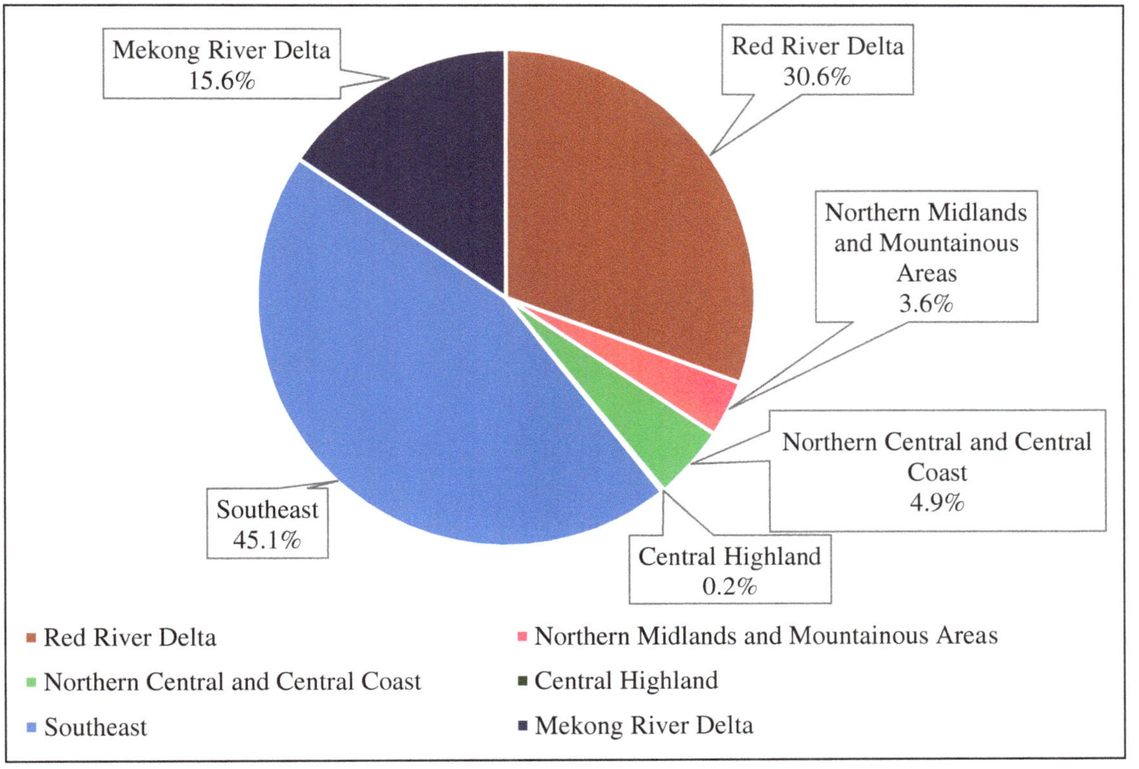

Note: Includes total registered capital of new FDI project licensed in 2015 and increase in registered capital of projects licensed in previous years.

Source: Vietnam's GSO

Table 2.10: Average Individual's Monthly Income and Poverty Headcount Ratio by Region, 2015

Region	Average Individual's Monthly Income (million Dong)	Poverty Headcount Ratio (percent of population)^
Northern Vietnam		
Red River Delta	3.8	3.2
Northern Midlands and Mountainous Areas	1.8	16
Central Vietnam		
Northern Central and Central Coast	2.3	9.8
Central Highland	2.2	11.3
Southern Vietnam		
Southeast	4.7	0.7
Mekong River Delta	2.6	6.5

Note: ^Based on national poverty lines: monthly expenditure of 615,000 Dong for rural areas and 760,000 Dong for urban areas.

Source: Vietnam's GSO

Figure 2.16: Average Infant Mortality Rates by Region, 2005–2016

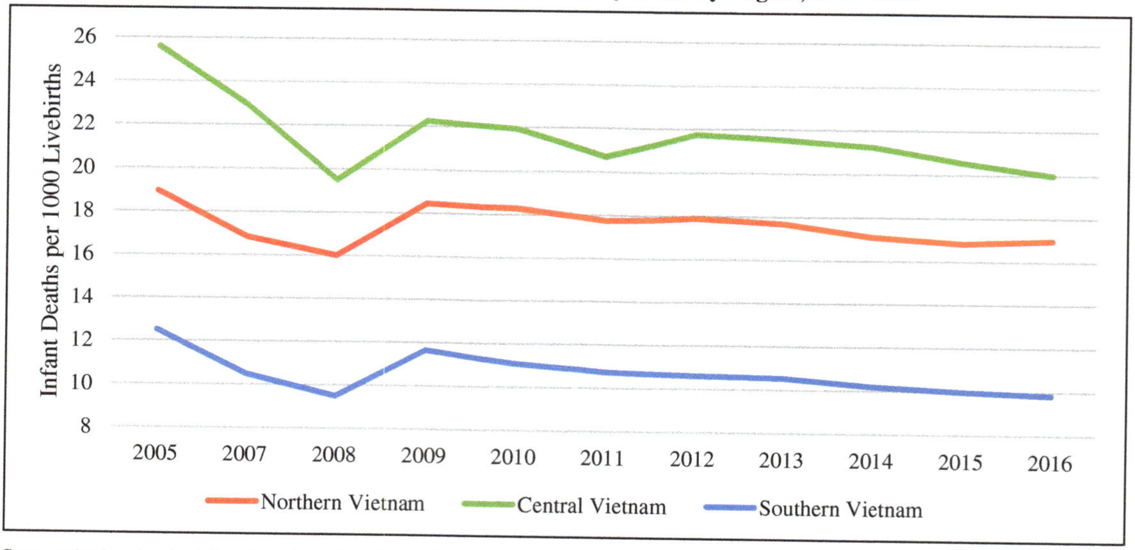

Source: Authors' calculation based on data from Vietnam's GSO

Figure 2.17: Average Life Expectancies at Birth by Region, 2005–2015

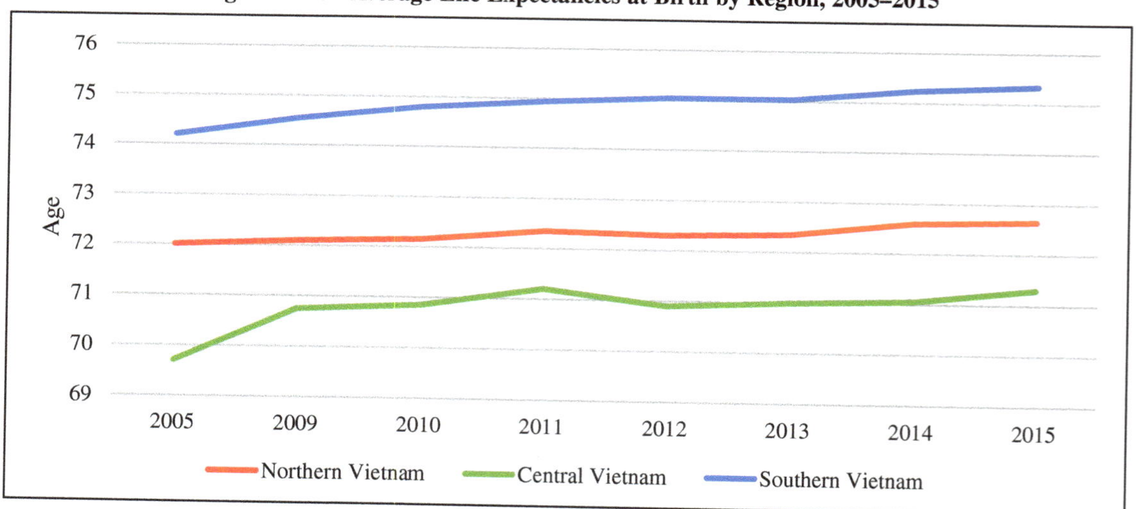

Source: Authors' calculation based on data from Vietnam's GSO

As the region with the highest living standards, the Southeast has experienced positive net migration over the past decade between 2005 and 2016 despite the declining trend since 2009 (see Figure 2.18). At 8.4 people per 1,000 population, the net migration rate in 2016 was higher than its 2005 level at 7.2 people per 1,000 population. Meanwhile, in spite of migration from the Northern Midlands and Mountainous Areas into the Red River Delta, the net migration rate of the latter region has fluctuated around zero, reflecting a significant outflow of people.

Figure 2.18: Average Net Migration Rates by Region, 2005–2016

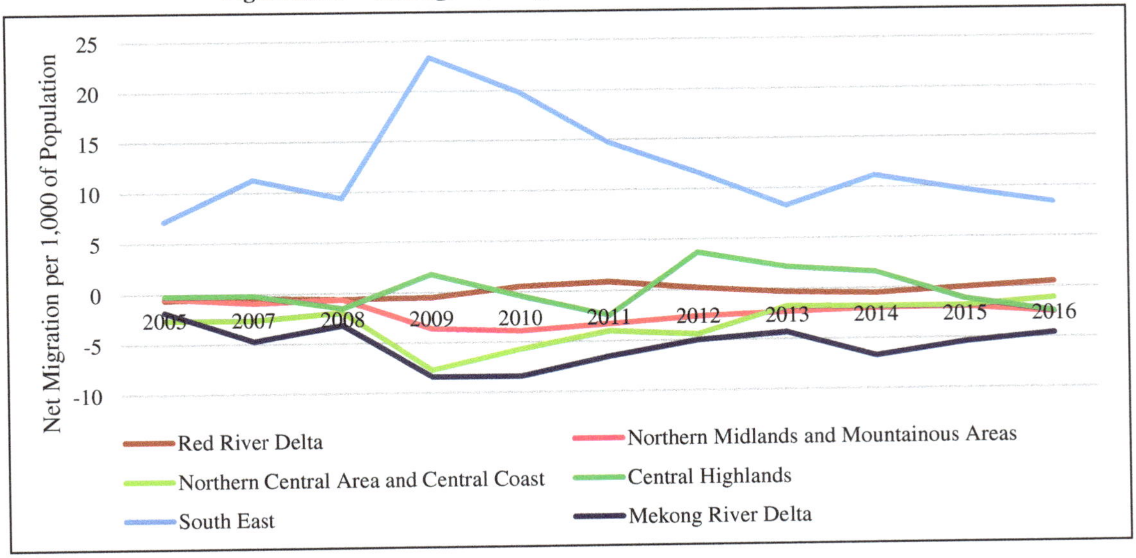

Source: Vietnam's GSO

Interestingly, the net migration rate of the Central Highlands has displayed occasional positive spikes throughout 2005–2016. This was largely due to active policies by the government to encourage population growth and relocation to this highly strategic region.

The above analysis has demonstrated that there are persistent and widening gaps in terms of economic opportunities, income and quality of life between Northern, Central and Southern Vietnam. If these imbalances are not addressed, Vietnam is at risk of becoming one country with two unequal economies: the advanced South and the less developed Central and North. The subsequent Sections 2.4.2 and 2.4.3 shall further illustrate entrenched regional disparities in Vietnam through a case study which compares Hanoi and Ho Chi Minh City, the two largest cities in the country.

2.4.2 Geographic, Demographic and Economic Overview of Hanoi and Ho Chi Minh City

As a result of its merger with Ha Tay province in 2008, Hanoi is almost 60 percent bigger than Ho Chi Minh City in terms of total land area. As of 2015, the area of Hanoi was 3,300 square kilometres as compared to 2,100 square kilometres for Ho Chi Minh City (see Table 2.11). However, Hanoi is less populous than Ho Chi Minh City. As a result, Ho Chi Minh City is more densely populated than Hanoi, with the former being almost 1.7 times as dense as the latter.

In terms of economic development. Ho Chi Minh City is more dynamic than the capital city. In 2015, Ho Chi Minh City's GDP was 67.9 percent larger than that of Hanoi. In fact, as shown in Figure 2.19, the gap in GDP between the two cities has widened over the past 10 years. In addition, we also observe an increasing divergence between Hanoi and Ho Chi Minh City in terms of their GDP per capita (see Figure 2.20). As of 2015, the GDP per capita of Ho Chi Minh

Table 2.11: Key Facts about Hanoi and Ho Chi Minh City, 2015

Indicators	Hanoi	Ho Chi Minh City
Nominal GDP (billion Dong)	570,046	957,359
Land Area (thousand km^2)	3.3	2.1
Population (million people)	7.4	8.2
Population Density (people per km^2)	2,223	3,936

Source: Vietnam's GSO and CEIC

Figure 2.19: Nominal GDP of Hanoi and Ho Chi Minh City, 2005–2015

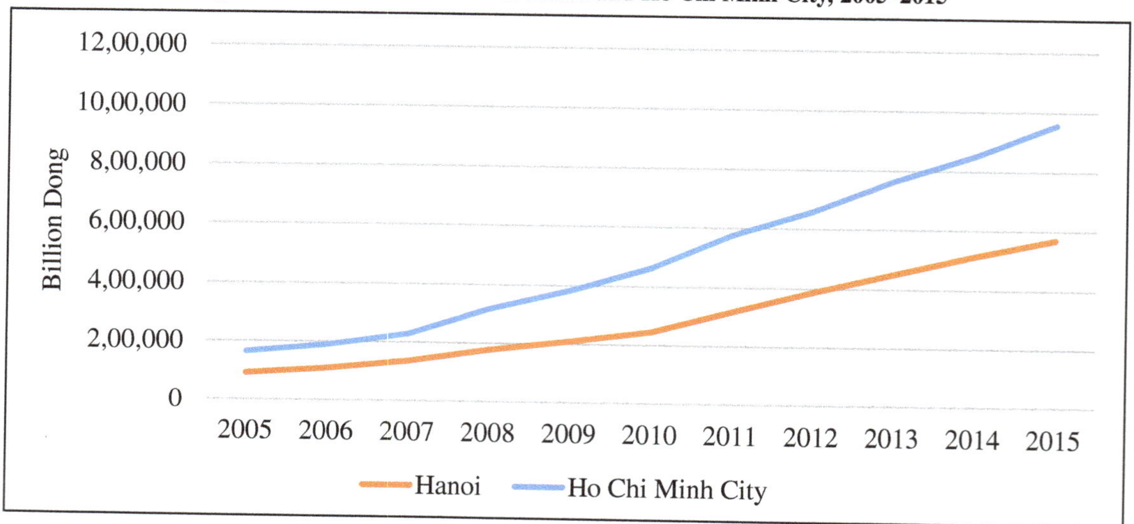

Source: CEIC

Figure 2.20: Nominal GDP per Capita of Hanoi and Ho Chi Minh City, 2005–2015

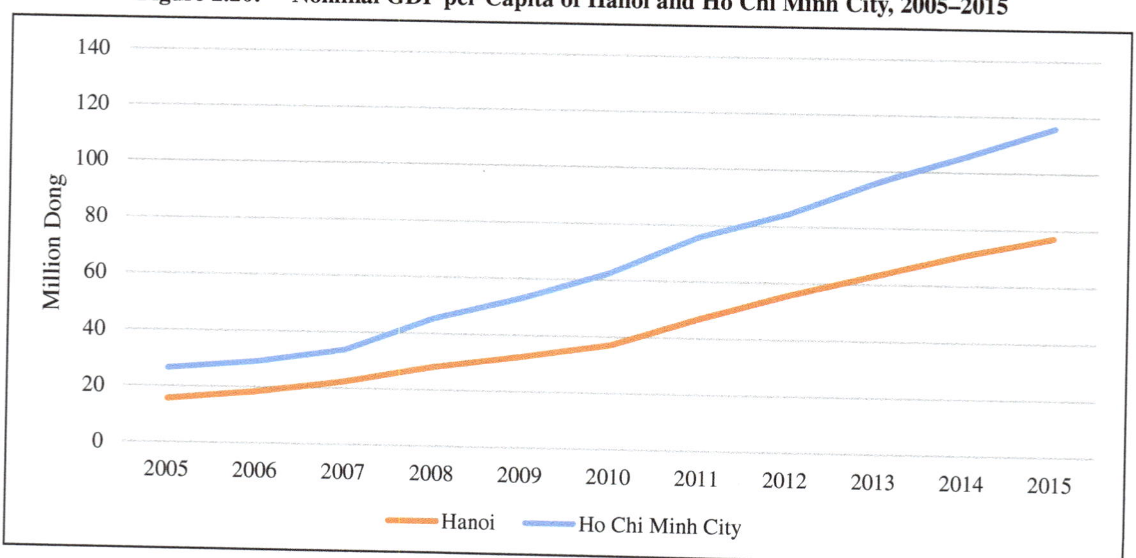

Source: CEIC

City was 50.5 percent higher than that of Hanoi. The disparity in economic development may be partly due to Ho Chi Minh City's greater attractiveness to investors. As mentioned in Section 2.4.1, Ho Chi Minh City is among the top FDI-receiving provinces/municipalities in Vietnam.

2.4.3 On Liveability, Cost of Living, Wages and Purchasing Power for Hanoi and Ho Chi Minh City

Leveraging on ACI's Global Liveable Cities Index (GLCI) and Cost of Living, Wages and Purchasing Power Indices for Ordinary Residents, this section makes a holistic comparison of the living standards and quality of life of ordinary residents in Hanoi and Ho Chi Minh City. The indices employed also allow us to benchmark their performances against other global cities.

The GLCI was first released in 2012 to quantitatively assess the liveability of a city from ordinary residents' point of view.[36] ACI's GLCI framework draws inspiration from the US President Franklin D. Roosevelt's 1941 State of the Union Address, in which he espoused on four basic human freedoms: freedom from want, freedom from fear, freedom to worship and freedom of speech.

"Freedom from want" captures the right to have a decent livelihood. More broadly, this dimension emphasises people's desire for comforts and material abundance. The degree that this is satisfied is in large part determined by the availability of economic opportunities for the people. The terminology adopted in the GLCI framework that represents this dimension is "Economic Vibrancy and Competitiveness".

"Freedom from fear" stresses the natural right of people to live in safety through the rule of law, the alleviation of natural disasters, and the prevention of wars by the state. The absence of such psychological pressures in a city increases its liveability in the same way that an improvement in the economic prospects do. The terminology adopted in the GLCI framework that captures this dimension is "Domestic Security and Stability".

"Freedom to worship" is subsumed within the broader dimension of "Socio-Cultural Conditions". This dimension emphasises the level of social comfort experienced by a city's residents (e.g. the degree of income inequality, social harmony, and social mobility), the physical ease afforded to the city's residents (e.g. adequacy of mass transit, healthcare, and education), and the cultural richness that can be tapped on to (e.g. social diversity, the degree of tolerance towards different religious beliefs, and access to museums and cultural performances).

"Freedom of speech" is subsumed within the broader dimension of "Political Governance". This dimension covers the effectiveness of the government in providing public services (e.g. the extent of corruption and the quality of the judiciary system), the responsiveness of the government (e.g. degree of transparency and accountability), and the openness to political participation (e.g. regular elections that are free and fair).

The framework is further supplemented by the inclusion of another important dimension of city liveability, which is "Environmental Friendliness and Sustainability". This dimension captures not only their desire of human beings for the responsible stewardship of the

[36] See Tan *et al.* (2017c).

environment, but also their aesthetic appreciation of nature. This dimension reflects the aspiration for sustainable development. Essentially, it is development that meets our own needs without compromising the ability of future generations to meet their needs through the responsible utilisation of natural resources.

In short, the GLCI conceptualises ordinary residents' liveability according to five environments: (i) Economic Vibrancy and Competitiveness, (ii) Environmental Friendliness and Sustainability, (iii) Domestic Security and Stability, (iv) Socio-Cultural Conditions, and (v) Political Governance. Subsumed under these environments are 18 sub-environments which are measured by 86 indicators. Figure 2.21 provides a summary of the GLCI framework, clearly demonstrating the links with Roosevelt's four freedoms.

The statistical method of standardised score was used to aggregate 86 indicators into a meaningful measure of liveability. The final GLCI index reflects the cities' liveability *vis-à-vis* the average performance of all 63 cities in the sample. These 63 cities were selected to be studied based on their status as megacities, major cities in most developed economies or major cities in most of the important emerging economies.

Additionally ACI has also constructed a Cost of Living for Ordinary Residents which tracks the living costs, wages and purchasing power for ordinary residents for 103 of the world's major

Figure 2.21: ACI's GLCI Framework

Inspired Themes of City Liveability	GLCI Environments	GLCI Sub-Environments
Satisfaction with "the freedom from want"	Economic Vibrancy and Competitiveness	➤ Economic Performance ➤ Economic Openness ➤ Infrastructure
Satisfaction with the status of natural environment and its management	Environmental Friendliness and Sustainability	➤ Pollution ➤ Depletion of Natural Resources ➤ Environmental Initiatives
Satisfaction with "the freedom from fear"	Domestic Security and Stability	➤ Crime Rate ➤ Threats to National Stability ➤ Civil Unrest
Satisfaction with the socio-cultural conditions, i.e. "the freedom to worship"	Socio-Cultural Conditions	➤ Medical & Healthcare ➤ Education ➤ Housing, Sanitation & Transportation ➤ Income Equality & Demographic Burden ➤ Diversity & Community Cohesion
Satisfaction with political governance, i.e. "the freedom to speak"	Political Governance	➤ Policy Making & Implementation ➤ Government System ➤ Transparency & Accountability ➤ Corruption

Source: Tan *et al*. (2017c)

Figure 2.22: 10 Consumption Categories for Ordinary Residents

Source: Tan *et al.* (2017a)

cities in a comprehensive manner.[37] Ordinary residents are assumed to follow local consumption preferences, which differ from country to country. Cost of living is measured according to a basket of 10 consumption categories, comprising 165 products and services and 283 price data entries for each city (see Figure 2.22).

As with other studies on cost of living such as the World Cost of Living Survey by the Economist Intelligence Unit, ACI's study has used New York as a base city. Other cities are benchmarked against it. As such, the index values for New York are always 100.00.

Using the Cost of Living Index and a Wage Index, the ACI computes the Purchasing Power Index for Ordinary Residents. This index measures the number of baskets of goods and services that ordinary residents in a given city can enjoy if they work for an hour, benchmarked against their counterparts in New York. An index value over 100.00 shows that ordinary residents in the city enjoy a higher purchasing power than New York.

The latest 2016 GLCI study, which utilised 2013 data, revealed that Ho Chi Minh City is more liveable than Hanoi, with the former being placed at the 42nd position out of 63

[37] See Tan *et al.* (2017d).

Figure 2.23: Cost of Living Index and Ranking for Ordinary Residents in Hanoi and Ho Chi Minh City, 2013–2015

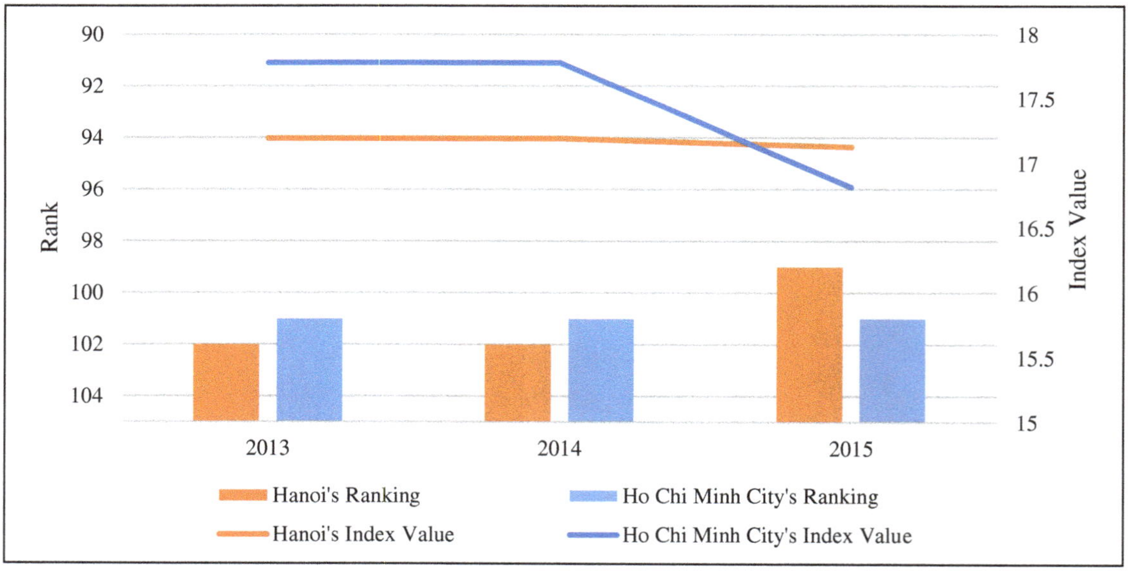

Source: Authors' computation

cities while the latter occupied the 48th place in the ranking. In terms of cost of living for ordinary residents, the two cities are relatively similar. Figure 2.23 shows the performances of Ho Chi Minh City and Hanoi in terms of cost of living for ordinary residents *vis-à-vis* the 103 cities covered by ACI's cost of living research. In 2013 and 2014, Ho Chi Minh City was ranked higher than Hanoi, which indicates that the cost of living was higher in Ho Chi Minh City. However, in 2015, Hanoi overtook Ho Chi Minh City as the more expensive city. Out of 105 cities, Hanoi was ranked 99th, while Ho Chi Minh City was ranked 101st (see Figure 2.23).

Similarly, as seen in Figure 2.24, ordinary residents in Hanoi initially had lower purchasing power than Ho Chi Minh City's residents in 2013 and 2014. However, in 2015, Ho Chi Minh City was ranked higher at 98th, while Hanoi was ranked 99th out of 105 cities. This implies that ordinary residents of Ho Chi Minh City have been able to enjoy higher purchasing power than their counterparts in Hanoi.

To put our findings for Hanoi and Ho Chi Minh City in perspective, we benchmark them against other global cities, especially the ASEAN cities. Aside from the two Vietnamese cities, other ASEAN cities covered in this research include Bangkok, Jakarta, Kuala Lumpur, Manila and Singapore. Median values of the GLCI as well as the Cost of Living and Purchasing Power Indices for Ordinary Residents may be used to categorise cities into different types as shown in Figures 2.25 and 2.26.

Figure 2.24: Purchasing Power Index and Ranking for Ordinary Residents in Hanoi and Ho Chi Minh City, 2013–2015

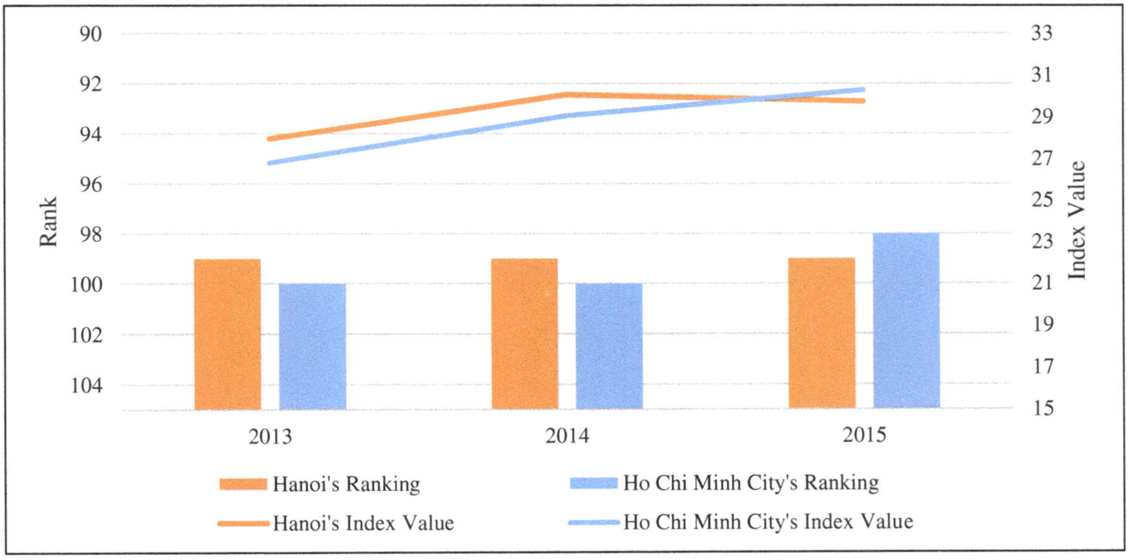

Source: Authors' computation

Figure 2.25: Four Categories of Cities Based on the GLCI and Cost of Living Index for Ordinary Residents

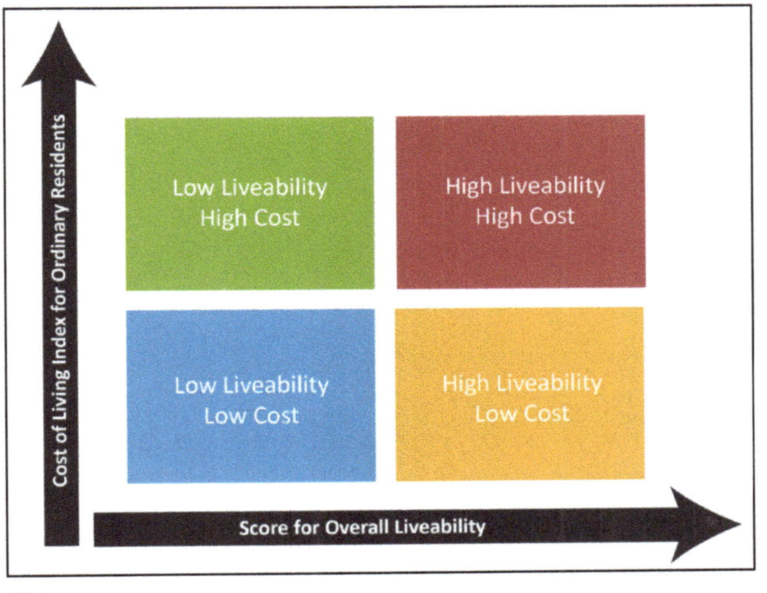

Source: Authors' compilation

Figure 2.26: Four Categories of Cities Based on the GLCI and the Purchasing Power Index for Ordinary Residents

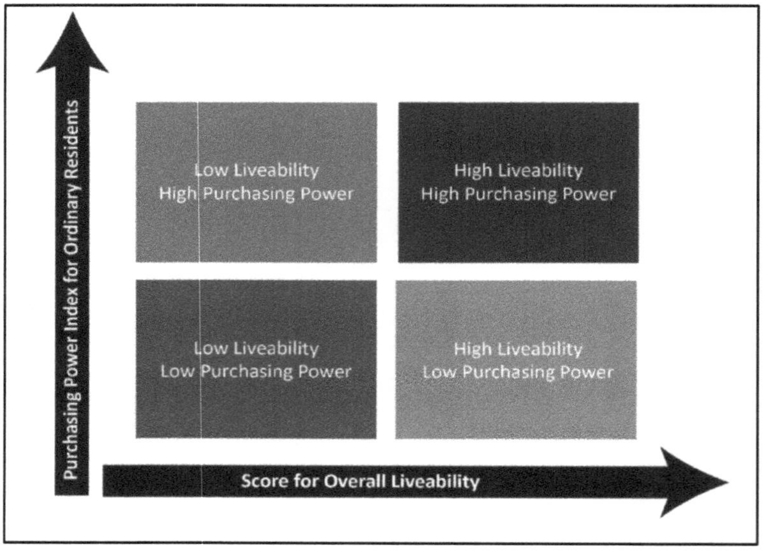

Source: Authors' compilation

Figure 2.27 shows the scatterplot of 49 global cities in terms of cost of living and liveability based on 2013 data. The ASEAN cities are highlighted. We observe that Hanoi and Ho Chi Minh City occupied the lower end of the Low Liveability–Low Cost quadrant. The cost of living for ordinary residents in both Vietnamese cities was lower than that in the other ASEAN cities. In terms of liveability, both cities were ranked below Kuala Lumpur and Singapore, but higher than Manila and Jakarta.

Indeed, this finding is consistent with the cities' performances when compared with indicators that are more specific to key public services. Figure 2.28 highlights the cities' relative performance in terms of housing, while Figure 2.29 covers education. Healthcare performances are showcased in Figure 2.30. In all of these figures, Hanoi and Ho Chi Minh City are rooted to the bottom left quadrant of Low Standards–Low Cost.

Figure 2.31 shows the scatterplot of the Purchasing Power Index for Ordinary Residents against the score for Overall Liveability. As seen in the figure, Hanoi and Ho Chi Minh City were above Manila and Jakarta in terms of ordinary residents' purchasing power. In contrast, though Bangkok, Kuala Lumpur and Singapore were more expensive than the two Vietnamese cities. In other words, ordinary residents in these cities earn much higher wages and enjoy greater purchasing power.

Overall, the comparison between Hanoi and Ho Chi Minh City reinforces the key message in Section 2.4.1 about persistent regional disparities in Vietnam. Even among these two top-tier cities, there are considerable imbalances as Ho Chi Minh City leads Hanoi in terms of economic vibrancy and liveability despite their relative similarities in cost of living for ordinary residents.

Figure 2.27: Scatterplot of Cost of Living Index for Ordinary Residents against Score for Overall Liveability

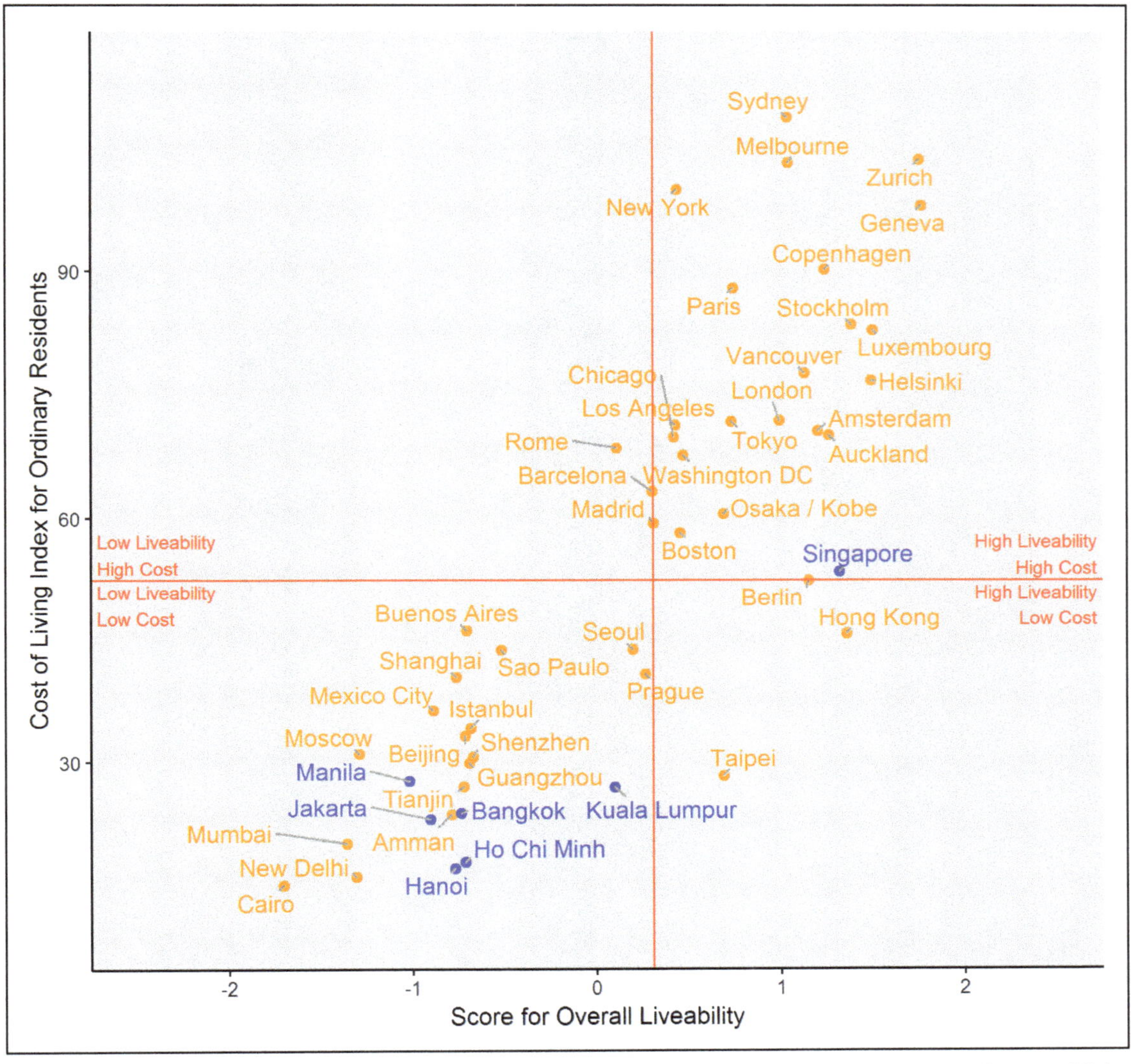

Note: The vertical and horizontal red lines represent, respectively, the median overall liveability score and the median cost of living index for ordinary residents of the 49 cities in the analysis.

Source: Authors' computation

At the same time, our analysis clearly shows that there is room for improvement for both cities. Hanoi and Ho Chi Minh City has indeed surpassed Manila and Jakarta in terms of liveability and purchasing power for ordinary residents. However, they are still deeply rooted in the Low Liveability–Low Purchasing Power quadrant, lagging behind many other cities in the developing world such as cities in China, Bangkok and Kuala Lumpur. More must be done to bridge these gaps.

Figure 2.28: Scatterplot of Housing Rents, Utilities and Transport Cost Index for Ordinary Residents against Score for Public Service Standards in Terms of Housing, Sanitation and Transportation Provision

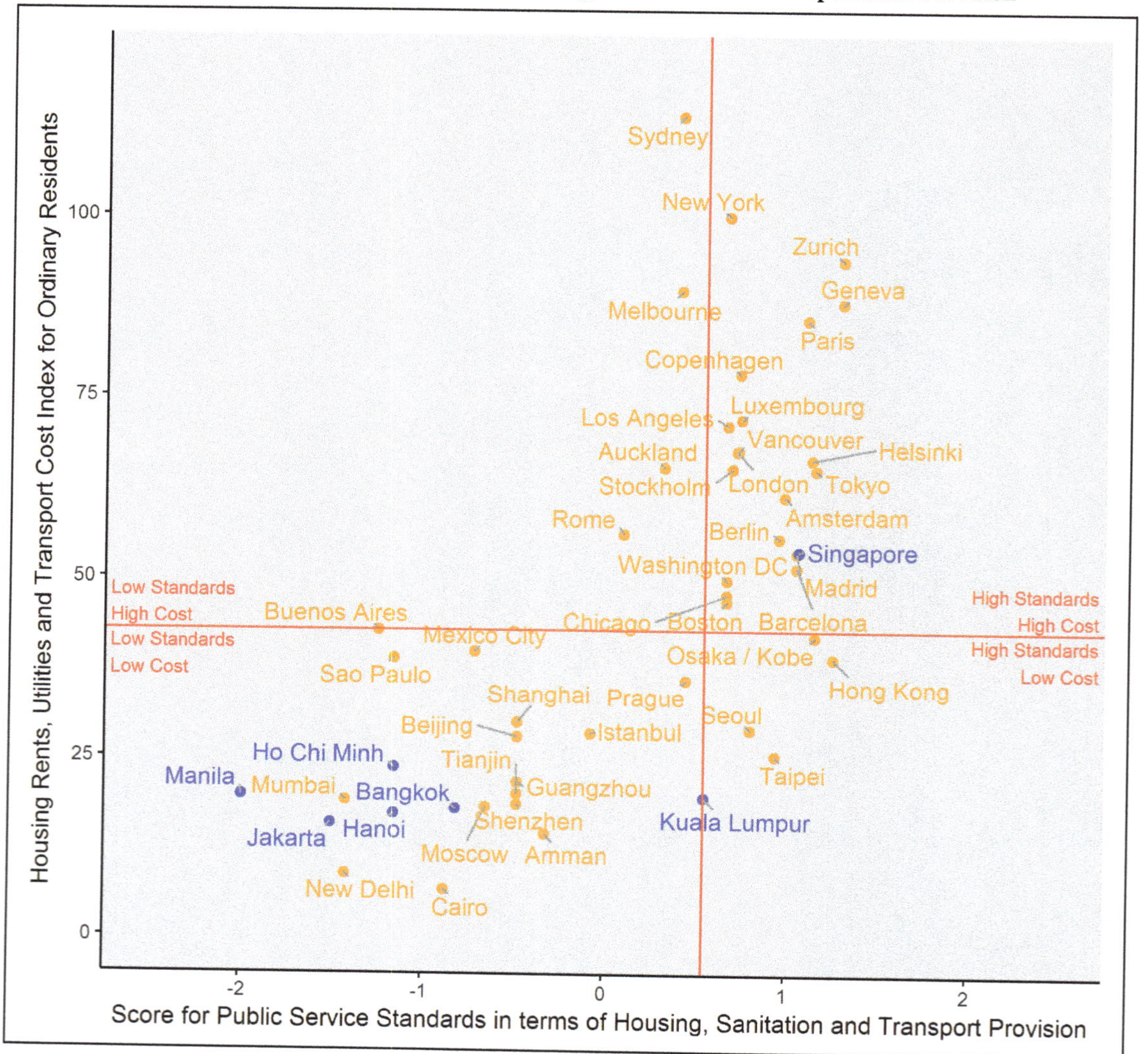

Note: The vertical and horizontal red lines represent, respectively, the median score for public service standards in terms of housing, sanitation and transportation provision and the median housing rents, utilities and transport cost index for ordinary residents of the 49 cities in the analysis.

Source: Authors' computation

Figure 2.29: Scatterplot of Education Cost Index for Ordinary Residents against Score for Public Service Standards in Terms of Education Provision

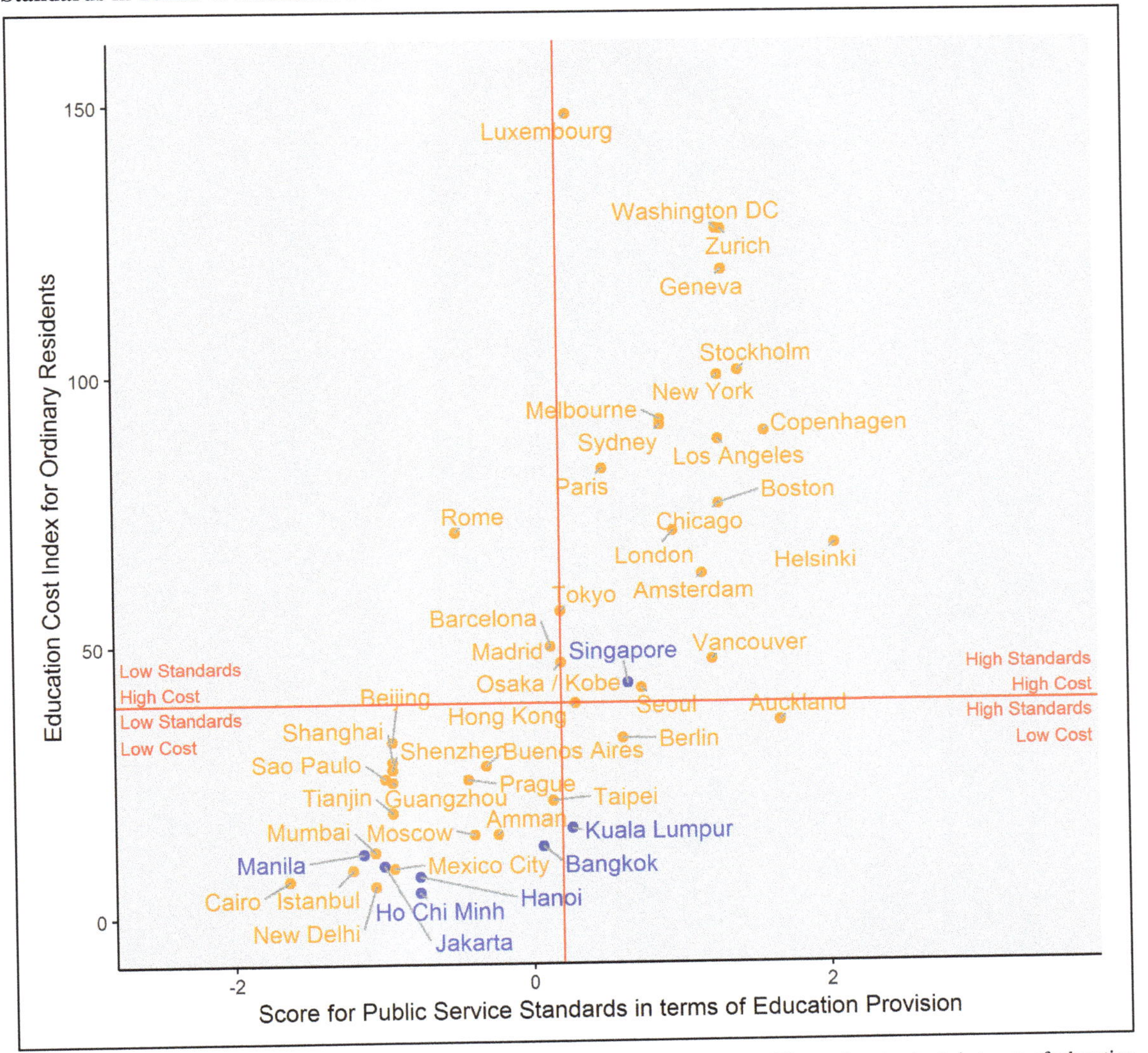

Note: The vertical and horizontal red lines represent, respectively, the median score for public service standards in terms of education provision and the median education cost index for ordinary residents of the 49 cities in the analysis.

Source: Authors' computation

Figure 2.30: Scatterplot of Health Cost Index for Ordinary Residents against Score for Public Service Standards in Terms of Healthcare Provision

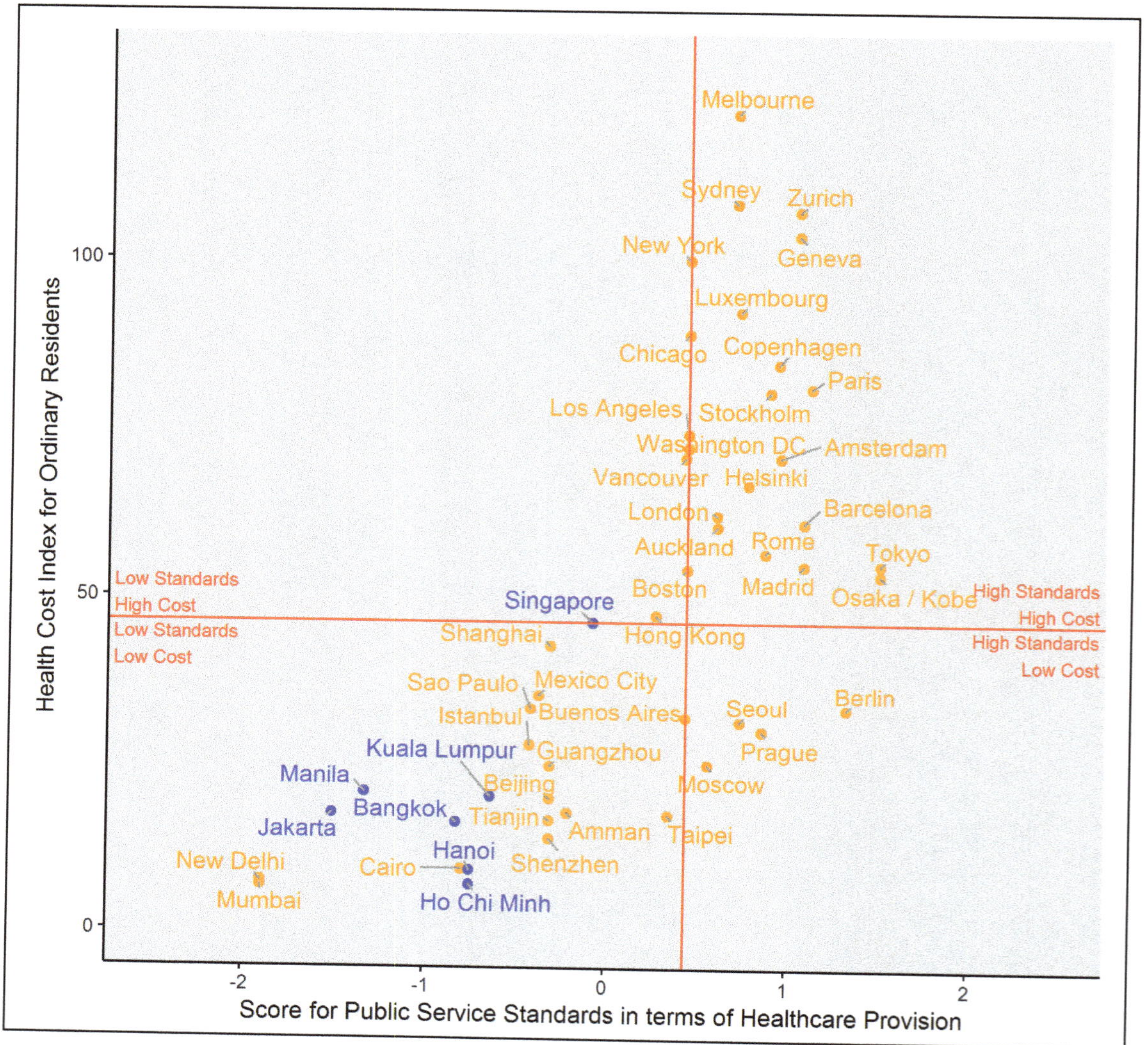

Note: The vertical and horizontal red lines represent, respectively, the median score for public service standards in terms of healthcare provision and the median health cost index for ordinary residents of the 49 cities in the analysis.

Source: Authors' computation

Figure 2.31: Scatterplot of Purchasing Power Index for Ordinary Residents and Score for Overall Liveability

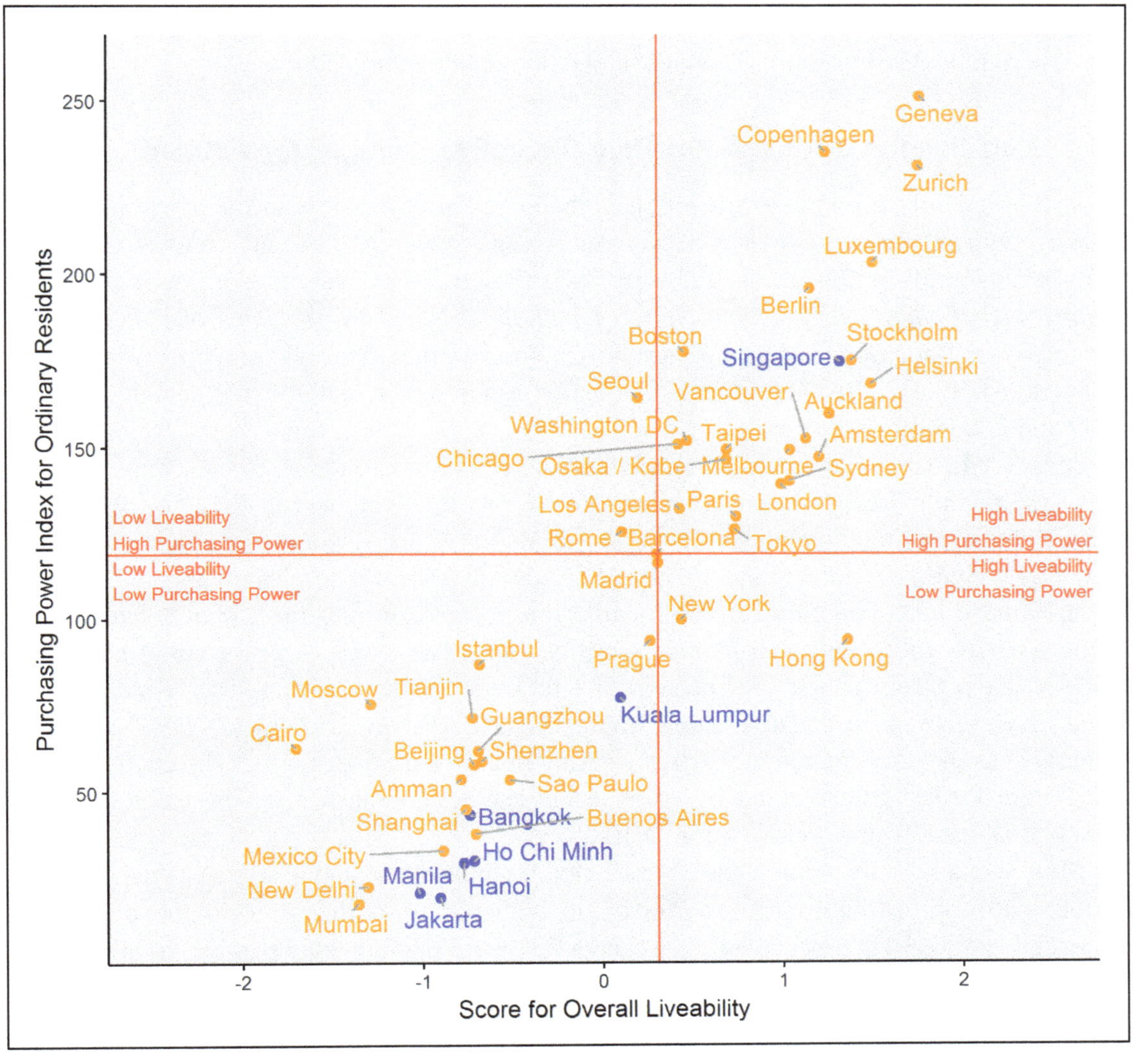

Note: The vertical and horizontal red lines represent, respectively, the median overall liveaiblity score and the median purchasing power index for ordinary residents of the 49 cities in the analysis.

Source: Authors' computation

2.5 Vietnam's Challenges and Opportunities in the International Context

The discussions in the previous sections have shed light on the importance of FDI and trade as important drivers of growth for Vietnam at both the national and sub-national level. With ongoing negotiations of trade agreements and partnerships, cross-border cooperation will continue to act as a catalyst for Vietnam's future development. Nevertheless, the adverse impacts of globalisation should also be acknowledged and addressed. This section examines potential challenges and opportunities arising from Vietnam's integration to the world economy.

2.5.1 Globalisation Drive and Potential Disruptive Changes for Vietnam

"New Normal" or "growth slowdown" have become the buzzwords in the aftermath of the Global Financial Crisis. Almost a decade has passed since then, but the residual effects of this crisis can still be felt today. Recovery from the crisis has been slow in many industrial countries, particularly the US and United Kingdom (UK), with prospects of sluggish economic growth[38] compounded by a persistently high unemployment rate of over seven percent on average between 2010 and 2015 as compared to an average rate of five percent between 2000 and 2007 before the crisis.[39]

Meanwhile, China has emerged as a key driver of global economic growth. Thus, it is not surprising that the drop in China's nominal growth rate to 7.9 percent in 2012[40] — the lowest since 2000 — and the continuous fall in the following years have created concerns about a sustained Chinese slowdown and its potential adverse spillover effects. While the ASEAN countries have been benefiting from globalisation, integration into the global economy also heightens their vulnerability to global volatility. Being the single largest trading partner of ASEAN, having contributed 15.2 percent of total trade in the region in 2015, China's slowdown may create some negative ripple effects in ASEAN.[41] In particular, CLMV are more vulnerable as they depend more heavily on China in terms of trade flows.[42] The challenges for CLMV are further compounded by rising economic uncertainties after the election of US President Donald Trump and Brexit in 2016.

More fundamentally, while trade liberalisation has indeed resulted in aggregate gains, it may also have adverse distributive effects. Workers in industries where there is a lack of comparative advantage may lose out, especially if they cannot easily transition to other sectors. As an example, recent empirical studies show that employment in export-competing industries in the US has been adversely affected by China's rise as an export powerhouse. More importantly, such losses have not been offset by gains in non-tradable sectors, export-oriented industries and industries which use imported inputs.[43] In turn, China may have to grapple with similar problems as the US with regards the transition of its workforce in the near future as manufacturing matures and labour costs rise. Indeed, the need for structural transformation is ubiquitous and it will affect all economies, including those who will succeed China as Asia's next manufacturing hub, such as Vietnam.

Thus, as Chapter 3 shall elaborate in more detail, it is important to foster a balanced economic structure even as Vietnam continues to ride the export-oriented manufacturing wave.

---

[38] See El-Erian (2010).

[39] See World Development Indicators database of the World Bank.

[40] Data on nominal GDP growth is obtained from World Development Indicators database of the World Bank.

[41] See ASEANStats, http://data.aseanstats.org/.

[42] See Salidjanova *et al.* (2015).

[43] See Autor *et al.* (2013, 2015).

Measures to develop a modern, high value-added service sector must be put in place so as to prepare the economy for future transition. In addition, fostering SMEs is another key step to realise inclusive growth in the age of globalisation.

2.5.2 Deepening International Integration for Further Development

The prior discussion on the challenges of globalisation does not imply that Vietnam should turn its back on economic integration. Deepened integration gives Vietnam access to larger markets and allows it to tap into regional economies of scale. Furthermore, technology spillovers and inflows of additional capital from FDI will help bolster development. More importantly, deepened integration creates the impetus for more wide-ranging domestic reforms. Against the backdrop of rising vulnerability and dampened reform momentum, integration initiatives including the ASEAN Economic Community (AEC), the Comprehensive and Progressive Agreement for Trans-Pacific Partnership (CPTPP), the Regional Comprehensive Economic Partnership (RCEP) and the Belt & Road Initiative (BRI) will be instrumental in propelling Vietnam forward. This section briefly discusses the significance of each initiative to Vietnam.

The AEC

Regional integration in ASEAN has become increasingly economically driven especially after the Asian Financial Crisis. The ASEAN Free Trade Area was instituted by the end of the 2000s, and with it came significant tariff reductions and eliminations. In addition, ASEAN also forged new and closer economic ties with other economies with the establishment of new partnerships including ASEAN+1, ASEAN+3 and ASEAN+6.

ASEAN has taken regional economic integration to new heights with the official establishment of the AEC on 31 December 2015. Since its conception, the AEC has widely been regarded as a highly ambitious project which aims to transform ASEAN into (i) a single market and production base, (ii) a highly competitive economic region, (iii) a region of equitable economic development and (iv) a region fully integrated into the global economy.[44] The creation of a single market with 630 million people presents Vietnam with many opportunities in terms of trade and investment. Petri *et al.* (2012) estimated that the full realisation of the AEC may raise Vietnam's GDP by US$2.4 billion, or 2.8 percent as compared to the baseline scenario.

Vietnam has actively supported and pursued the integration initiatives set out under the AEC blueprints. For instance, it has contributed to the establishment of the ASEAN Single Window (ASW)[45] by being the first among the CLMV to successfully develop a National Single Window and connect it to the ASW. However, more efforts from all member states are needed to complete key initiatives which remain outstanding despite the official formation of the AEC.

---

[44] See ASEAN Secretariat (2015).

[45] The ASEAN Single Window is a digital platform comprising ten National Single Windows of the individual member states. It is envisaged to expedite customs clearance, reduce transaction costs and thus facilitate a more seamless intraregional flow of goods.

Another major challenge to Vietnam's participation in the AEC is the lack of awareness about the AEC among the Vietnamese business community. In a 2013 survey conducted by the ADB and the Institute of Southeast Asian Studies, the percentage of Vietnamese respondents indicating that they were not aware of the AEC was a whopping 76 percent, much higher than regional average of 55 percent. Indeed, the resources allocated by the Vietnamese government to raise awareness among local enterprises, professionals and the general populace about the AEC and its benefits have been inadequate.[46]

The CPTPP

The US' withdrawal from the Trans-Pacific Partnership (TPP) was among the first few executive orders signed by President Trump on his first day in office. Spearheaded by Japan and Australia, the remaining 11 countries regrouped to protect the gains made in the original TPP negotiations. On 11 November 2017, a Ministerial Statement was issued following talks in Da Nang, heralding the resurrection of the TPP under a new name and reaffirming the commitment of all negotiating parties to open markets, combat protectionism and advance regional economic integration.

Under the new pact, the remaining 11 members, which include Australia, Brunei, Canada, Chile, Japan, Malaysia, Mexico, New Zealand, Peru, Singapore, and Vietnam, agreed to keep the core elements of the original deal. However, 20 provisions, mostly related to property rights and pertinent to US' interests, were temporarily suspended. Additionally, four specific items were slated for further negotiation. These items constitute sensitive issues for Brunei (coal), Canada (cultural exception), Malaysia (SOEs) and Vietnam (trade sanctions). It is also noteworthy that the ratification threshold for the new agreement has been reduced. Accordingly, the CPTPP only requires six out of 11 members to ratify before coming into force and not 85 percent of combined GDP as per the original deal.

Clearly, the withdrawal of the US is a blow to the economic impact and significance of the CPTPP as the US represents almost 60 percent of the combined GDP under the old agreement. Nonetheless, Vietnam will still benefit from the CPTPP. Together, the 11 signatories to the CPTPP form a bloc with a total population of 500 million people and total output of US$10 trillion.[47] In addition, the agreement offers Vietnam access to new markets including Canada, Mexico and Peru. By the projections of the Vietnam's National Centre for Information and Forecasting, the CPTPP stands to raise Vietnam's GDP by 1.3 percent and boost export growth by four percent.[48]

Meanwhile, the provisions regarding digital economy in which member countries are required to allow cross-border free flow of data[49] may facilitate the development of Vietnam's digital sector. Furthermore, the CPTPP is a high-quality trade agreement. Clauses regarding rules for SOEs, the protection of labour rights and the environment and most notably the investor-state

---

[46] See Vo (2015).

[47] See Helble and Xie (2017).

[48] See *Vietnamnet* (2017).

[49] See Donnan (2017).

dispute settlement system have remained intact. These obligations may act as a catalyst for deeper reforms in Vietnam. Finally, together with the RCEP, the CPTPP may serve as the pathway to a larger and more ambitious agenda — the Free Trade Area of the Asia-Pacific (FTAAP).

The RCEP

The RCEP was introduced by ASEAN at the 19th Summit in Bali in November 2011 with the goals of untangling the "spaghetti bowl" of existing ASEAN+1 FTAs as well as deepening economic integration between ASEAN and its six FTA partners including China, Japan, South Korea, India, Australia and New Zealand. The RCEP negotiation is conducted with the main objective of achieving a modern, comprehensive, high-quality and mutually beneficial economic partnership agreement for all participating economies.[50] The six prospective partners are growing in their significance as a source of FDI in ASEAN. In 2015, FDI from these countries accounted for 30 percent of total FDI inflows to ASEAN, or US$40 billion in absolute terms. With regards to CLMV, the four countries received a combined US$17.4 billion in FDI inflows, with a large proportion coming from the six ASEAN's FTA partners especially Japan and China.[51]

While the CPTPP is more ambitious in terms of harmonising standards and regulations, the RCEP is more pragmatic and practical in allowing the prospective members to participate in accordance to their needs for market access and acceptable levels of commitment. The RCEP's coverage includes trade in goods, trade in services, investment, intellectual property, competition, dispute settlement, and economic and technical cooperation. The last component, economic and technical cooperation, which is not part of the CPTPP, reflects the development orientation of the RCEP and the acknowledgement of the diverse economic circumstances of member countries.[52] The less demanding commitments required and potential benefits from technical cooperation certainly make RCEP an appealing option for Vietnam.

RCEP negotiations were formally initiated in November 2012 and have gone through 20 rounds thus far. Time-consuming negotiation is an inevitable feature of any plurilateral or multilateral partnerships, and the RCEP is not an exception. While there are existing FTAs between ASEAN and its partners, to merge these respective FTAs into a single comprehensive agreement is not an easy task. The RCEP negotiations are further impeded by the same problem faced in the establishment of AEC, namely the development gap among ASEAN members. ASEAN is leading the RCEP negotiation as a single bloc, and hence the disparities in the levels of economic development among ASEAN member states pose critical challenges to harmonisation of domestic rules and policies. While a flexibility clause has been built into the RCEP framework, which helps to protect disparate national interests and thus resolve deadlocks, it might compromise the main objective of establishing a high-quality partnership and reduce cooperation to the lowest common denominator.

---

[50] The guiding principles for negotiating RCEP are accessible from http://dfat.gov.au/trade/agreements/rcep/Doc uments/guiding-principles-rcep.pdf (accessed on 17 January 2018).

[51] See ASEAN Secretariat (2016).

[52] See Tan *et al.* (2017e).

Upon successful completion, the partnership will cover 30 percent of the global economy, providing tremendous opportunities for growth. Vietnam should also tap on the RCEP for new sources of foreign investment which will not only bring in economic benefits but also facilitate infrastructure and skill upgrading — two major structural challenges faced by Vietnamese economy. Furthermore, the realisation of the ASEAN-led RCEP will complement the CPTPP considering that not all ASEAN countries are signatories to the latter. More importantly, it is a stepping stone towards deeper economic integration and shall pave the way for the FTAAP.

The BRI

The idea of the Silk Road Economic Belt was first proposed during China's President Xi Jinping's visit to Kazakhstan in September 2013. It was reiterated a month later when President Xi visited Indonesia. Concrete steps are taken subsequently with the adoption of the proposal, which is officially termed as One Belt, One Road Initiative and subsequently the BRI, as one of the key policy priorities of the Chinese Central Committee. Formulation of BRI gained momentum after the endorsement of 57 economies in establishing the Asian Infrastructure Investment Bank (AIIB). The potential stakeholders used to only be able to acquire clues about the initiative from the reports of China's State Council and National Congress, and speeches of Chinese leaders on multiple occasions. It was not until March 2015 during the Boao Forum that an action plan revealing the principles, framework, and cooperation priorities and mechanisms was announced by President Xi.

The BRI will be covering the continents of Africa, Asia and Europe, which account for more than 60 percent of world population.[53] Against the backdrop of rising uncertainties in the global landscape, the BRI has outlined five cooperation priorities, namely (i) policy coordination; (ii) facilitating connectivity; (iii) unimpeded trade; (iv) financial integration; and (v) people-to-people bonds.[54] In sum, this global initiative has gone beyond economic integration and includes the elements of mutual social, political and cultural interests.

International scholars and pundits have reacted differently to the BRI. However, it is clear that the BRI is significant for Vietnam with regard to infrastructure development, which is also the main feature distinguishing the BRI from other international cooperation initiatives. The connectivity vision which is the main driver of BRI envisages a common prosperity built on an efficient and integrated network of land, sea and air transportation.

The creation of the AIIB and the Silk Road Fund under the BRI will certainly add to the current financing options which usually come from the limited national budget or international organisations such as the World Bank and the ADB. As the BRI acknowledges the central role of infrastructure in generating inclusive growth, Vietnam together with the other ASEAN countries must leverage on their positions as founding members of the AIIB to shape its policy agenda and channel this new infrastructure funding mechanism towards projects which foster connectivity and serve their development needs.

[53] See Huang (2016).

[54] See Tian (2015).

2.6 Concluding Notes

Decades of wars had hampered economic development in Vietnam. It was not until the late-1980s that the momentum of economic reforms has intensified, leading to major structural transformations of the Vietnamese economy. The *Doi Moi* reform in general can be encapsulated as a transition from centrally-planned to a more market-oriented system as well as modernisation from an agrarian to an industrial and service-based economy, driven by export-led industrialisation and integration into the world economy. Vietnam soon emerged as a darling of investors, and was regarded as the new frontier of growth in Asia.

While the positive progress that resulted from *Doi Moi* is indisputable, the sustainability of economic growth remains questionable. As analysed in Section 2.2.2, Vietnam is beset with seven pertinent challenges to its growth model. Specifically, ageing population and rapid technological advancements are two megatrends which may prove disruptive to Vietnam's development trajectory as they undermine the country's advantage in low labour cost. Against this backdrop, it is worrisome that labour productivity growth in Vietnam has slowed, especially in terms of agricultural productivity. Sluggish productivity growth is worsened by inefficiencies in a bloated state sector and lack of synergies between the FDI sector and local enterprises. In addition, institutional reforms have lagged behind economic reforms. Gaps in institutional quality have hampered the implementation of reforms aimed at addressing Vietnam's economic malaises. Meanwhile, issues related to governance and the overreach of the state in commercial activities through SOEs have resulted in wastages and inefficiencies.

By benchmarking Vietnam's economic competitiveness against other countries in ASEAN, we found that Vietnam has been performing well below the regional average in many aspects in ACI's competitiveness framework, as reflected through its negative standardised scores. As a result, it has not been able to catch up with the ASEAN-6. In fact, Vietnam's overall competitiveness score has been relatively stagnant since 2011. By deep-diving into the sub-environment and the indicator levels of the ACI competitiveness index, we found that Vietnam's relative weaknesses *vis-à-vis* its ASEAN peers include low productivity, weak competition and regulatory standards, inadequate human capital development as well as infrastructure bottlenecks. These weaknesses, which are manifestations of the fundamental impediments to Vietnam's growth model, must be addressed. The urgency of doing so can be gleaned from our competitiveness analysis which shows that Vietnam is gradually losing its cost competitiveness and attractiveness to investors.

Adding to the set of challenges faced by policy-makers is the problem of regional disparities among Vietnam's sub-national economies. Fuelled by FDI, the Southern provinces have developed markedly faster than their Northern and Central counterparts. Therefore, Southern Vietnam leads the other two regions in many socio-economic indicators, including individual's incomes, progress in poverty reduction and healthcare outcomes. The same pattern is also borne out at the city-level where Ho Chi Minh City outperforms Hanoi in terms of economic vibrancy and liveability. The stark contrast between unequal development and relatively equal distribution of population means that regional imbalances will adversely affect a great number of people in Vietnam. Without concerted effort to promote more balanced development, Vietnam risks becoming "One Country-Two Economies" where the gaps between Southern Vietnam and the other two regions become too large to bridge.

More challenges and opportunities arise from Vietnam's pursuit of deepened integration. On the one hand, the economy is exposed to more external risks beyond its control as it becomes more open. The residual effects from the Global Financial Crisis, rise of protectionist sentiments and the spectre of a Chinese growth slowdown will cause mounting unpredictability and drags on Vietnam's growth momentum. More fundamentally, globalisation and the constant emergence of low-cost competitors require Vietnam to prepare for economic transformation in which productivity and efficiency are improved, SME growth is fostered, and services and manufacturing are developed in tandem supported by a highly productive agriculture sector. On the other hand, multilateral initiatives such as the AEC, CPTPP, RCEP and BRI continue to offer unique benefits to the Vietnamese economy. As such, they should be leveraged on to spur domestic economic reforms and bring about upgraded development.

References

ASEAN Secretariat. 2015. *ASEAN Economic Community Blueprint 2025*. Jakarta: ASEAN Secretariat.

ASEAN Secretariat. 2016. *ASEAN Investment Report 2016*. Jakarta: ASEAN Secretariat.

Autor, David H., David Dorn, and Gordon H. Hanson. 2013. "The China Syndrome: Local Labour Market Effects of Import Competition in the United States". *American Economic Review* 103 (6):2121–2168.

Autor, David H., David Dorn, and Gordon H. Hanson. 2015. "The China Shock: Learning from Labour Market Adjustment to Large Changes in Trade". NBER Working Paper No. 21906. National Bureau of Economic Research (NBER), Massachusetts.

Beresford, Melanie, and Angie Ngoc Tran. 2004. *Reaching for the Dream: Challenges of Sustainable Development in Vietnam*. Denmark: NIAS Press.

Bristow, Gillian. 2010. *Critical Reflections on Regional Competitiveness: Theory, Policy, Practice (Routledge Studies in Human Geography)*. Oxon: Routledge.

Camagni, Roberto. 2002. "On the Concept of Territorial Competitiveness: Sound or Misleading?" *Urban Studies* 39 (13):2395–2411.

Coxhead, Ian, Kim N.B. Ninh, Vu Thi Thao, and Nguyen Thi Phuong Hoa. 2010. *A Robust Harvest: Strategic Choices for Agricultural and Rural Development in Vietnam*. San Francisco: The Asia Foundation.

Donnan, Shawn. 2017. "Long Live the TPP — Pacific Trade Pact Survives Largely Intact". *Financial Times*, 14th November, available at https://www.ft.com/content/c5cdd3aa-c82d-11e7-ab18-7a9fb7d6163e (accessed on 17 January 2018).

Duong, Thi Nhi. 2015. "Vietnam Country Report". In *Financing ASEAN Connectivity*, edited by Fauziah Zen and Michael Regan. Jakarta: Economic Research Institute for ASEAN and East Asia (ERIA).

El-Erian, Mohamed. A. 2010. *Navigating the New Normal in Industrial Countries*. Washington DC: Per Jacobsson Foundation.

Government of Vietnam. 2016. *Báo cáo tình hình cổ phần hóa doanh nghiệp nhà nước giai đoạn 2011–2015 và 9 tháng 2016, giải pháp đẩy mạnhcổ phần hóa doanh nghiệp nhà nước giai đoạn tới* [Report on the equitization of SOEs in the phase of 2011–2015 and the first 9 months of 2016, and measures to accelerate

SOE equitization in the coming period], available at http://vietnamfinance.vn/bao-cao-cua-chinh-phu-ve-co-phan-hoa-giai-doan-2011-2016-20161023201944748.htm (accessed on 20 October 2017).

Hallward-Driemeier, Mary, and Gaurav Nayyar. 2017. *Trouble in the Making? The Future of Manufacturing-Led Development*. Washington DC: World Bank.

Helble, Matthias, and Yizhe Daniel Xie. 2017. "Is the CPTPP a Risky Gamble?". *East Asia Forum*, 23rd December, available at http://www.eastasiaforum.org/2017/12/23/is-the-cptpp-a-risky-gamble/ (accessed on 17 January 2018).

Hong, An. 2016. "Vietnam May be Missing Out on "Golden Population": UNDP". 28th April, *VN Express International*, available at https://e.vnexpress.net/news/news/vietnam-may-be-missing-out-on-golden-population-undp-3394794.html (accessed on 20th October 2017).

Huang, Yiping. 2016. "Understanding China's Belt & Road Initiative: Motivation, Framework and Assessment." *China Economic Review* 40: 314–321.

Kitson, Michael, Ronald Martin, and Peter Tyler. 2004. "Regional Competitiveness: An Elusive yet Key Concept?" *Regional Studies* 38 (9):991–99.

Krugman, Paul. 1994. "Competitiveness: A Dangerous Obsession." *Foreign Affairs* 73 (2):28–44.

Le, Hoang Cuong, Helen Cabalu, and Ruhul Salim. 2014. "Winners and Losers in Vietnam Equitization Programs." *Journal of Policy Modeling* 36 (1):172–184.

Le, Hong Hiep. 2017. "Vietnam's New Wave of SOE Equitization: Drivers and Implications." ISEAS Perspective No.57. Institute of Southeast Asian Studies (ISEAS), Singapore.

McKinsey Global Institute. 2012. "Sustaining Vietnam's Growth: The Productivity Challenge", available at https://www.mckinsey.com/global-themes/asia-pacific/sustaining-growth-in-vietnam (accessed on 20 October 2017).

Nakamura, David. 2016. "Buoyed by U.S. Firms, Vietnam Emerges as an Asian Manufacturing Powerhouse." *The Washington Post*, 21st May, available at https://www.washingtonpost.com/politics/buoyed-by-us-firms-vietnam-emerges-as-an-asian-manufacturing-powerhouse/2016/05/21/6f117876-1b6a-11e6-b6e0-c53b7ef63b45_story.html?utm_term=.1531000517d9 (accessed on 20 October 2017).

Nguyen, Van Thang, and Nick J. Freeman. 2009. "State-owned Enterprises in Vietnam: Are They 'Crowding Out' the private sector?". *Post-Communist Economies* 21(1):227–247.

Petri, Peter, Michael Plummer, and Fan Zhai. 2010. "The Economics of the ASEAN Economic Community." Brandeis Working Papers No. 13, Brandeis University, Department of Economics and International Business School, Massachusetts.

Porter, Michael E. 1980. *Competitive Strategy: Techniques for Analyzing Industries and Competitors*. New York: Free Press.

Salidjanova, Nargiza, Iacob Koch-Weser, and Jason Klanderman. 2015. *China's Economic Ties with ASEAN: A Country-by-Country Analysis*. Washington DC: US-China Economic and Security Review Commission.

Tan, Khee Giap, Nguyen Trieu Duong Luu, and Xiao Lian. 2017a. "Empirical Analysis on Growth Slowdown in ASEAN" 2017. *The Journal of Developing Areas* 51(3):363–376.

Tan, Khee Giap, Le Phuong Anh Nguyen, and Nguyen Trieu Duong Luu. 2017b. *2016 Annual Competitiveness Analysis and Growth Slowdown Analysis for ASEAN-10*. Singapore: World Scientific.

Tan, Khee Giap, Tongxin Nie, and Shinae Baek. 2017c. *2015 Greater China Liveable Cities Index: Ranking Analysis, Simulation and Policy Evaluation*. Singapore: Whioce Publishing.

Tan, Khee Giap, Nguyen Trieu Duong Luu, Diviya Chandran, and Kong Yam Tan. 2017d. *2016 Annual Indices for Expatriates and Ordinary Residents on Cost of Living, Wages and Purchasing Power for World's Major Cities*. Singapore: World Scientific.

Tan, Khee Giap, Le Phuong Anh Nguyen, Sasidaran Gopalan, and Nguyen Trieu Duong Luu. 2017e. *2015 Annual Competitiveness Analysis, Agricultural Productivity and Development Vision for ASEAN-10*. Singapore: World Scientific.

Taussig, Markus D., Chi Hieu Nguyen, and Thuy Linh Nguyen. 2016. *From Control to Market: Time for Real SOE Reform in Vietnam?* Singapore: Centre for Governance, Institutions and Organisations (CGIO).

The Economist. 2010. "Plus One Country". 2nd September, available at http://www.economist.com/node/16953208 (accessed on 17 January 2018).

Thời Báo Tài Chính. 2017. "Nhà đầu tư chưa mặn mà với cổ phần hóa DNNN" [Strategic investors are not yet keen on equitization of SOEs], 30th October, available at http://thoibaotaichinhvietnam.vn/pages/kinh-doanh/2017-10-30/nha-dau-tu-chua-man-ma-voi-co-phan-hoa-dnnn-49740.aspx (accessed on 17 January 2018).

Tian, Shaohui. 2015. "Full Text: Vision and actions on jointly building Belt and Road". *Xinhua*, 28th March, available at http://news.xinhuanet.com/english/china/2015-03/28/c_ 134105858.htm (accessed on 21 February, 2017).

UN DESA. 2017a. *World Population Prospects: The 2017 Revision, Volume I: Key Findings and Advance Tables*. New York: United Nations Department of Economic and Social Affairs (UN DESA).

UN DESA. 2017b. *World Population Prospects: The 2017 Revision, Volume II: Demographic Profiles*. New York: United Nations Department of Economic and Social Affairs (UN DESA).

UNFPA. 2011. *The Ageing Population in Viet Nam: Current Status, Prognosis, and Possible Policy Responses*. Hanoi: UNFPA Viet Nam.

Vietnamnet. 2017. "What Does Vietnam Expect From the 'TPP Without the US'?". 20th November, available at http://english.vietnamnet.vn/fms/business/190385/what-does-vietnam-expect-from-the--tpp-without-the-us--.html (accessed on 17 January 2018).

Vo, Tri Thanh. 2015. "Managing Domestic Consensus Building for ASEAN Community Building in Vietnam". *Journal of Southeast Asian Economies* 32 (2):275–288.

VTV News. 2017. "Gần hết năm 2017, cổ phần hóa DNNN chưa đạt 50% kế hoạch" [Equitization of SOEs Has Not Met 50 Percent of Annual Targets], 26th December, available at http://vtv.vn/kinh-te/gan-het-nam-2017-co-phan-hoa-dnnn-chua-dat-50-ke-hoach-20171226150522764.htm (accessed on 17 January 2018).

World Bank. 2013. *Vietnam Development Report 2014 — Skilling up Vietnam: Preparing the Workforce for a Modern Market Economy*. Washington DC: World Bank.

World Bank and Ministry of Planning and Investment. 2016. *Vietnam 2035: Toward Prosperity, Creativity, Equity, and Democracy*. Washington DC: World Bank.

World Bank. 2017. *Vietnam at a Crossroads: Engaging in the Next Generation of Global Value Chains*. Washington DC: World Bank.

World Economic Forum. 2017. "Country/Economy Profiles Viet Nam", available at http://wef.ch/2wcPmeh (accessed on 17 January 2018).

Chapter 3

Achieving Balanced and Sustainable Development for Enhanced Economic Competitiveness

3.1 Introductory Notes

Chapter 2 has raised concerns about the future efficacy of Vietnam's current growth model and highlighted Vietnam's low economic competitiveness relative to several other countries in Southeast Asia. Despite the success of *Doi Moi*, the Vietnamese economy still suffers from major weaknesses including stagnating productivity growth, prevalence of market distortions, weak institutional capacity, inadequate human capital and physical infrastructure development, and persistent imbalances at the sub-national level, among others. Thus, instead of just "renovating" the economy as during the past 30 years, Vietnam now has to focus on "revitalising" it with a new wave of wide-ranging reforms.

This chapter outlines a comprehensive policy roadmap for Vietnam to achieve balanced and sustainable development for enhanced economic competitiveness. We call on the Vietnamese government to ensure the following:

(i) **Facilitate private sector development** by intensifying the reforms of state-owned enterprises (SOEs) and strengthening market mechanisms for a level playing field;
(ii) **Prevent the emergence of "One Country-Two Economies"** by enhancing intracountry connectivity and pursuing the upgraded development of Hanoi as a catalyst for the broader development of Northern Vietnam;
(iii) **Nurture small and medium enterprises (SMEs) through market-oriented policy initiatives** which foster synergies between SMEs and multinational corporations (MNCs), to enhance the former's productivity, efficiency and internationalisation potentials, and improve the business environment. These policies must be **supported and informed by evidence-based, policy-oriented research on SMEs' strengths and weaknesses as well as the ease of doing business**;
(iv) **Build digital capacity for SMEs** to prepare them for the Fourth Industrial Revolution;
(v) **Promote the holistic development of the workforce** through the Skills Future Initiative which encompasses the Tripartite and Targeted Industrial Internship Model with Placed-Trained-Employed Scheme (IIM-PTE) as well as policies to foster data literacy, soft skill and language skill development, among others;
(vi) **Transform Vietnam into a vibrant, diversified and sustainable economy** whereby Vietnam shall become a leading manufacturing hub and excellent centre for services, with a highly productive and sustainable agriculture sector;
(vii) Formulate a comprehensive strategy with clear targets, performance metrics and monitoring of processes to **ensure the viability of special economic zones (SEZs) as the engine for growth and test-beds for policy reforms**.

The rest of this chapter is organised as follows. The aforementioned policy area (i) is discussed in Section 3.2, while (ii) is presented in Section 3.3. Section 3.4 then provides concrete recommendations associated with (iii) and (iv). Section 3.5 describes the initiatives mentioned in (v). Section 3.6 sets out the necessary policy measures to achieve (vi), while Section 3.7 discusses (vii). This new wave of reforms will only be successful if the government can mobilise popular support and public participation. In light of this, Section 3.8 presents the Singapore's People's Association (PA) model on public policy communication, articulation and acceptance, which may offers useful insights for the Vietnamese government. Finally, Section 3.9 concludes.

3.2 Facilitating Private Sector Development

As explained in Chapter 2, a bloated state sector has impeded private sector development due to the severe market distortions it has created. Thus, it is exigent for Vietnam to quicken the pace of its SOE reforms and move towards a rule-based, transparent and competitive economic environment.

3.2.1 Revitalising State-owned Enterprise Reforms

The government must seize the momentum of recent successful deals such as the US$4.8 billion sale of the majority stake in Sabeco to ThaiBev to accelerate the equitisation and divestment of SOEs. Under the current SOE restructuring plan, 137 more SOEs are slated for equitisation by 2020. To achieve this goal, the equitisation process and the valuation of SOEs must be made more transparent and efficient. In addition, larger holdings of stakes must be put up for sale so that equitisation will indeed result in divestment of state resources from non-essential sectors. There should also be more concerted effort to engage strategic investors with industry expertise to ensure the viability of SOEs after privatisation.

In particular, speedy implementation of Decree 126 will be crucial to the success of the next wave of equitisation. Formulated in November 2017, the Decree contains new specific provisions aimed at attracting strategic investors such as cutting the investment lock-in period from five to three years and providing more detailed guidelines on SOE valuation. Most notably, the Decree introduces book-building as an initial public offering (IPO) method on top of the three existing ones, which are auction, underwriting and private placement. Book-building involves creating a book of institutional investors' orders of SOE stocks with clear records of the quantities demanded and corresponding prices. Such information is then used to determine the eventual IPO price. This method is expected to facilitate more market-sensitive pricing, thus improving the appeal of the equitisation process to prospective investors.[1] In addition, to tackle SOEs' reluctance to be listed on the stock exchange, Decree 126 now mandates SOEs to file for listing with the UPCoM exchange within 90 days of completing an IPO. Overall, if properly implemented, Decree 126 will enhance the legal framework for equitisation, making it more efficient.

[1] See Nguyen and Weisblatt (2017).

At the same time, it is vital that the management of state assets is centralised under a specialised agency. Currently, state capital in SOEs is overseen by different ministries and a multitude of both central and local government bodies. This results in a situation whereby government agencies act as both the player and the referee: overlaps in their SOE-related responsibilities and their primary role as regulators create conflicts of interest, incentivise favouritism and engender inefficiencies. The establishment of a specialised agency to oversee the SOEs will help to separate the ownership and regulatory functions of the state and promote greater accountability.

The Vietnamese government has undertaken to create a "super committee" under the direct supervision of the Cabinet to oversee 30 major state-owned conglomerates. These consist of industry giants such as the Vietnam Oil and Gas Group (PetroVietnam), the Vietnam National Coal–Mineral Industries Holding Corporation Limited (Vinacomin), the Vietnam Posts and Telecommunications Group (VNPT) and the Airports Corporation of Vietnam (ACV), among others. The combined state capital in these 30 firms is estimated to be 5,000 trillion Vietnam Dong, or more than US$200 billion.

While the move to centralise management of the government's stakes in major SOEs is a step in the right direction, the success of the proposed "super-committee model" will largely hinge on the organisational structure and operational framework of the committee, the details of which are still being hammered out by a working group recently set up by the government. Incorporating business and industrial expertise in the committee will be essential given the operational complexities and the sheer scale of the SOEs under its portfolio. In addition, there should be clear assignment of roles and responsibilities such that committee members do not interfere with business operations of the SOEs. More importantly, it is critical that the committee does not engage in passing regulations and is kept independent from the various ministries in order to avoid the pitfalls of the current system. It is hard to imagine how this would be achieved if the committee is to be staffed and led by officials from the various ministries. Depending on the outcome of this initiative, Vietnam may need to revisit the professional investment fund model similar to that of Singapore's Temasek Holdings, and the government-linked company model, which allow the management of state capital to be carried out at arms-length.

3.2.2 Strengthening Institutional Governance and Market Mechanism

The government's push for greater SOE equitisation and a centralised capital management system must be accompanied by more concerted effort to enhance the market mechanism and improve institutional quality. In particular, market distortions in favour of SOEs must be eliminated to level the playing field. As described in Section 2.2.2 of Chapter 2, SOEs are still given undue privileges in terms of land, credit and market access, at the expense of private enterprises.

Additionally, strengthening corporate governance across all sectors is crucial to improve the competitiveness of Vietnamese enterprises and achieve a healthy market economy. However, corporate governance in Vietnam remains problematic notwithstanding the rapid development of the legal and regulatory framework for investor protection. For instance, new laws on independent audit were enacted in 2011, and in 2013 the State Securities Commission of Vietnam (SSC) revised the Corporate Governance Regulations as well as Model Charter detailing good practices for listed companies. Nonetheless, weaknesses remain in terms of poor disclosure, outdated accounting standards, lack of internal control mechanisms and limited accountability of firm management. In fact, current practices in many public enterprises fall far short of what is required in the revised Corporate Governance Regulations, which also highlights the government's difficulties in enforcing the rule of law.

The roles and functions of the SSC could actually be enhanced as an independent supervisory body to ensure compliance of corporate laws and regulations. Furthermore, incentives for firms to uphold accountability to investors should be introduced. For example, corporate governance scorecard with detailed firm rankings can be published for investors to monitor the listed firms as well as for the firms to improve their management. At the same time, an organisation dedicated to providing training and technical support to firms could be established, ideally with local and international industry experts on the board or acting as advisors.

3.3 Mitigating Regional Disparities to Prevent the Emergence of "One Country-Two Economies"

Building on the analysis in Section 2.4 of Chapter 2, this section highlights the importance of mitigating regional disparities in Vietnam to manage income inequality, prevent Vietnam from becoming one country with two economies and forestall potential negative socio-economic consequences of interregional migration. Policy-makers should seek to enhance intracountry connectivity so that distanced, less-developed provinces can share in the fruits of growth through better connection to production chains and markets. Another key policy initiative is to leverage on Hanoi's advantage as the national capital of Vietnam for its upgraded development. Hanoi's rise as a business and financing hub will catalyse the broader development of Northern Vietnam, and help bridge its gap with Southern Vietnam.

3.3.1 The Need for More Balanced Regional Development

Balanced regional development is important for managing inequality. Unlike most other fast-growing economies, the sustained period of prosperity in Vietnam over the past 20 years was successfully attained without significant increases in income inequality. As seen in Figure 3.1, the Gini coefficient of Vietnam has never surpassed 0.4 between 1992 and 2014. After the sharp spike in 2010, the coefficient has been on a downward trend. By 2014, Vietnam's Gini coefficient was at 0.348, lower than its 1992 level at 0.357.

Nevertheless, past performance is not indicative of future success, and the Gini coefficient is only one method to examine inequality. A study by Oxfam in 2017 has warned that inequality in Vietnam is currently on the rise. According to this report, the richest households in Vietnam have been experiencing stronger growth in income than the poorer households. In the three provinces of Lao Cai, Nghe An and Dak Nong, income disparity between the 20 percent richest and 20 percent poorest households was as high as 21 times in 2016.[2] The 2010 Vietnam Household

[2] See Lefur (2017).

Figure 3.1: Vietnam's Gini Coefficient, 1992–2014

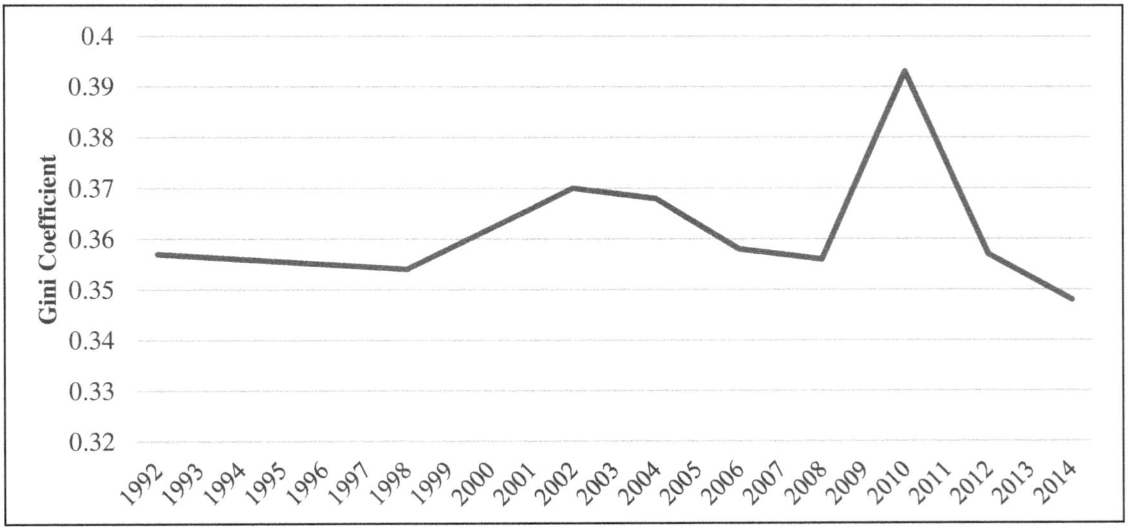

Source: World Bank, World Development Indicators

Living Standards Survey also revealed that nation-wide, the gap in monthly average income per capita between these two groups of households has increased from 8.1 to 9.2 times between 2004 and 2010.

Moreover, Vietnam has been able to suppress growing inequality due to the government's emphasis on pro-equity spending and income transfers. However, continuous social spending limits the government's ability to finance large-scale development programmes, especially infrastructure development which is crucial to sustain Vietnam's growth momentum. It is also questionable if the current pro-equity policies are fiscally sustainable in the long run. Given rising public debt, it is critical that Vietnam reconsiders its approach to tackle inequality.

A key driver of inequality in Vietnam is regional disparities. As we have shown in Section 2.4 of Chapter 2, differences in development level and availability of economic opportunities have engendered persistent gaps in living standards between the Northern, Central and Southern regions. In general, Southern provinces have been able to attract more foreign direct investment (FDI) than Northern and Central provinces. As a result, they have experienced stronger economic expansion, which helped to create more well-paying jobs and facilitate faster poverty reduction. In addition, the South has achieved better basic healthcare than the North and the Central as evident in its lower average infant mortality rate and higher average life expectancy. Regional disparities become even more salient as we compare Hanoi and Ho Chi Minh City, the largest cities in the North and the South, respectively. The latter leads the former in terms of economic development and liveability.

Should such gaps continue to widen, Vietnam is at risk of becoming "One Country-Two Economies" with Southern provinces pulling too far ahead of their Northern and Central counterparts. This is a serious concern, particularly from a political point of view. People tend to assess their well-being in comparison with others; groups which fall behind will become disgruntled if the income and welfare gaps grow too fast and too large. Therefore, an emergence of "One Country-Two Economies" will weaken national cohesion.

Furthermore, from a socio-economic perspective, large geographic differences in income and standards of living may be problematic to both the sluggish and more dynamic regions. Provinces with lower economic growth may struggle to provide ordinary residents with meaningful employment and adequate access to high-quality public services including housing, transport, education and healthcare. This is likely to encourage internal migration, which may further hinder the development of poorer provinces. At the same time, the influx of migrants may strain the service provision systems in richer regions, while also posing challenges in terms of social problems among migrant groups who could not obtain employment. As a result, policy-makers should seek to address regional imbalances in the next phase of Vietnam's development.

3.3.2 Enhancing Intracountry Connectivity

Enhancing intracountry connectivity is an important policy pillar for achieving more balanced regional development. Over the past 30 years, Vietnam has made progress in reducing economic disparities between its regions though there is still room for improvement. On the one hand, investment in physical infrastructure has helped to reduce internal trade costs. As a result, Vietnam's logistics industry has outperformed many economies at similar levels of development (World Bank and Ministry of Planning and Investment, 2016). Within the Association of Southeast Asian Nations (ASEAN), Vietnam has decidedly surpassed Cambodia, Laos and Myanmar, and even Brunei and Philippines in terms of the Logistic Performance Index (see Figure 3.2). In 2016, Vietnam was neck-to-neck with Indonesia and was only below the three most advanced economies in ASEAN (Singapore, Malaysia and Thailand).

On the other hand, the interregional transport networks in Vietnam still face persistent weaknesses. Despite high demands in movements of goods and passengers, Vietnam has not developed a railway system with trains capable of running at 100 kilometres per hour. Additionally, according to the World Bank's assessment, the country's total length of operational international-standard expressways in 2016 fell far short of its targets of over 2,500 kilometres by 2020 and over 3,000 kilometres by 2030.[3] Furthermore, in 2011, 87 percent of freight trips in Vietnam were short-distance trips of 200 kilometres or less and the majority of road journeys were less than 100 kilometres.[4]

Lack of adequate infrastructure has hampered urbanisation in more geographically isolated regions and limited their participation in supply chains, thus holding back their economic development. Furthermore, it also hinders regions from developing synergies with one another for mutual gains. Another challenge relates to the decentralised and fragmented nature of infrastructure planning in Vietnam. Lack of coordination between regional

[3] See World Bank and Ministry of Planning and Investment (2016).

[4] See World Bank (2011).

Figure 3.2: Logistic Performance Index for ASEAN Countries, 2016

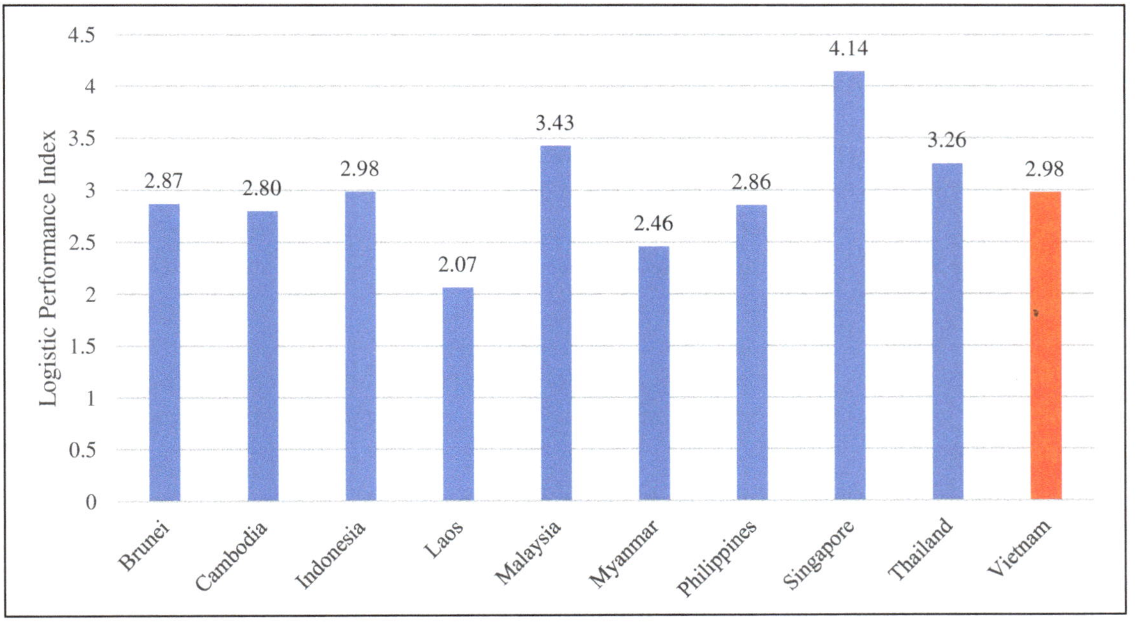

Source: World Bank

authorities and government agencies may result in highly inefficient outcomes where infrastructure projects misalign with each other. This can be seen in seaport development, where the World Bank has consistently warned of overcapacity.[5] The Cai Mep-Thi Vai port in Ba Ria-Vung Tau province is a case in point. This new, modern port complex is located only 80 kilometres away from inner-city river ports in Ho Chi Minh City. Partly due to competition from these existing facilities, the Cai Mep port is only able to utilise less than 30 percent of its container-handling capacity.[6]

Going forward, addressing weaknesses in connective infrastructure must be a top policy priority. The focus should be on key projects to enhance the efficiency of interregional transport and logistics. For instance, the railway and highway system to link the poorer provinces in the Northern Midlands and Mountainous Region to major markets, ports and border gates should be upgraded to stimulate their development. Besides, more should be done to build strategic interregional corridors between the Central Highlands, the Mekong River Delta and production centres in other regions so that their potentials in large-scale agriculture production and other primary industries can be maximised through seamless connection to supply chains.

In addition, to prevent fragmented development with projects cannibalising one another, the government should adopt integrated planning which fosters collaboration between regions and different public-sector functions. There must also be strong fiscal discipline through suitable auditing and reporting mechanisms to minimise wastage in investment.

---

[5] See *Thanh Nien News* (2014).

[6] See World Bank and Ministry of Planning and Investment (2016).

3.3.3 Raising the Status of Hanoi as Truly the Capital of Vietnam

In the quest to prevent Vietnam from becoming one country with two economies, Hanoi has a special role to play as a growth centre which will create the impetus for the rapid development of Northern Vietnam. Hanoi should be embedded in a system of towns and cities with complementary functions where it serves as the key node connecting Northern regional cities and the hinterland provinces to regional and global value chains as well as international service markets. In other words, Hanoi should become the gateway of North Vietnam to the world.

To this end, Hanoi's advantage as the national capital should be fully leveraged. The government may look to the following:

(i) Encourage MNCs in Vietnam to set up representative offices in Hanoi to facilitate better business consultation as well as administrative service supports with relevant governing authorities;
(ii) Develop Hanoi as a business and financing hub;
(iii) Develop advanced urban transport systems in Hanoi and good infrastructural linkages with other Northern industrial centres such as Bac Ninh province and especially the port city of Hai Phong;
(iv) Modernise airport facilities for greater international connectivity. This will enhance ease of doing business in Hanoi while also increasing its potentials for tourism;
(v) Leverage on Hanoi's rich cultural heritage to make it an attractive tourist destination;
(vi) Improve connectivity and transport services to other tourist hotspots in the North such as Sa Pa, Ha Long Bay and Ninh Binh province to stimulate the tourism sector in the North;
(vii) Promote urban diversity to encourage creativity and innovation; foster entrepreneurship among the young population.

These policies will promote the upgraded development of Hanoi, which will in turn spur the establishment of more industrial parks in the North to exploit infrastructure, logistics and administrative advantages from being closely linked with the national capital. Furthermore, as a communication and transport hub with enhanced domestic and international connectivity, Hanoi has the potential to facilitate the development of services, especially tourism, in the North. This will serve to create more jobs, raise wages and narrow the gap in living standards between Northern and Southern Vietnam.

Hanoi is well-placed to achieve these development objectives. As the capital city, it enjoys distinctive regulations and status as stipulated in the Law on National Capital of 2012. In addition, it is a vibrant city with an increasingly favourable business environment. Figure 3.3 showcases Hanoi's performance in terms of the Provincial Competitiveness Index (PCI), which assesses the quality of economic governance by local authorities in facilitating private sector development. Jointly constructed by the Vietnam Chamber of Commerce and Industry (VCCI) and the United States Agency for International Development (USAID), the PCI comprises 10 categories.[7]

[7] The 10 categories, or sub-indices, include (i) entry costs; (ii) land access and security of tenure; (iii) transparency and access to information; (iv) time costs and regulatory compliance; (v) informal changes; (vi) policy bias; (vii) proactivity of provincial leadership; (viii) business support services; (ix) labour training and (x) legal institutions. See http://eng.pcivietnam.org/phuong-phap-c9.html (accessed on 24 December 2017).

Figure 3.3: Hanoi's Overall PCI Score and Ranking, 2010–2016

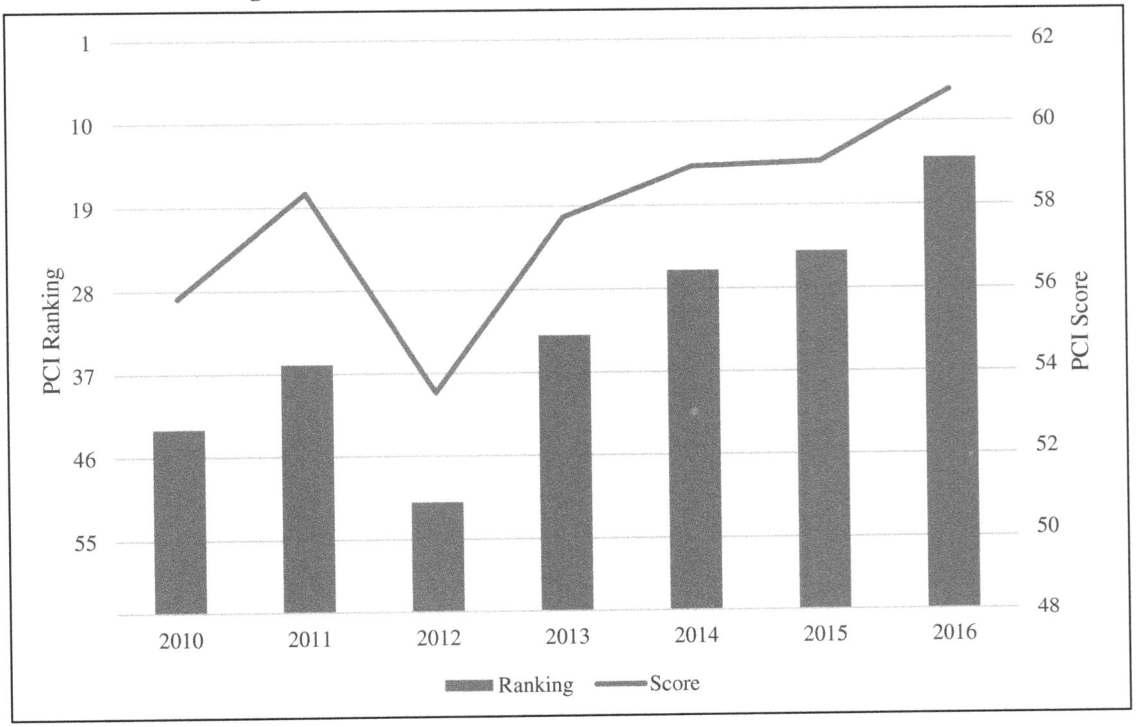

Source: VCCI and USAID (2017)

As shown in Figure 3.3, Hanoi's PCI ranking has steadily improved over the past seven years, from being 43rd out of 63 provinces and cities in 2010 to 14th in 2016. With a score exceeding 60 points, Hanoi has also broken into the "High" PCI tier consisting of provinces/cities with good economic management in 2016. In particular, the capital city has demonstrated its strength in labour training and provision of business support services, being ranked second out of 63 provinces and cities in both of these categories in 2016.[8] High-quality human capital and wide availability of business services will facilitate Hanoi's rise as a regional and international business hub.

3.4 Nurturing Small and Medium Enterprises (SMEs) for Inclusive Growth

Fostering SME growth is a key step to realise the vision of inclusive growth and develop a vibrant private sector. In this section, we contend that it is far more important for the government to play a facilitative role instead of relying on direct interventions such as hand-outs and tax breaks as the primary channel to assist SMEs. Accordingly, the government should seek to alleviate information asymmetries which hinder linkages between SMEs and MNCs, foster cross-learning between SMEs and industry captains, as well as improve the ease of doing business.

[8] See VCCI and USAID (2017).

To help the government effectively perform its facilitative role, we propose an Enterprise Future Initiative with a key focus on evidence-based research which will guide the formulation of actionable plans to enhance the efficiency, productivity and internationalisation potentials of Vietnamese SMEs. This shall be complemented by empirical studies to identify challenges to ease of doing business faced by SMEs for concrete policy interventions. In addition, we shall highlight the importance of building digital capacity as a necessary condition for SMEs to thrive in the upcoming Fourth Industrial Revolution.

3.4.1 SMEs as the Backbone of the Economy

The performance of local firms, especially SMEs, underpins sectoral and national competitiveness as well as productivity.[9] An increasing number of studies in the economic literature have identified SMEs as a potential channel for fostering growth in an economy. This has also been partly driven by shifts in the global governance structures where state-dominant economies have gradually been giving way to ones led by entrepreneurship, which in turn has concomitantly established the importance of SMEs in modern economies. In fact, the latter half of the 20th century witnessed a surge in entrepreneurship rates globally, which consequently led to the growth of small and new firms. While smaller and newer firms are experiencing transitional dynamics, it is pivotal to recognise the significant employment potential and contribution of SMEs in an entrepreneurial economy.[10]

Figure 3.4 succinctly summarises the importance of SMEs, as gleaned from the related literature. SMEs create a virtuous cycle of development by generating employment, facilitating income growth and promoting competition, innovation and entrepreneurship in an economy.[11] According to the Asian Development Bank (ADB), SMEs are believed to create dynamic efficiencies as they tend to be more flexible and adaptable with a greater willingness to innovate relative to large and established enterprises.[12]

A plethora of studies show that SMEs contribute significantly to the total employment in an economy. A study by the International Labour Organisation and the German Agency for International Cooperation, for instance, examined 99 countries and showed that SMEs contributed to a large share of employment across all these countries, with the corresponding shares being especially high in developing countries.[13] According to the United Nations Economic and Social Commission for Asia and the Pacific, SMEs act as a catalyst in the structural transformation of an economy and help it advance up the value chain. They help in achieving the twin goals of economic growth and job creation, and thus are considered a key engine of growth, especially for developing economies.[14]

---

[9] See Porter (1980) and Altomonte *et al.* (2011).

[10] See Audretsch and Roy (2001).

[11] See Fritsch and Mueller (2005) and Beck *et al.* (2005).

[12] See ADB (2009).

[13] See ILO (2015).

[14] See Stel and Suddle (2005); Garikai (2011) and Katua (2014).

Figure 3.4: The Economic Importance of SMEs

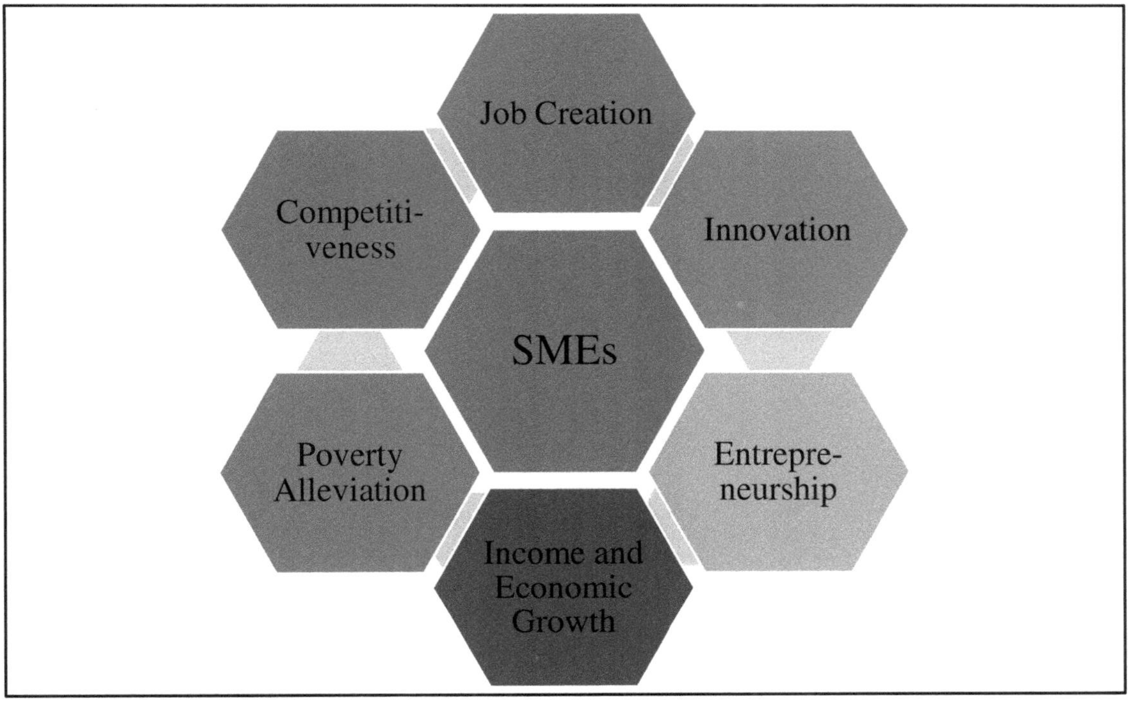

Source: Tan *et al.* (2017c)

SMEs play a decisive role among ASEAN countries and Vietnam in particular. Figures 3.5–3.7 highlight three different dimensions of SMEs' economic significance in Vietnam *vis-à-vis* the ASEAN-6 (Brunei, Indonesia, Malaysia, Philippines, Singapore and Thailand). The first pertains to SMEs' contribution to national output. The second relates to SMEs' share of total employment, while the third is their share of total establishments.

Figure 3.5 shows SMEs' contribution to national output in Vietnam and the ASEAN-6. It is observed that SMEs' output made up of 45 percent of Vietnam's Gross Domestic Product (GDP) in 2015, only below the corresponding share in Singapore at 47 percent and that in Indonesia at 58 percent. Moreover, according to estimates by the Ministry of Planning and Investment (MPI), Vietnamese SMEs contributed more than 205 trillion Vietnam Dong, or US$12.8 billion, to the state's budget in 2014, which represented 34 percent of the total contribution by the enterprise sector.[15]

Meanwhile, Figure 3.6 shows that SMEs' share of total employment in Vietnam has reached 51.7 percent by 2014, reflecting the importance of SMEs as a source of job creation. This share is expected to increase as the Vietnamese economy continues to industrialise and modernise, which will fasten the shift of labour from agricultural production to industrial and service sectors.

---

[15] Ministry of Planning and Investment (2014).

Figure 3.5: SMEs' Share of GDP in Selected ASEAN Countries, 2015

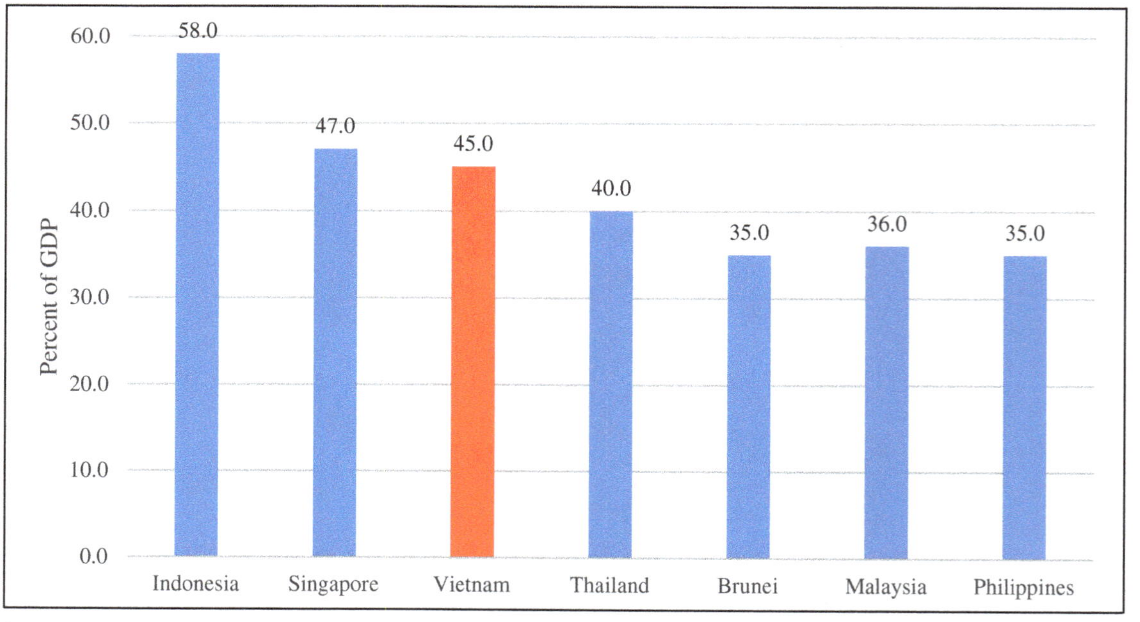

Source: Tan *et al*. (2017c) based on data from the World Bank and different country sources[16]

Figure 3.6: SMEs' Share of Employment in Selected ASEAN Countries, 2014

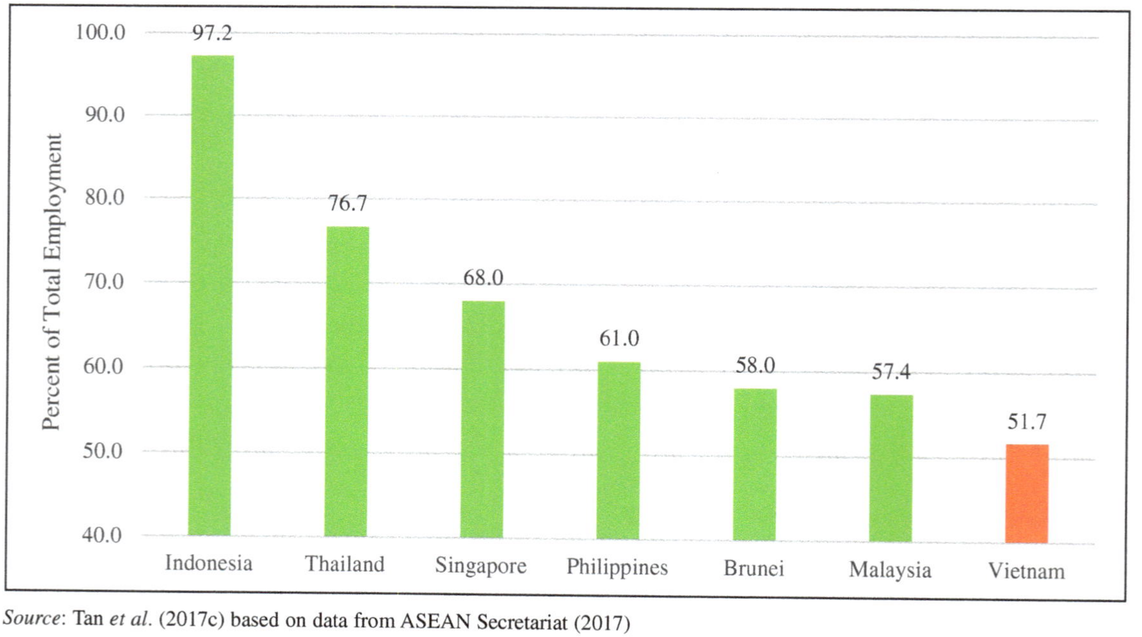

Source: Tan *et al*. (2017c) based on data from ASEAN Secretariat (2017)

[16] Ministry of Planning and Investment (Vietnam), Office of SME Promotion (Thailand), Ministry of Industrial Development (Brunei), Department of Trade and Industry (Philippines).

Figure 3.7: SMEs' Share of Establishments in Selected ASEAN Countries, 2014

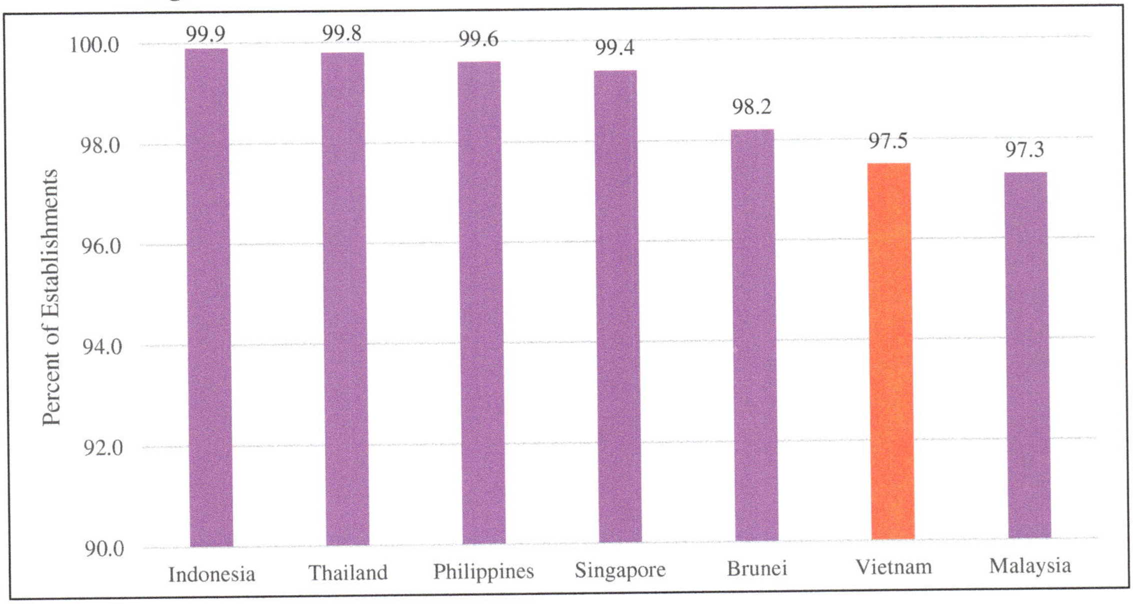

Source: Tan *et al*. (2017c) based on data from the OECD[17]

Last but not least, SMEs constitute the overwhelming majority of business establishments in Vietnam. Based on data from the Organisation for Economic Co-operation and Development (OECD), the share of Vietnamese SMEs in total establishments has reached 97.5 percent in 2014 (see Figure 3.7). This may seem surprising at first blush given the dominant positions of MNCs and SOEs in terms of market share and access to capital resources. Nevertheless, the large share of SMEs in total establishments and their significant contribution to GDP as well as total employment emphasise the need to foster SME development to achieve inclusive growth.

3.4.2 Alleviating Information Asymmetries to Forge Closer Linkages between SMEs and Multinational Corporations

The literature has pointed out that SMEs must contend with myriad challenges that have to be addressed to ensure their sustainability. As Figure 3.8 summarises, some of the major problems faced by SMEs include credit constraints and higher cost of capital, lack of access to new markets and skilled labour, as well as lack of economies of scale. In general, SMEs face more productivity challenges compared to larger firms as higher costs of capital and fewer capital resources tend to make them less productive, which in turn affects their efficiency.[18]

On top of these challenges, the majority of SMEs in Vietnam are microenterprises and small-scale business households. Most do not have meaningful participation in the global value chain

[17] See OECD (2017).

[18] See ESCAP (2012). Also see Tan and Tan (2014) for the various interactions between FDI flows, productivity spillovers and SMEs in Asia and beyond.

Figure 3.8: Challenges for SMEs as Highlighted by the Literature

Source: Tan *et al.* (2017c) based on different sources[19]

despite Vietnam's success in attracting FDI and the presence of many MNCs in Vietnam. The current government has made supporting SMEs a key priority of its policy-making agenda. In June 2017, the National Assembly passed the Law on Supporting SMEs, the first of its kind in Vietnam.

Under the new law, the government has committed to give SMEs better access to credit by encouraging banks and other financial organisations to loan to SMEs, institutionalising credit ratings of SMEs, and establishing an SME Credit Guarantee Fund. Second, SMEs stand to enjoy corporate income tax rates which are lower than the standard rate as well as simpler accounting and tax administrative procedures. Third, SMEs shall be granted land use rent subsidies from local governments. Fourth, organisations which set up incubation centres, technical facilities and common working areas for SMEs to improve their technological capacity shall enjoy tax breaks and subsidies in land use rents. Fifth, to allow SMEs to gain more market access, the government shall grant the same incentives to businesses with at least 80 percent of their supply chains being made up of SMEs. Sixth, the government pledges to help in improving SMEs' access to information on support programmes and legal services. Seventh, SMEs shall also be granted subsidies for labour training costs. Finally, the government has identified three groups of SMEs qualified for special support measures, namely business households converting to become formal enterprises, innovative start-up businesses, and SMEs participating in value chains in production and processing industries.

[19] See Harvie and Lee (2005); Asasen *et al.* (2003) and ESCAP (2012).

The 2017 SME Law marks a departure from the primary focus on the state sector under previous governments. It has provided the guiding principles and outlined a comprehensive, multi-pronged approach to help SMEs in Vietnam. Nevertheless, the devils are in the details, and it remains to be seen if the support programmes under this law will deliver tangible benefits to SMEs. Some of the policy initiatives are in fact not new. For instance, it is unclear whether the SME Development Fund proposed under the new SME Law will substitute or complement the current fund of the same name under the MPI. In addition, regarding credit guarantees to help SMEs to obtain credit, such services are already available through the credit fund by the Vietnam Development Bank or the various local funds administered by the Ministry of Finance (MOF). In fact, as of 2014, 21 local credit guarantee funds have been set up across the country.[20] However, the problem is that these funds have been operating inefficiently and remain underutilised despite high demand.[21]

Most importantly, the SME Law demonstrates that the Vietnamese government still seems to rely on traditional fiscal measures, namely subsidies and tax breaks, as the key policy tools to support SMEs. Developing economies such as Vietnam may have difficulties sustaining these programmes in the long run because they impose significant strains on the government's budget. For instance, the feasibility of having local governments to grant SMEs land use rent subsidies is questionable given the importance of land rent as a major revenue stream in many provinces, especially the poorer ones. Additionally, there are concerns over the effectiveness of direct interventions through fiscal measures. Due to the large number of SMEs in the economy, the actual benefits available to individual SMEs may be too small to create any noticeable impact.

While fiscal interventions do play a role in alleviating the immediate constraints faced by SMEs, the strategy to develop SMEs in the next phase of Vietnam's development requires a paradigm shift. The government should focus on playing a facilitative role. This entails levelling the playing field and establishing market institutions required for SMEs, and private enterprises in general, to flourish. Streamlining bureaucracy, improving bureaucratic capabilities and enhancing ease of doing business should also be prioritised.

Moreover, governments should seek to amend information asymmetries in the market. Despite the financial incentives offered in the SME Law to entice large companies to integrate SMEs into their supply chains, SMEs may still miss out on opportunities arising from FDI like in the past because investors and prospective business partners lack information about them. Therefore, policy-makers should encourage the development of an information platform for SMEs in order to enable these firms to connect with global MNCs for greater synergies through outsourcing, joint production, mergers and acquisitions. Furthermore, the government should fund empirical firm-level research to identify SMEs' weaknesses and promote dialogue between SMEs and industry captains to address these shortcomings through cross-learning. Market-based initiatives such as these are more sustainable, and perhaps also more effective, than fiscal interventions in the long run as they assist SMEs in developing their internal capacity over time.

---

[20] See ADB (2015).

[21] See *Viet Nam News* (2016a) and Le (2016).

3.4.3 Enterprise Future Initiative and Improving Ease of Doing Business for SMEs

Evidence-based, policy-oriented research on SMEs is critical for the Vietnamese government to fulfil its facilitative role, especially to alleviate information asymmetries. The Asia Competitiveness Institute (ACI) can assist in advancing empirical research on Vietnamese SMEs, given its experience in SME research and contribution to SME development in Singapore.[22] We propose the establishment of the Enterprise Future Initiative for Vietnam (EFIV) where ACI will work closely with VCCI, Vietnamese think-tanks, and business chambers to strengthen and deepen knowledge capabilities of SMEs. The purpose is to encourage SMEs to innovate, go digital and scale up in the age of technology disruptions which compound the existing challenges faced by them.[23]

They key pillar of the EFIV will be the adaptation of the Productivity Tracking and Efficiency Monitoring (PTEM) index of SMEs to the Vietnamese context. Developed by ACI in joint research collaboration with SPRING Singapore, the PTEM index takes a comprehensive, holistic and multi-dimensional approach, therefore complementing the existing literatures which tend to focus on particular dimensions of SME performance. The PTEM index framework has drawn on and extended the technical framework established by the European Central Bank Competitiveness Network, which has been analysing competitiveness from a comprehensive perspective, encompassing the macro-, firm-level and cross-country dimensions, using a firm-level database (see Box 3.1).[24] Apart from a time-series hard dataset, survey data has been collected on an ongoing basis to ensure a comprehensive database, enabling ACI to conduct in-depth firm-level studies in Asian economies. The PTEM index will prove to be instrumental in helping Vietnamese SMEs to grow as it:

(i) Facilitates information acquisition process for SMEs by building up a business information matrix;
(ii) Enables SMEs to identify their relative strengths and weaknesses through competitiveness rankings and simulation analysis;
(iii) Helps the Vietnamese government engage industry experts to provide customised consultation as to how SMEs can enhance their digital capabilities, innovate and scale up;
(iv) Assists in designing training courses which are better suited to SMEs' needs;
(v) Enables cross-country benchmarking and comparison with SMEs in other Asian economies upon the integration of the Vietnam dataset to the database on Asian SMEs managed by ACI.

Furthermore, data collected for the PTEM index will also allow ACI to deep-dive into interesting policy-relevant research topics on Vietnamese SMEs for impactful policy

[22] See Shafeeq (2017) and *The Business Times* (2017).
[23] See Kwek and Tan (2017) and Tan and Ng (2017).
[24] Box 3.1 provides a summary of the PTEM Index framework. See Tan *et al.* (2017c) for a more detailed description of the methodology.

Box 3.1: ACI's PTEM Index Framework

The PTEM Index is made up of four sub-indices of "environments" that appear as quadrants within a circle (see Figure 3.9). The quadrants represent an attempt to provide a holistic view of SMEs' productivity and efficiency through four environments: (1) Financial and Business Statistics; (2) Human Capital, Manpower Investment and Productivity; (3) Internationalisation, Marketing, Branding, and Innovation; and (4) Corporate Governance, Management and Execution.

Figure 3.9: PTEM Index Framework

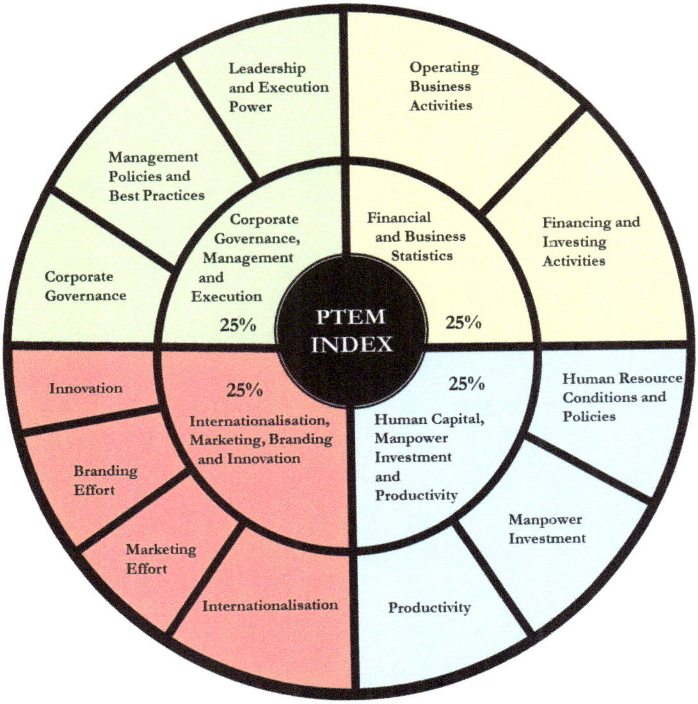

Source: Tan *et al.* (2017c)

These four environments are assumed to have the same magnitude of impact on the overall index. In other words, each environment accounts for 25 percent of the entire index. As mentioned in Tan *et al.* (2017c), the intertwining factors affecting the productivity and efficiency of SMEs indicate that it is arbitrary and contentious to assign different weights to different environments. Hence, an equal distribution of weight reflects a balanced view towards the different factors that contribute to an overall notion of PTEM index.

There are in total 12 sub-environments under the four environments, as displayed in Figure 3.9. Each sub-environment is given the same weightage as other sub-environments which fall under the same respective environment. The overall index is made up of 86 indicators which are distributed among the different environments and sub-environments. There are 19 indicators for Financial and Business Statistics, 22 indicators for Human Capital, Manpower Investment and Productivity, 23 indicators for Internationalisation, Marketing, Branding, and Innovation and 22 indicators for Corporate Governance, Management and Execution.

Source: Summary based on Tan *et al.* (2017c)

recommendations. For instance, based on the data of the prototype PTEM index for Singapore, econometric models have been developed to investigate the determinants for a firm's decision to become an exporter and factors affecting its likelihood to have an overseas presence. From a policy point of view, it is worth noting that SMEs' internationalisation activities, be it in the form of exporting or establishing an overseas presence, tend to be positively associated with raising overall productivity which generates positive spillovers to the economy at large. Moreover, it was found that sound management of exchange rates that prevents excessive currency fluctuations and financial sector development which allows SMEs to build hedging capabilities to shield themselves against exchange rate risks and would encourage SMEs to internationalise.[25] Similar studies can be conducted for Vietnamese SMEs after the successful construction of the Vietnam PTEM index.

As mentioned in Section 3.4.1, improving ease of doing business is crucial for SME development. First and foremost, the government has to be committed to cutting red tape. Regulations are important for balancing the needs of society and the private sector, but they should not unnecessarily add to business costs or hinder commerce. To this end, concerted effort to implement administrative reform is key. Government rules and regulations should increasingly gear towards *ex post* outcomes rather than an *ex ante* rule-based approach. In other words, regulations should be based on actual practices, not devised in a vacuum based on theory.[26]

At the same time, it is worth remembering that a conducive business environment is not the only necessary condition for SMEs to thrive. They need business opportunities from domestic and foreign investment. Even with business-friendly regulations, an economy will still be unable to attract investors if it is lacking in infrastructure resilience, market potential and cost effectiveness, all of which determine the profitability of investment. In this sense, the government's role in improving ease of doing business must be understood broadly as not only facilitating business operations but also planning and implementing policies aimed at enhancing the competitiveness of the economy.

ACI has developed a holistic and comprehensive Ease of Doing Business Index framework: the EDB Index ABC. This index looks beyond the regulatory aspects which are the focus of the World Bank's Doing Business survey. Instead, it measures ease of doing business of an economy according to three environments: (i) Attractiveness to Investors; (ii) Business Friendliness, and (iii) Competitiveness Policies (see Box 3.2).[27] Another unique feature of the EDB Index ABC as compared to the World Bank's index is its emphasis on collecting extensive survey data at the sub-national level. This is important as several constraints that businesses, especially SMEs, face lie under the purview of local governments. Adapted to the Vietnamese context, the EDB Index ABC shall complement the PCI constructed by the VCCI and USAID, which focuses on economic governance at the provincial level, as a useful tool to identify province-specific hindrances to ease of doing business for policy interventions.

---

[25] See Tan *et al.* (2017c).

[26] See Kwek and Tan (2017).

[27] Box 3.2 provides a summary of the EDB Index ABC framework. See Tan *et al.* (2017a, 2017b) for more details.

Box 3.2: ACI's EDB Index ABC Framework

ACI's EDB Index ABC takes into account three major aspects or 'environments' of doing business: (1) Attractiveness to Investors, (2) Business Friendliness and (3) Competitive Policies. Our bottom-up approach takes into account the various operational issues that firms face at the ground level, with the emphasis being on *de facto* issues. Figure 3.10 succinctly captures the conceptual framework of EDB index ABC.

Figure 3.10: Framework for EDB Index ABC

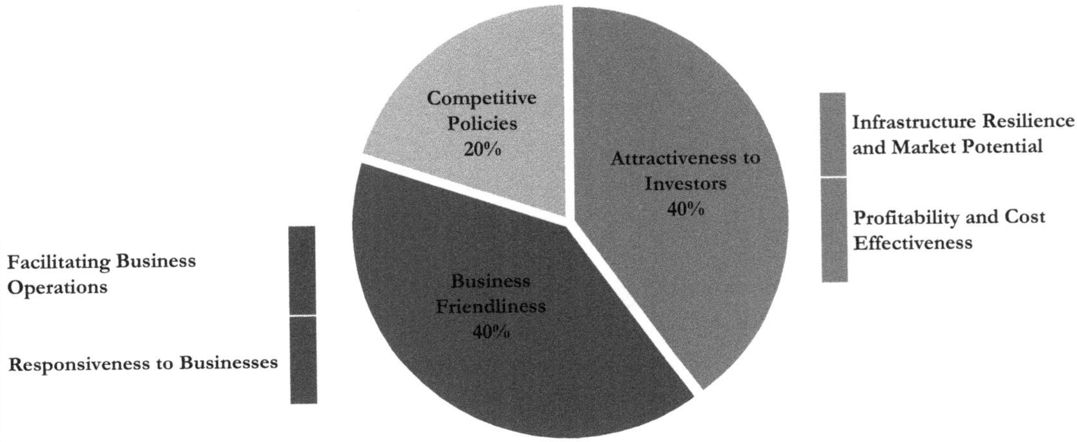

Source: Tan *et al.* (2017a, 2017b)

First, Attractiveness to Investors (A) measures the comparative advantage of a location that comes into consideration when firms are considering where to invest. These are the factors that a firm would compare and contrast as *ex ante* factors, before it decides or makes a commitment to invest in said location. This environment captures basic factors that make a sub-national economy attractive as an investment destination. From investors' point of view, the sub-environment "Infrastructure Resilience and Market Potential" stands out as the key considerations when making decisions on where to invest. The other sub-environment is "Profitability and Cost Effectiveness", which includes cost of labour, ease of obtaining land and property, as well as taxation matters.

Second, Business Friendliness (B) measures the ease of functioning that comes into consideration when firms are already committed to an investment, but still may pull out, albeit with some costs. These are the factors that a firm would scrutinise as *ex post* factors, after it made the commitment to invest. This environment extensively covers factors that create a friendly ecosystem for businesses. The first sub-environment, "Facilitating Business Operations", includes ease of getting favourable labour supply, accessing financial services, and obtaining reliable local suppliers. Also, investors value security where businesses are isolated from disruptions triggered by crime, violence, and political instability. The second sub-environment, "Responsiveness to Businesses", describes firms' assessment on the regulatory procedures and bureaucracy imposed by the government.

The third environment, Competitive Policies (C) evaluates the existence of policies and practices that facilitate ease of doing business at the provincial level, making the sub-national economy more competitive compared to its peers from a regulatory point of view. Environment C is not broken down into any further sub-environments. Instead it is composed of indicators which captures whether related business procedures are in place.

Source: Summary based on Tan *et al.* (2017a, 2017b)

3.4.4 Building Digital Capacity for SMEs

Another critical policy priority is to prepare SMEs for future disruptions arising from the Fourth Industrial Revolution. Rapid breakthroughs in robotics, artificial intelligence, the Internet of Things (IoT), big data and their synergies with new technologies in other fields including 3-D printing, nanotechnology, biotechnology and materials science are expected to transform entire systems of production, management and governance.[28]

In particular, digitalisation stands to have major impacts on businesses in all industries. It offers new avenues for companies to reach into the global market, enables cost-saving improvements in operations and transforms the ways in which goods and services are delivered to consumers. A key trend is the emergence of technology-enabled platforms which have facilitated sharing economies in a plethora of services, ranging from travel to transport, shopping to start-up financing. Moreover, the IoT and big data will allow companies to gain unprecedentedly detailed insights about consumers' behaviour, creating new opportunities for growth.

In this context, developing strong digital capacity will be crucial for the future development of Vietnamese SMEs. On the one hand, digital technologies are more "scale-neutral" than other technologies which have driven previous Industrial Revolutions; they are accessible to both big and small firms since they do not require large investment in physical capital. Thus, nimble SMEs and innovative start-ups can leverage on new technologies to improve their productivity and efficiency, carve out niche markets, internationalise, and scale up rapidly. On the other hand, firms which fail to adjust to the changing technological landscape may find themselves ill-equipped to compete with both the large companies and their more adaptable peers.

To help SMEs develop their digital capabilities, the government may look to the following:

(i) Increase investment in information and technology (ICT) infrastructure, not only in the metropolises but throughout the country to ensure equal access to telecommunication and Internet services;
(ii) Implement an appropriate regulatory framework which facilitates innovation and the adoption of technology;
(iii) Set up an agency dedicated to promoting digitalisation, providing advice and helping SMEs to adopt suitable digital technologies based on their business needs;
(iv) Specifically, this agency may partner with reputable domestic and international ICT vendors and consultants to compile a reference list of sector-specific, proven digital solutions for SMEs to consider adopting;
(v) Encourage telecommunication service providers to offer one-stop digital packages which bundle Internet connectivity services with digital solutions, cybersecurity and data analytic tools to reduce search costs;
(vi) Through partnerships with banks and other financial institutions, provide SMEs with access to loans to defray the cost of acquiring or developing new digital capabilities;

[28] See Schwab (2016).

(vii) Cooperate with key industry players to provide training to upgrade the workforce for the digital economy;
(viii) Develop deep capabilities in cybersecurity and network management as these issues will become increasingly pertinent as digitisation takes place throughout the economy.

Finally, it is worth noting that trade associations and business chambers have a key role to play in helping SMEs transform. As advocates for their industries, these organisations are well-positioned to put forth clear facts and figures for their members, outlining the opportunities for growth and, more importantly, what is at stake if transformation fails to happen. In addition, they may also guide SMEs forward by highlighting success stories and filling any information gaps about government's support programmes.[29]

3.5 Human Resource Investment and Capacity Building

After 30 years of *Doi Moi*, skill mismatch is still prevalent. Firms still find it hard to find skilled workers to fill the jobs, particularly professionals, managers, executives and technicians (PMETs). Moreover, the need for human resource investment and capacity building is even more pertinent if Vietnam is to successfully transform its economy and raise the living standards of its citizens in the age of the Fourth Industrial Revolution.

Thus, we call for the implementation of the Skills Future Initiative to promote skill deepening while emphasising the role of public policy in achieving better labour productivity with rising wages for workers. Furthermore, we propose a German variant of an Industrial Internship Model (IIM) for Vietnam under a flexible market-oriented Placed-Trained-Employed (PTE) Scheme to support industry internships for Vietnamese students, especially those in vocational schools. At the same time, we highlight the enhancement of data literacy, language skills, soft skills as well as innovation capacity as key targets for the holistic development of the workforce.

3.5.1 Skills Future Initiative and Nexus for Labour Productivity Upgrading

The Vietnamese government should kickstart the Skills Future Initiative, a national movement aimed at galvanising the workforce to pursue skill deepening throughout their career. The central thrusts of the Initiative include encouraging individuals to make well-informed decisions regarding their education and training; aligning education and technical training with industry needs; promoting skill-based career development and fostering a culture of lifelong learning among the workforce.[30] These objectives call for the implementation of the following policies:

(i) Emphasise career guidance and support in universities and vocational schools;
(ii) Profile and disseminate information on key growth areas and skills required for future jobs;

---

[29] See Kwek and Tan (2017).

[30] Singapore's SkillsFuture programme may serve as a useful model. See http://www.skillsfuture.sg/AboutSkillsFuture (accessed on 26 December 2017) for more details.

(iii) Foster closer collaboration between higher-learning institutes, industry associations, and companies to ensure curriculum aligns with industry demands;
(iv) Through financial incentives and subsidies, provide support for company-led training programmes and nudge workers to upgrade their skills throughout their career;
(v) Encourage universities and other higher-learning institutes to offer part-time skill-based modular courses for individuals looking to acquire new skills or deepen relevant skills;
(vi) Support industry internships by implementing the proposed IIM-PTE. IIM-PTE is envisioned to be a comprehensive, targeted and private sector-driven programme aimed primarily at students with vocational qualifications or lower. The proposal for the IIM-PTE shall be explained in more detail in Section 3.5.2;
(vii) Finally, promote data literacy, soft skills, language skills development and encouraging innovation as elaborated on in Section 3.5.3.

Human capital development and productivity improvement are expected to raise ordinary residents' real wages in the long run. Nonetheless, in the short to medium run, progress may be hindered, and a variety of scenarios may come to pass. Tan and Tan (2014) explored the wages–productivity nexus which is summarised in Figure 3.11.

Ideally, Vietnam would move steadily and directly from Quadrant A, which exhibits low wage-low productivity stalemate towards the high wage-high productivity Quadrant D of

Figure 3.11: Wages–Productivity Nexus

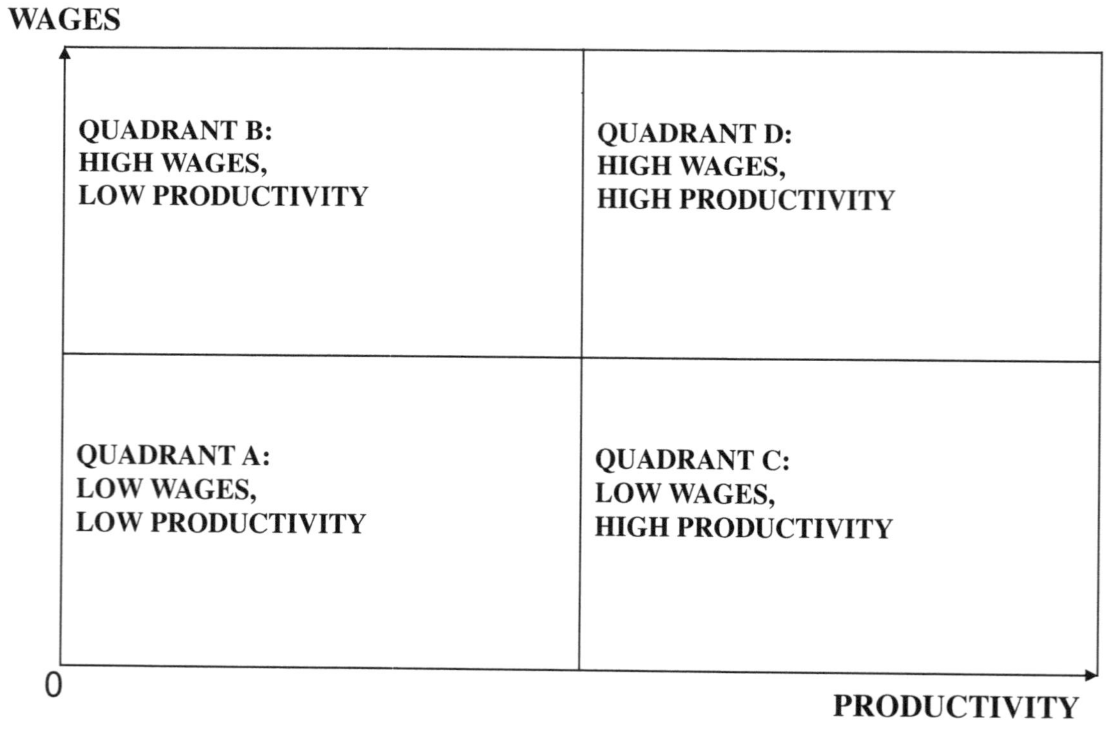

Source: Tan and Tan (2014)

inclusive competitiveness. However, Quadrant B, or the high wage-low productivity trap,[31] is also a possible outcome. As shown through the experience of several crisis-ridden European economies, the country will be caught in this least desirable scenario if labour unions aggressively pursue an agenda of maximising short-term wage gains without regard for the long-run competitiveness of the economy. Meanwhile, the country may also end up in Quadrant C, i.e. the low wage-high productivity hybrid, where it suffers from mismatch in productivity and wage growth as well as low and stagnant wages among low-income workers. This may arise because there is a lack of equal access to opportunities across classes or sub-national regions.

Thus, aside from encouraging human capital development, it is imperative that the government also takes on a facilitative role and corrects labour market failure to shepherd labour upgrading and economic transformation. The government should seek to foster tripartite collaboration between itself, unions and employers for harmonious labour-management relations in order to avoid the high wage-low productivity trap. At the same time, it should provide targeted income-supplement transfers to augment the wages of low-income individuals without reducing their incentives to work. Moreover, the government should ensure that the opportunities for upgrading are extended to all classes and strive for more balanced regional development.

3.5.2 The Proposed Tripartite Targeted Industrial Internship Model with Placed-Trained-Employed Scheme

Internships and apprenticeships play a vital role in supplementing graduates' knowledge with technical skills through hands-on training, cultivating a keen awareness of current industry needs and increasing their future employability. It is therefore essential that the government makes concerted effort to support targeted industry internship programmes. With this objective in mind, we propose the IIM-PTE.

The IIM-PTE scheme will primarily cover students with vocational qualifications or lower. Despite the acute shortage of skilled workers, and the fact that university graduates are finding of increasingly difficulty to land a suitable job upon graduation due to skill mismatch and limited university places,[32] vocational schools still struggle to enrol students.[33] If appropriately implemented, the IIM-PTE would serve to fill a big gap on productivity enhancement, increase the attractiveness of vocational schools as a viable pathway to secure good jobs, thus resulting in positive socio-economic effects. In addition, the scheme may be extended to university students, though only as a complementary measure to the main focus on revamping university curriculum to suit industry needs and placing a stronger emphasis on career guidance as espoused on in Section 3.5.1.

To implement the IIM-PTE, an agency dedicated to workforce development and productivity enhancement initiatives should be set up under the Ministry of Labour, Invalids and Social Affairs (MOLISA). In addition, a Pro-tem Committee should be established which would later

---

[31] See Rajan *et al.* (2014).

[32] See *Tuoi Tre News* (2017) and *Vietnamnet* (2017b).

[33] See *Viet Nam News* (2018).

evolve into an Industrial Internship Productivity Enhancement Council (IIPEC) to monitor, fine-tune and improve the IIM-PTE Scheme throughout its implementation. The IIPEC would be led by top political leaders assisted by presidents of business federations and associations, academic representatives and the Executive Director of the newly-established workforce development agency who would administer the IIM-PTE Scheme. In addition, committee members would consist of senior representatives from the MOF, MOLISA, Ministry of Education and Training (MOET), Ministry of Industry and Trade (MOIT) as well as the Vietnam General Confederation of Labour. Principals from vocational schools and high schools would serve as resource persons to provide linkages to educational establishments. Additionally, IIPEC would be advised by a team of Advisory Panellists consisting of industry captains from diverse industries where donations would be sought for to kick-start the IIM-PTE.

The main features of the IIM-PTE include the following:

(i) **Market-based curriculum structure re-adjustments:** The IIM-PTE scheme shall implement programmes for employment placement with employer-driven in-house skill development training modules validated by vocational schools;

(ii) **Seamless coordination among tripartite stakeholders:** The IIM-PTE would enable the realisation of Vietnam's productivity potential with employment stability especially for SMEs by proactive effort from employers, employees and the government in terms of public policy fine-tuning with supports from education institutions and close coordination of public policies across ministries;

(iii) **Tax incentives with matching grants:** A proactive role of the government is critical in ensuring the success of the IIM-ITE scheme by giving appropriate tax incentives with matching grants for companies participating in the proposed scheme. The detailed formulae can be finalised among ministries and government agencies involved;

(iv) **A centralised-interactive multi-party IIM-PTE platform:** An inclusive approach to centralise existing highly selective internship coverage of vocation school students and high school leavers will be pursued;

(v) **Identifying inspiring role models:** The agency administering the IIM-PTE should set up an Advisory Committee consisting of industrial leaders who had humble family upbringings and with vocational school qualifications or lower. These successful entrepreneurs shall be invited to provide guidance on pragmatic initiatives. Their active participation would serve as a clear signal that one can realise their full potentials notwithstanding low education qualifications;

(vi) **Better-informed career path expectation and mapping:** The IIM-ITE enables Vietnamese students to choose, embark on and follow through an internship program with better and clearer understanding of the job scope or job content which they are committing to at the early stage of their career development;

(vii) **Positive social–political–economic dimensions:** The IIM-ITE would help to mitigate income disparity, improve low or stagnated salary caused by low productivity and ensure better upward social mobility.

Specifically, under the IIM-PTE Scheme:

A. Through a centralised, interactive IIM-PTE online platform, potential employers from different industries or sectors would list their job openings, on-the-job training requirements, in-house training programmes certified by vocational schools and the newly-established workforce development agency, information on the period of internship and future remuneration when successful interns eventually join as full-time employees upon graduation. Secondary and high school leavers are also eligible to participate for the certified in-house, on-the-job training programmes.
B. Potential employers whose interests are matched by those of students who indicate interests to participate in the scheme would provide funding upfront to pay for their remaining tuition fees at vocational schools as well as stipends and salary when students undertake in-house on-the-job training. Upon certification by respective vocational schools and the workforce development agency, these employers would receive training subsidies to offset up to 90 percent of their initial payment of interns' tuition fees.
C. Tax incentives in the form of deductions on taxable revenue for employers who participate in the IIM-PTE scheme, the specifics of which are to be worked out by the MOF, would also be helpful to businesses. In addition, the government would also provide matching grants, to be calculated by MOF and managed by the newly-established workforce development agency, which shall be used to fund certified training modules for interns under the IIM-PTE scheme.
D. Upon successful completion of the in-house internship program, should the intern decide to join the company, a "sign-on bonus" would be awarded, depending on his or her performance during the internship. This sign-on bonus shall be paid out from the matching grants provided by the government.
E. Interns participating in the IIM-PTE who have joined the company and found to be outstanding would be encouraged to go for higher and more structured training modules. This pool of workers will eventually augment Vietnam's PMET workforce.

3.5.3 Promoting Data Literacy, Soft Skill, Language Skill Development and Encouraging Innovation

Data is at the heart of the fast-approaching Fourth Industrial Revolution. Datasets have been growing rapidly as they are gathered in increasingly larger quantity at cheaper costs through software logs, wireless sensory networks, mobile devices and various other IoT appliances. This trend has also been augmented by rapid advancements in data storage technologies: the world's information storage capacity per capita has doubled roughly every 40 months since the 1980s.[34] The result is voluminous and complex datasets, commonly known as big data, which hold the promise to help businesses optimise their operations, unlock new insights about consumer behaviour and innovate on their products and services.

[34] See Hilbert and López (2011).

In the future, managers and business analysts in all sectors will be required to conduct data-driven experiments and draw business-relevant insights from data. To ensure their future competitiveness, it is critical that young Vietnamese professionals should develop critical thinking, numerical skills and most importantly data literacy in collecting, managing, processing and interpreting data of all types.[35] Institutes of higher learning including universities and vocational schools should partner with leading technology MNCs to design relevant courses to serve this need. Moreover, the government should look to train its public administrators in data skills to ensure that regulators are kept abreast of the latest technological developments so that they are equiped to apply data-driven solutions to improve the quality and efficiency of public services. Programmes on data analytics, cybersecurity and their applications to urban planning are particularly helpful given Vietnamese policymakers' ambition to transform its metropolises into smart cities.[36]

Another key area for holistic development of the workforce is soft skill and language enhancement. This has become all the more important as Vietnam deepens its integration into the regional and global market, particularly in the context of its participation in the ASEAN Economic Community (AEC). Strong interpersonal skills and a good command of English are crucial for Vietnamese professionals to gain a competitive advantage in the AEC integrated labour market. Furthermore, as the service sector becomes more prominent as an engine of growth and a source for employment creation, these skills will be vital.

In the recently-published English Proficiency Index by Education First (EF), a global language training company, Vietnam was ranked seventh out of 20 Asian countries and 34th among 80 countries globally with a "moderate" proficiency rating.[37] However, such ranking may have been inflated as it is based on online tests of only reading and listening skills.[38] Vietnam's language training system suffers from chronic weaknesses in terms of an overt focus on mastery of grammar and vocabulary without sufficiently preparing students to use English as business language. In particular, the workforce's general competency in formal writing and conversational English leaves much to be desired.

Since 2008, MOET has been pursuing reforms to align the English curriculum to international standards and upgrade the quality of English teachers at all levels under the National Foreign Language Project for the 2008–2020 period. However, this initiative, commonly known as Project 2020, is in danger of failing to meet its targets by the deadline.[39] Challenges include overly ambitious targets, low awareness of the importance of English proficiency and lack of incentives for English teachers to take up further training above the minimum requirements.[40] These gaps need to be addressed, perhaps through the implementation of a more transparent structured incentive system for English teachers to upgrade their proficiency. In addition, alternative approaches outside formal education reforms should be explored. For instance, universities

[35] See Harris (2012).

[36] See *Vietnam Economic Times* (2017).

[37] See *Vietnamnet* (2017a).

[38] See https://www.ef.sg/epi/regions/asia/vietnam/ (accessed on 10 January 2018).

[39] See *Viet Nam News* (2016b).

[40] See Parks (2011) and *Viet Nam News* (2016b).

and youth associations may look to support grassroot programmes which allow students to use English in real-life settings, such as the walking tour model whereby students volunteer as local tour guides for foreign visitors.

Finally, in the long run, the capacity to innovate will be a prime driver of growth. At higher levels of development, the returns from adapting imported technology will diminish and growth through factor accumulation as well as exploitative use of resources will certainly not be sustainable. Instead, growth will have to be generated through innovations by a high-quality and productive workforce. As such, we echo the World Bank's suggestion in the *Vietnam 2035* report for the government to lay the foundation for the innovation-driven economy on top of pursuing short- and intermediate-term growth targets. This will require critical adjustments which will take a long time to come to fruition.[41]

Specifically, on the demand side, improving national innovation capacity is intimately linked to developing vibrant and competitive domestic enterprises as they create the market demand for new technologies and production processes. On the supply side, there is a need to step up investment in both basic and market-oriented thematic research through merit-based funding allocation. Moreover, tertiary and post-tertiary education should be reformed to sharpen the focus on innovation and self-learning. Vietnam must also shore up its regulation regarding intellectual property rights protection, including building a credible patent system in order to protect innovators' and investors' interests as well as to establish trust in the local business environment.

3.6 Fostering Vibrant, Diversified and Sustainable Economic Clusters

This section places the policy recommendations in this chapter in the context of an overarching development strategy for Vietnam. Section 3.6.1 shall elaborate on the importance of state intervention in resolving the bottlenecks to development and facilitating catch-up industrialisation. Next, Section 3.6.2 will describe our holistic development vision for Vietnam to become a highly integrated manufacturing hub and excellent regional centre for services as well as a productive agriculture sector.

3.6.1 Resolving the Bottlenecks to Development

Since the inception of *Doi Moi*, Vietnam has sought to emulate the East Asian development model of export-led growth. Central to the success of this model is the role of the government in resolving bottlenecks in financing, infrastructure and production. This is illustrated in the experiences of Japan and China, where the governments used export earnings to finance infrastructure development. Such investment helped to unlock the production bottleneck and further enhanced the performance of their export machines.

Though Vietnam's export performance has steadily improved over the years, its success in terms of exporting is still modest as compared to Japan, China or other successful Newly-Industrialised Economies. At the same time, the government is hamstrung by burgeoning fiscal

---

[41] See World Bank and Ministry of Planning and Investment (2016).

deficits and mounting public debt. This has translated into difficulties in overcoming the financing bottleneck. As a result, an infrastructure bottleneck has developed, which in turn has caused a production bottleneck whereby economic activities are hampered. Indeed, the World Bank has estimated that Vietnam's infrastructure investment needs over the next several decades could reach tens of billion dollars a year.[42] State budget is unlikely to be able to meet this demand, and funding from official development assistance may be scaled down as the economy develops.

In this context, it is important that Vietnam leverages on its cooperation with multi-lateral development banks including the World Bank, the ADB and the Asia Infrastructure Investment Bank to partly cover the financing gap. Moreover, Vietnam should look to encourage more private sector participation in infrastructure development through public–private partnerships. In 2015, the government issued Decree 15 which provided a single, transparent legal framework for public–private investment and clarified regulations regarding the identification, preparation and implementation of such projects. This is a step in the right direction, and the effort to facilitate public–private partnerships should be intensified.

More generally, the government's role is crucial in facilitating "catch-up industrialisation". Figure 3.12 showcases the different development stages which an economy may go through as explained by Ohno (2009). Countries which have gone through war or political turmoil are

Figure 3.12 Different Stages of Catching-up Industrialisation

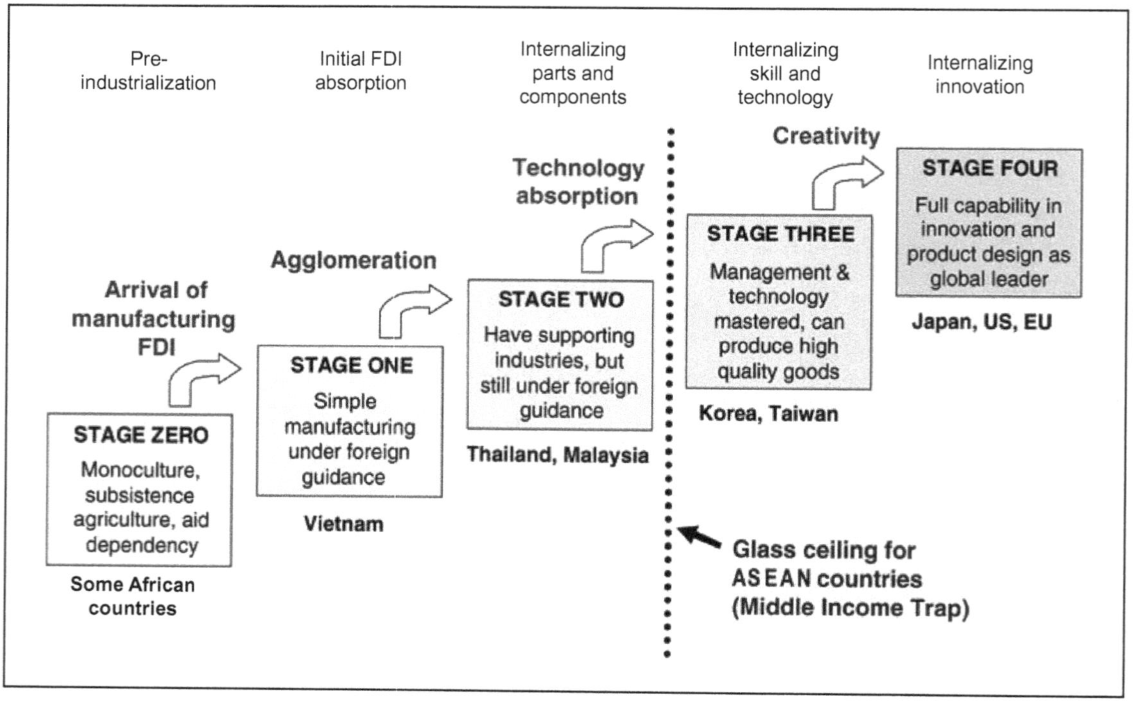

Source: Ohno (2009)

---

[42] *Ibid.*

usually characterised by a fragile economic structure highly dependent on aid, subsistence agriculture and other extractive resources. This is stage zero, or pre-industrialisation. As with East Asian and ASEAN economies, economic development starts with the arrival of manufacturing FDI firms which focus on simple assembly or processing of products for export. At this stage one, the value-added contribution of the domestic economy only lies in unskilled labour and land, with most of the production processes and technologies provided by foreign investors.

As FDI accumulates, domestic supporting industries gain a larger share of the value chain and domestic assembly firms become more competitive (stage two). The next challenge is to internalise skills and knowledge, gain mastery of management and technology thus developing the capabilities to compete with more advanced competitors in a range of high-quality manufactured products (stage three). Finally, countries at the fourth stage are leaders of global market trends fully capable of creating new products and services. Per this schema, Vietnam is transitioning from stage one to two. Its fellow ASEAN members Thailand and Malaysia are at stage two, while Singapore, Hong Kong, South Korea and Taiwan are at stage three. However, progress is not guaranteed and failure to make the transition from stage two to three constitutes being caught in the "middle-income trap".

As shown through the development experience of the East Asian economies, the government plays a critical role as an economic facilitator, social equaliser and political stabiliser in the quest for upgraded development. It enables free trade and competition to work by providing technological, physical and soft infrastructure in anticipation of demand; ensuring adequate provision of public goods and merit goods; setting up an overall conducive macroeconomic environment with greater ease for doing business operating under minimum regulations and rules; assisting to reduce the pain of structural transformation arising from industrial restructuring, diversification and obsolescence of jobs; and ensuring upward social mobility for the mass majority which in turn contributes to political stability.

More specifically, a proactive industrial policy is necessary for Vietnam and other late-developers to transition from stage two to stage three and avoid the so-called "middle-income trap".[43] Such a policy marries the acceptance of market mechanism and globalisation with a cooperative, symbiotic relationship between the public and private sectors. Its key elements include the following:

(i) Strong commitment to global integration and private sector-driven growth;
(ii) A wise and strong government guiding the private sector;
(iii) Securing sufficient policy tools for latecomer industrialisation;
(iv) Constant policy learning through concrete projects and programs;
(v) Internalisation of knowledge, skills and technology as a national goal;
(vi) Effective public–private partnerships;
(vii) Collection and sharing of sufficient industrial information between government and businesses.

[43] See Ohno (2009).

3.6.2 Vietnam as Asia's Manufacturing Hub and Excellent Centre for Service-based Industries

As mentioned in Chapter 2, Vietnam has been very successful in attracting FDI and increasing the technological content of exports. Going forward, Vietnam's active participation in multi-lateral integration initiatives will allow it to leverage on synergies with regional partners to enhance its attractiveness to investors. At the same time, Vietnam stands to benefit from the southward relocation of manufacturing facilities from China. This offers an invaluable opportunity which, if harnessed well, will propel Vietnam to become a leading manufacturing base in the world.

Nevertheless, the window for manufacturing-led growth for Vietnam may be considerably smaller than what China has enjoyed. Disruptive technological changes, particularly in automation and 3-D printing, as well as diminishing demographic dividends due to rapid growth of Vietnam's aging population will erode Vietnam's current advantage in low-cost manufacturing in due time. Thus, it is critical that the government intensifies its effort to implement the following policy measures, which are formulated according to the principles of proactive industrial policy as explained in Section 3.6.1, to ensure Vietnam's viability as Asia's manufacturing hub with high value-added and adaptable industries:

(i) Identifying opportunities for the upgrading of manufacturing capabilities within regional and global value chains;
(ii) Developing cost-effective manufacturing clusters through partnership with industrial partners in Japan, South Korea, Greater China, the United States (US) and the European Union;
(iii) Building a conducive investment climate through streamlining rules and regulations and substantially reducing the costs of doing business;
(iv) Levelling the playing field between state-owned and local private sectors, removing barriers to entry and promoting healthy competition among all firms as per Section 3.2;
(v) Fostering local SMEs to become reliable suppliers of MNCs and able to absorb technologies and adopt global best practices through the measures put forth in Section 3.3;
(vi) Promoting technology and knowledge transfers from MNCs to local enterprises;
(vii) Encouraging interindustry linkages for deepening the value chains;
(viii) Developing high-quality human capital capable of undertaking increasingly technology- and knowledge-intensive activities in regional and global value chains through the measures proposed in Section 3.4;
(ix) Improving transportation networks and increasing accessibility to inland production centres through maintenance and expansion of strategic roads, highways, sea ports and airports;
(x) Designate special industrial and economic zones with preferential tax treatment for MNCs as a springboard for regulatory, corporate and institutional development, thereby paving the way for deepening structural reforms.

In addition, Vietnam's future as a manufacturing hub is intertwined with that of ASEAN. A highly integrated ASEAN is crucial to the decisions of MNCs to relocate and expand. According to the 2014 ASEAN Business Outlook Survey conducted by the US Chambers of Commerce, about three-fourths of the survey respondents from US companies operating in ASEAN view ASEAN integration as vital to their business in ASEAN. Likewise, the Federation of Japanese Chambers of Commerce and Industry in ASEAN has highlighted to the Secretary General of ASEAN that deepening of production networks by Japanese firms would be better executed if ASEAN becomes more integrated.[44] In light of this, Vietnam should continue to support strategies for future ASEAN integration by playing a leading role among the Cambodia–Laos–Myanmar–Vietnam (CLMV) sub-grouping to complete integration initiatives under the AEC blueprint.

At the same time, it is also crucial for Vietnam to prepare for reforms to ensure that the economy can cope with structural challenges and future disruptions. As noted in Tan and Luu (2017), a key policy priority is to develop the service sector in tandem with the manufacturing sector. The economic literature suggests that services increase in importance as an engine of growth and a source of employment creation as the economy develops. Nonetheless, the development of the service sector is not a natural progression achieved solely through market forces. The government has an important role to play in:

(i) Formulating the appropriate regulatory framework which fosters competitive and efficient service markets;
(ii) Investing in infrastructure which is essential for service industries to grow, specifically in the case of logistics and tourism;
(iii) Facilitating the development of the ICT sector through market liberalisation and upgrading the telecommunication and broadband networks. ICT serves to make other services tradable, creating large positive spillover effects on other sectors of the economy.

3.6.3 Developing a Highly Productive and Climate-resilient Agriculture Sector

As the factors of production continue to be shifted to the manufacturing and service sectors, improving agriculture productivity is vital to ensure food security. Moreover, productivity enhancement will enable the agriculture sector to become another robust channel for growth, contributing to a well-diversified vibrant economy.

Having the third largest ratio of arable land to total land area in ASEAN,[45] Vietnam is bestowed with diverse topography and high latitude range which is conducive for a variety of crops. In particular, the mountainous and hilly soils are suitable for afforestation and cultivation of perennial crops and fruit crops. The delta soils form the country's centre of food production. These regions are typically amply moisturised and less prone to soil degradation. Institutional reforms as part of *Doi Moi* programme in 1986 in rural areas unleashed the country's potential in agricultural production, enabling its remarkable transformation from a recipient of emergency food assistance to a net agricultural exporter since the early 1990s. This was followed by major

[44] See Intal *et al.* (2014).
[45] See Tan *et al.* (2017d).

public investments in irrigation and fertiliser, which contributed to higher crop intensity and yield. As a result, Vietnam's agricultural exports increased substantially at an average annual growth rate of 12.6 percent between 1995 and 2010,[46] ranging from rice and coffee to fishery, pepper, cashew nuts, rubber, fruits and wood products.

Notwithstanding these impressive achievements, agriculture productivity growth over the past 10 years for Vietnam has been sluggish. ACI has conducted an empirical assessment of agricultural productivity in eight ASEAN countries based on a total factor productivity (TFP) growth accounting exercise complemented by the Malmquist Index Data Envelopment Analysis (DEA) methodology. We estimated agricultural productivity in individual ASEAN countries for the 2000–2011 period and decomposed it into technological change (TC) and technical efficiency change (TEC). We found that Vietnam's agriculture TFP has grown by only 0.5 percent p.a. between 2000 and 2011, as compared to the ASEAN's average of 1.4 percent p.a.[47]

In particular, estimation from the Malmquist Index DEA methodology shows that Vietnam experienced robust growth in TC but a decline in TEC, which indicates a need for a more efficient and effective allocation of agricultural resources to achieve higher agricultural productivity. The case of Vietnam implies that investment in agricultural research and development (R&D) may not bring about significant growth in TFP without improved resource allocation and utilisation. While R&D efforts may shift a country's production frontier forward, better resource management can increase productivity for a substantially lower cost, which has important policy implications for Vietnam, and more generally low-income and lower middle-income countries.

Going forward, Malaysia may serve as an informative case study to emulate as it tops the region in agriculture TFP growth in our analysis. The case of Malaysia underscores the fact that agriculture can be integral to the industrialisation process in a dual economic structure by bolstering the overall national competitiveness and economic development. In fact, Malaysia's success in agriculture can be attributed to its concerted efforts in four areas: fostering a competitive agribusiness industry; close partnership between government agencies, agribusiness firms and research institutes; and integrating smallholders into agro-based value chains and provision of infrastructure, credit and extension services. The following important policy lessons can be drawn for Vietnam:

(i) Identifying and developing agricultural niches based on climate, natural endowment and core competencies, with a goal of becoming internationally competitive in those particular products;
(ii) Fostering strong linkages between agriculture and resource-based manufacturing in a dual economic structure;
(iii) Developing agro-based industries through nurturing the growth of competitive agribusiness companies and public–private partnerships;

[46] See Ministry of Agriculture and Rural Development and FAO (2013).
[47] See Tan *et al.* (2017d).

(iv) Identifying opportunities for vertical fragmentation of the agro-based industry and integrating smallholder producers into the agribusiness value chains, thereby raising their incomes and alleviating rural poverty;
(v) Upgrading agricultural infrastructure including drainage and irrigation systems as well as roads, sea ports and electricity to improve farmers' access to the market;
(vi) Promoting and incentivising public and private agricultural R&D to develop productivity-enhancing, environmentally friendly and sustainable technologies and practices, such as creating new varieties of crops with increased resistance to pests;
(vii) Improving resource management for stimulating agricultural TFP growth;
(viii) Providing preferential credit schemes and extension services to farmers to enhance their access to capital and new technologies, thereby augmenting their productivity and capability to tackle climate change.

3.7 Special Economic Zones (SEZs): Concept, Development and Execution

From the experiences of the East Asian economies, SEZs are important engines for trade and investment. SEZs are a cornerstone of the strategy to attract FDI in many developing economies, including Vietnam. In fact, the Vietnamese government has resolved to set up three new special administrative-economic zones (SAEZs) in Van Don, Bac Van Phong and Phu Quoc which offer investors greater incentives and more conducive business environment than existing zones. In this section, we examine factors leading to the success or failure of SEZs as illustrated through the experiences of China and India. We then discuss the Vietnamese government's current plan for the three new SAEZs. We call to attention the need for a comprehensive strategy with constant monitoring to ensure the successful execution of the SEZ model. In particular, we suggest the formulation of an SEZ index to assess viability of proposed SEZ locations, track their operations and evaluate SEZs' outcomes.

3.7.1 Overview of SEZs and the Experiences of China and India

In the economic literature, SEZs can be broadly defined as "demarcated geographic areas where the rules of business are different from those that prevail in the national territory".[48] The business environment in SEZs is intended to be more liberal with a more effective public administration when compared to other parts of the country. To this end, these zones enjoy preferential policies in terms of investment conditions, customs, taxation and regulations. In fact, as shown in Figure 3.13, "SEZ" is an umbrella term which encompasses different types of zone setups.

Among the sub-classes of SEZs, Free Trade Zones (FTZs) generally refer to areas offering warehousing, storage and distribution facilities for trade and re-export operations under specific customs regulations whereby goods are generally exempted from duty. Export Processing

[48] See Farole and Akinci (2011).

Figure 3.13: Different Types of Economic Zones

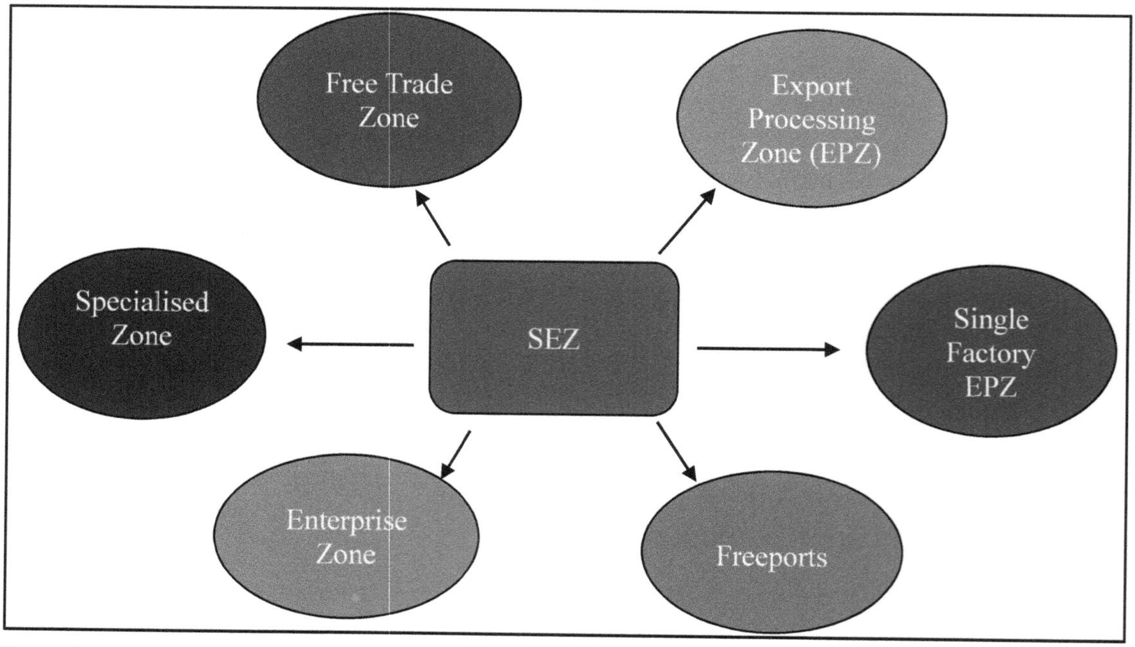

Source: Authors' compilation based on FIAS (2008)

Zones (EPZ) are specific FTZs and industrial estates aimed at serving foreign markets. For instance, China differentiates EPZs from general FTZs through an export quota requirement for the former. In some instances, Single Factory EPZs are created. Meanwhile, Freeports typically encompass larger areas than FTZs or EPZs as they accommodate more types of activities which may include residence, tourism and retail on top of manufacturing and exporting. Enterprise Zones are usually set up to revitalise economic activities in designated urban or rural areas through tax-incentives and financial grants to the private sector. Finally, Specialised Zones are those established to promote specific sectors. Examples include logistics parks, petrochemical zones or science parks.

As summarised by Farole and Akinci (2011) as well as FIAS (2008), SEZs often aim to fulfil at least one of the following objectives: (i) to attract FDI; (ii) to alleviate massive unemployment; (iii) to support a wider economic reform strategy; or (iv) to serve as testbed of new policies and governing approaches. Other aims of SEZs may include to generate foreign exchange reserves and to promote domestic interregional competition. In certain historical contexts, the establishment of SEZs may also be an attempt to quarantine economic liberalisation to specific corners of a country, reflecting the political leadership's resistance to economic reforms on a wider scale.[49] Nevertheless, in general, SEZs in the modern era are expected to deliver both immediate

[49] Consider, for instance, the limited trade outpost of Dejima in Nagasaki during the closed-door policy enacted by the Tokugawa Shogunate in Japan from the mid-17th to mid-18th century.

gains in jobs, trade and investment as well as dynamic long-term economic benefits including facilitating technological transfers and industrial upgrading, sparking structural economic transformation with the emergence of new growth industries, and catalysing large-scale economic reforms.

The track record of the SEZ model is mixed[50] as seen through the contrasting experiences of China and India. In China, the term "SEZ" would often bring to mind eight specific areas: Shenzhen, Zhuhai, Shantou, Xiamen, Hainan, Shanghai Pudong New Area, Tianjin Binhai New Area and the recently announced Xiong'an economic zone. However, it also encompasses a myriad of FTZs, EPZs and specialised zones. By many yardsticks, SEZs in China have been a resounding success. They are estimated to account for more than 20 percent of national GDP, more than 45 percent of FDI, 60 percent of exports and generate in excess of 30 million jobs.[51] In addition, SEZs have made significant contributions to technological progress and innovation. The average commercialisation rate of industrial parks in China was estimated to be six times the overall level for the economy. In particular, in the agriculture sector, agriculture demonstration zones and agro-tech parks have driven technological development and improved agricultural productivity, thus raising farmers' income.[52] Most importantly, SEZs have fulfilled their role as laboratories for new economic policies, creating the momentum for the reform and liberalisation of the Chinese economy which has propelled China's meteoric rise over the past three to four decades.

The success of Chinese SEZs is due to a number of factors. First, these areas are established at advantageous locations with good infrastructure networks. Second, they offer attractive investment incentives, including concessionary tax rates, rapid customs clearance and flexible labour policies.[53] This is complemented by greater institutional autonomy whereby SEZs were given authority to craft suitable laws to pursue new development policies. Third, land reforms have played a crucial role in SEZs' success. Starting from Shenzhen, the central government allowed SEZs to lease land to investors, initially for a tenure of 20–50 years. This was followed by the promulgation of a land auction system for commercial land in 2002 and 2007.[54] Fourth, SEZs have managed to attract not only low-skilled but also high-skilled labour through a slew of incentives such as housing provision and education subsidies. Coupled with the abundance of FDI as a result of the above-mentioned preferential policies and the opening up of China, the influx of skilled labour has allowed these zones to transform into centres for technology diffusion, imitation, adaptation, and ultimately innovation.[55] Fifth and most importantly, the Chinese government has shown strong commitment to experiment market-oriented reforms in SEZs and executed a sound, systematic SEZ strategy. The central

[50] See Farole and Akinci (2011).

[51] See Zeng (2015).

[52] *Ibid.*

[53] See Enright *et al.* (2005).

[54] See Shen and Xu (2011).

[55] See Zeng (2012).

government has decentralised power to enable local governments to build a conducive legal and policy environment for SEZs. In addition, SEZs were established in batches, with clear performance metrics to track their development. The model was only replicated after the first zones proved to be successful.[56] Moreover, the SEZs are closely linked to the rest of the domestic economy through value chains, and they are sometimes made to compete against one another to enhance their efficiency.

In contrast, SEZs in India have failed to take off. As of January 2018, there are 423 SEZs which have received formal approvals by the Indian government. However, only slightly less than half (210 zones) are in operation[57] and their contribution to India's export performance as well as overall economic growth has been found to be disappointing.[58] The biggest hindrance to the development of SEZs in India is difficulty in obtaining land. The lack of an effective land acquisition policy has generated political backlash to SEZs which weakens state governments' support for such projects, leading developers and banks to shun them altogether.[59] Inconsistent implementation of policies is also a reason for SEZs' failure. In particular, the rollback of the minimum alternate tax (MAT) and dividend distribution tax (DDT) incentives in 2012 dealt a massive blow to the attractiveness of Indian SEZs to investors.[60]

3.7.2 Vietnam's Proposed Special Administrative-Economic Zones (SAEZs) as Engines of Growth and Laboratories for Policy Reforms

The newly proposed SAEZs of Van Don, Bac Van Phong and Phu Quoc are located in Northern, Central and Southern Vietnam, respectively. Situated in Quang Ninh province, the Van Don island district is well known for its collection of islands and beautiful beaches. It has been slated for development of high-tech industries and associated support industries; namely eco-tourism, aviation services and retail services.[61] Many infrastructure projects are in the pipeline, most notably the construction of a new international airport, to enhance Van Don's connectivity to nearby Asian cities such as Shenzhen, Shanghai and Hong Kong as well as the major domestic growth centres of Hanoi, Hai Phong and Mong Cai. Meanwhile, the main focus of the Bac Van Phong SAEZ in the Central province of Khanh Hoa will be its port and related businesses. The government is looking to develop an industrial centre attached to the nearby seaport to create investment opportunities for various sectors ranging from logistics, shipbuilding, and sea freights to many more. Other sectors of interest include IT, electronics and precise engineering

[56] See Zeng (2015).

[57] See Ministry of Commerce and Industry of India (2018).

[58] See *Times of India* (2014) and Palit (2016).

[59] See Palit (2016).

[60] See Aggarwal (2016).

[61] See *VN Express* (2017) and Ariffin (2018).

industries, as well as financial, commerce and tourism services.[62] Finally, the Phu Quoc SAEZ in Kien Giang province is gearing up to develop eco-tourism, retail services, high-quality healthcare and education services as well as biotechnology.[63] Interestingly, there are plans to set up integrated resorts with casinos on all three SAEZs.

There are high hopes that the three SAEZs will help to close the gap between Vietnamese businesses and their overseas counterparts with regard to technology, engineering and ancillary service capabilities. Particularly, Vietnam plans to increase trade flows between foreign investors and local businesses by incentivising advanced technology companies to settle down in these new SAEZs. This is expected to speed up technology transfer and allow domestic firms to move up the value chain by prioritising larger investment initiatives on high-tech and clean-energy projects over low-cost manufacturing sectors.[64] Furthermore, the fact that service sectors play a major role in the proposed economic focuses of the SAEZs signifies the Vietnamese government's intention to foster services as an additional growth engine alongside manufacturing.

Though the final masterplans for the three SAEZs are still being hashed out, the government seems ready to roll out unprecedented incentives to realise its ambitious goals. Among others, these could include corporate tax exemptions for up to four years, and subsequent 10 percent preferential tax rate for up to 30 years, along with a 50 percent tax cut in the next nine years from the day firms have taxable income. It has also been proposed that the tax levied on income from investments in SAEZ real-estate projects could be as low as 17 percent.[65] There are also significant concessions on personal income tax to attract labour, especially skilled workers including managers, scientists and other experts. In terms of improving the business environment, the online one-stop service model for public administration is to be adopted. Furthermore, land-use rights may be extended to 99 years for development of certain priority sectors. In addition, foreigners may be allowed to own residential and resort properties.

However, the most significant proposal is perhaps to have administrative reform to create the post of SAEZ Chief Executive (or Head) to manage these zones in lieu of the usual People's Committee model. In fact, it has also been suggested that the position of SAEZ Party Secretary be consolidated with that of the Chief Executive to afford the latter full power in running the SAEZ. The SAEZ Chief Executive will answer to the central government and relevant provincial central authorities. Nevertheless, he or she is expected to have more power than the chair of the provincial People's Committee where the SAEZ is in.[66]

While the government's determination to set up the three SAEZs is indeed commendable, there will be considerable challenges which it has to overcome. The very choice of locations

---

[62] *Ibid.*

[63] *Ibid.*

[64] See De Freitas (2017).

[65] *Ibid.*

[66] See *Vietnamnet* (2017c).

for these zones may have raised eyebrows as they are less developed than other established growth centres, especially Ho Chi Minh City, Hanoi and Da Nang, which possess considerable infrastructure, market access and population advantages.[67] As a result, utmost care has to be devoted to planning these SAEZs to ensure their viability. Infrastructure investment to enhance connectivity must be a priority because services are a major focus in the development strategies of the zones. In particular, good air connectivity through modernised international airports is key. Meanwhile, as Hanoi and Ho Chi Minh City will remain the country's pre-eminent business, financing, and innovation hubs; the attempt to develop high-tech industries and business services on the SAEZs must seek to foster synergies between these zones and the two metropolises. It is necessary for the government to come up with a comprehensive masterplan clearly outlining how Hanoi and Ho Chi Minh City will complement the development of the SAEZs.

On the other hand, the SAEZs' status as up-and-coming areas instead of developed growth centres presents a unique advantage for them to be laboratories for new policies. Similar to China, policy innovations should be encouraged in SAEZs, and successful experiments can be replicated in a gradual manner so as to bring about widespread reforms throughout the country. Their relatively small size and current lack of economic and political importance make SAEZs ideal as testbeds for new governance models, land policies and industrial planning approaches. In fact, competitive pressure from existing economic zones within Vietnam as well as throughout the region demand actual policy breakthroughs if the new SAEZs are to be viable. For SAEZs to successfully spearhead growth and the next wave of reforms, it is imperative that the government adopt the long-term view for the proposed SAEZs. There should be legislations to ensure breakthroughs in administrative and tax policies will persist beyond the term of the current government. Consistency in policy-making is key because flip-flopping will damage investor sentiment to the detriment of the SAEZs, as seen through the Indian experience in Section 3.7.1.

Furthermore, another important lesson from the implementation of the SEZ model in China and India is that broad-based popular support is important for the success of Vietnam's three new SAEZs. Thus, it is not only important that SAEZs deliver on their economic promises, but they also have to do so without compromising on the living environment and workers' quality of life. Despite their success, Chinese SEZs have come under criticism for environmental degradation and imbalance between industrial development and social dimensions.[68] In Vietnam, public outcry over pollution by industrial zones, especially the 2017 Formosa environmental scandal in Ha Tinh province, must not be overlooked in planning the new SAEZs. At the same time, there must be concerted effort to achieve commensurate improvement in social and urban services as the SAEZs grow. In addition, as seen from the Indian experience, it is critical for the government to formulate an effective land acquisition policy. The government may want to consider giving land owners a stake in the SAEZs' development on top of the lump-sum compensation to entice them to support SAEZs.

---

[67] See *Vietnamnet* (2017d).

[68] See Zeng (2015).

3.7.3 ACI's SEZ Index: Tracking Viability, Operations and Outcomes of SAEZs in Vietnam

All in all, the SAEZs will be long-term projects which require constant monitoring and policy adjustments. To this end, ACI proposes an SEZ Index which track the viability, operations and outcomes not only of the proposed SAEZs but also future similar economic zones to be set up throughout the country. This index will serve as basis for detailed analysis to identify strategies to prioritise the development of these areas so that they may achieve a good level of competition and complementarity with one another. Furthermore, the SEZ Index may be used to map and inform the international community on various investment potentials and opportunities in Vietnam's SAEZs. More broadly, the Vietnam SEZ Index and its counterpart which the ACI is also developing for Indonesia will be pilot-tests for a general research framework on SEZs which could be replicated in other developing Asian countries. This research effort will enable cross-border comparison of SEZs across Asian economies, thus facilitating cross-country learning and promoting best practices in planning, managing and attracting investment to SEZs.

Drawing on the prevailing economic literature, the proposed SEZ Index will comprise five environments reflecting the different facets of SEZs which are as follows:

(i) **Sub-national Endowments and Constraints** which examines potentials and challenges that exist in the SEZs' location and host provinces;
(ii) **Zone Management, Services and Infrastructure Support** which scores SEZs on how they are managed, how their tenants are serviced and how their workers are treated;
(iii) **Role of Government and Regulatory Framework** which reflects special subsidies and constraints that apply in the zone, as well as policies to protect investors;
(iv) **Environmental and Ecological Sustainability** which tracks how pollution is controlled and ecological footprints may be minimised;
(v) **Zone Performance and Policy Outcomes** which measures the impacts of SEZs in terms of generating investment, creating jobs and contributing to the regional and national economy.

Subsumed under each environment is three to four sub-environments, leading to a total of eighteen as illustrated in Figure 3.14

Tentatively, the index shall be made up of 101 indicators from secondary data sources ("hard data") as well as propriety survey data ("soft data"). The list of potential indicators is presented in Table 3.1.

A variety of issues of interest to different stakeholders may be examined through the SEZ Index. From the government perspective, the index can be used to set policy objectives, not only in terms of growth, investment and employment but also environmental and social considerations, infrastructure development and financing, manpower plans as well as industrial relations. Meanwhile, customised reports based on the index research findings are useful tools to disseminate information on investment incentives, targeted industries specific to each SEZ, locational

Figure 3.14 Framework of ACI's SEZ Index

Source: ACI

and other advantages to potential investors. For investors already operating in the zone, the index shall provide a useful benchmark on the quality of services provided in terms of infrastructure and administrative support; perception of law and order, including protection of property rights, labour relations, and availability of upgrading programmes for domestic suppliers. Thus, the index will also spur zone operators to do better in these respects. Finally, the proposed SEZ Index shall reflect the conditions of zone employees in terms of workplace environment, accommodation and living facilities, salary expectation and job satisfaction and information regarding industrial harmony, safety and security.

Table 3.1: List of Indicators for the Proposed SEZ Index

1. Sub-national (provincial) Endowments and Constraints (4 Sub-environments, 24 indicators)							
1.1	**Natural Resources**	**1.2**	**Manpower Requirements**	**1.3**	**Access to Market**	**1.4**	**Access to Capital**
1.1.01	Gross Regional Domestic Product (GRDP)	**1.2.01**	Labour Force	**1.3.01**	GRDP	**1.4.01**	Bank Deposits
1.1.02	GRDP from Oil, Gas, Minerals	**1.2.02**	Employment Rate	**1.3.02**	Population	**1.4.02**	Bank Loans
1.1.03	GRDP from Agriculture Products	**1.2.03**	Minimum Wage (R)	**1.3.03**	Distance to Closest Regional Port (R)	**1.4.03**	Non-performing Loans per Total Bank Loans
1.1.04	Tourism Potential (S)	**1.2.04**	Life Expectancy	**1.3.04**	Distance to Closest Metropolitan Area (R)	**1.4.04**	Population per Number of Bank Branches
1.1.05	SEZ Land Area	**1.2.05**	Mean Years of Schooling	**1.3.05**	GRDP of Closest Metropolitan Area	**1.4.05**	Ease of Dealing with Banks (S)
		1.2.06	Number of Vocational Schools	**1.3.06**	Domestic Market Size Index		
		1.2.07	Labour Productivity	**1.3.07**	Foreign Market Size Index		

2. Zone Management, Services, and Infrastructure Support (4 Sub-environments, 34 indicators)							
2.1	**Ownership and Governance**	**2.2**	**Infrastructure and Utilities**	**2.3**	**Satisfactory Working and Living Condition of Labour**	**2.4**	**Administrative Efficiency and Responsiveness to Firms**
2.1.01	Private Share in Zone Equity	**2.2.01**	Quality of Transportation Access to / from Zone (S)	**2.3.01**	Deviation (improvement) from Minimum Wage	**2.4.01**	Ease of Exporting (S)
2.1.02	Foreign Share in Zone Equity	**2.2.02**	Distance to Deep Seaport (R)	**2.3.02**	Change in Salary (before and after)	**2.4.02**	Ease of Importing (S)
2.1.03	Private Representation in Zone Board	**2.2.03**	Capacity of Deep Seaport	**2.3.03**	Availability of Housing and Sanitation Facilities	**2.4.03**	Ease of Registering a Business (S)
2.1.04	Foreign Representation in Zone Board	**2.2.04**	Quality of Deep Seaport Services (S)	**2.3.04**	Quality of Housing and Sanitation Facilities (S)	**2.4.04**	Ease of Obtaining Construction Permit (S)
2.1.05	Union Representation in Zone Board (R)	**2.2.05**	Distance to Airport (R)	**2.3.05**	Availability of Healthcare Facilities	**2.4.05**	Ease of Paying Taxes (S)

(Continued)

Table 3.1: ***(Continued)***

2.1.06	Central Government Representation in Zone Board	**2.2.06**	Capacity of Airport	**2.3.06**	Bed to Patient Ratio	**2.4.06**	Ease of Closing a Business (S)
2.1.07	Independent Members in Zone Board	**2.2.07**	Quality of Airport Services (S)	**2.3.07**	Availability of Recreational Facilities		
2.1.08	Frequency of Board Meeting	**2.2.08**	Capacity of Warehouse Services				
		2.2.09	Quality of Warehouse Services (S)				
		2.2.10	Capacity of Installed Power				
		2.2.11	Quality of Power Transmission (S)				
		2.2.12	Capacity of Waste Treatment Plant				
		2.2.13	Quality of Waste Treatment Services (S)				
3. Role of Government and Regulatory Framework (3 Sub-environments, 21 indicators)							
3.1	**Ownership and Governance**	**3.2**	**Infrastructure and Utilities**	**3.3**	**Satisfactory Working and Living Condition of Labour**		
3.1.01	Income Tax Rate	**3.2.01**	Export Requirements	**3.3.01**	Quality of Property Rights Regulation (S)		
3.1.02	Import Duty Rate (R)	**3.2.02**	Import Limitations	**3.3.02**	Quality of Labour Regulation (S)		
3.1.03	Export Duty Rate (R)	**3.2.03**	Limitation to Sell to Domestic Market	**3.3.03**	Perception of Corruption (S)		
3.1.04	Extent (length) of Fiscal Subsidies	**3.2.04**	Limitation to Buy from Domestic Suppliers	**3.3.04**	Perception of Rule of Law (S)		
3.1.05	Incentives for Research and Development	**3.2.05**	Extent (length) of Policy Constraints	**3.3.05**	Crime Rate (R)		
3.1.06	Incentives for Firm Collaboration			**3.3.06**	Number of Law Enforcement Officers		

3.1.07	Training Programme for Tenant Firms			**3.3.07**	Labour Relations (S)		
3.1.08	Training Programme for Domestic Suppliers			**3.3.08**	Government Mediation of Labour Relations (S)		
4. Environmental and Ecological Sustainability (4 Sub-environments, 12 indicators)							
4.1	**Fiscal Subsidies and Incentives**	**4.2**	**Policy Initiatives and Constraints**	**4.3**	**Investor's Legal and Physical Protection**	**4.4**	**Ecological Footprint and Green Technology**
4.1.01	Air Quality Index	**4.2.01**	Water Quality Index	**4.3.01**	Soil Quality Index	**4.4.01**	Monitoring and Management of Environmental Impact (S)
4.1.02	Number of Respiratory Disease Cases (R)	**4.2.02**	Number of Waterborne Disease Cases (R)	**4.3.02**	Loss of Forest Cover (R)	**4.4.02**	Energy Consumed per Value Added (R)
4.1.03	Programmes to Safeguard Emission Standard (S)	**4.2.03**	Reclamation (re-use) Rate of Wastewater	**4.3.03**	Reforestation and Tree-planting Initiatives (S)	**4.4.03**	Incentives for Using Green Technology
5. Zone Performance and Policy Outcomes (3 Sub-environments, 11 indicators)							
5.1	**Attraction of Foreign and Domestic Investment**	**5.2**	**Employment Creation for Local and Migrant Workers**	**5.3**	**Contribution to Regional Economic Vibrancy**		
5.1.01	Foreign Direct Investment	**5.2.01**	Total Zone Workers	**5.3.01**	Exports from Zone to Other Countries		
5.1.02	Domestic Direct Investment	**5.2.02**	Number of Local Workers (from province)	**5.3.02**	Exports from Zone to Domestic Market		
5.1.03	Private Investment	**5.2.03**	Number of National Migrant Workers (from within the country, but outside the province)	**5.3.03**	Imports into Zone from Domestic Market		
		5.2.04	Number of International Migrant Workers	**5.3.04**	Zone Value Added		

Note: (S) denotes survey indicators while (R) denotes reverse indicators.

Source: ACI

3.8 The Singapore People's Association (PA) Model on Public Policy Communication, Articulation and Acceptance: Potential Lessons for Vietnam

An excellently formulated public policy with good intent and purpose may be rejected overwhelmingly by the people if it is not communicated effectively. The late Minister Mentor Lee Kuan Yew, founding father of Singapore, used to advise younger political leaders that this is the classic case where public debate fails and implementation of public policy derailed because the government of the day failed to carry the message properly to its constituency.

Concise articulation of public policies is increasingly challenging in the era of new media. The mode of public policy communication through the mainstream media and press are not sufficient either to say the least as many governments found it an uphill task and are in daily struggle as precious financial and manpower resources are being diverted to fight with fake or distorted news.

The most effective mode of communication and articulation of public policies still hinges upon direct regular people to people contact through well-informed agents, including both volunteers and salaried social workers, who have good comprehension of the key objectives, expectations and implementation aspects of the proposed public policy initiative. Singapore is a society with multiple national ethnicities in the setting of open accessibility to international press and new media and also a cosmopolitan city with widely travelled citizens. Thus, the government has fully recognised the difficulty of efficient public policy dissemination. Substantial government resources were invested since the early nation building to construct the bridge of communication between the people and the government and vice versa, which is known as the **Singapore People's Association (PA)**. As the current Prime Minister put it succinctly

... Peoples association is an organisation of "people". For PA to succeed, we must have good people. ...to click on that proud sense of identity and to unite Singaporeans. We should bring the volunteers to the ground, to give them an opportunity to serve, to test their ideas and to fulfil their dreams. We should help them improve their leadership skills and communication skills. ...to encourage them to innovate and to build communities in Singapore in a creative way. — **Prime Minister, Lee Hsien Loong**

PA's Mission is to build and to bridge communities in achieving the objective of "One People and One Singapore". The PA was conceptualised as an organisation that would bind the government of Singapore to the people, allowing them to connect and understand each other. It is dedicated to grassroots community and social work to promote social cohesion, which is undeniably important in implementing a cohesive national development plan.

3.8.1 Main Job Scopes of the PA

The role of community leaders is critical as it formed the background of PA. In support of the mission of the PA, community leaders of the PA will be expected to promote good neighbourhood relationships and overall community cohesiveness, while simultaneously strengthening the racial harmoniousness and sense of belonging that bind Singapore together. The PA must function as a bridge between the government and the people, facilitating the provision of feedback to the government directly from the people while at the same time helping to explain or execute government policy.

The PA can also help to understand and solve people's common everyday problems along with providing social aid to less-privileged residents. Another main role of the PA would be to strengthen the social fabric of Singapore by eliminating divisions that arise from issues such as race, income, education level and age. A culture of volunteerism, social responsibility and civic mindedness should also be cultivated by the PA.

In Figure 3.15, we can see a general overview of how the PA fits into the bigger public policy communication picture. The PA will serve as that middle organisation that helps reflect resident's feedback to the government while also helping residents better understand government policy.

In Figure 3.16, we can see a more detailed structure of how connection between government and people is actually achieved. Out of your everyday residents, there will be some that volunteer for grassroots work or partner with relevant organisations that provide these social services. These will form the second layer which is closest to the residents. From these volunteers and

Figure 3.15: Interconnections between the Government and the People

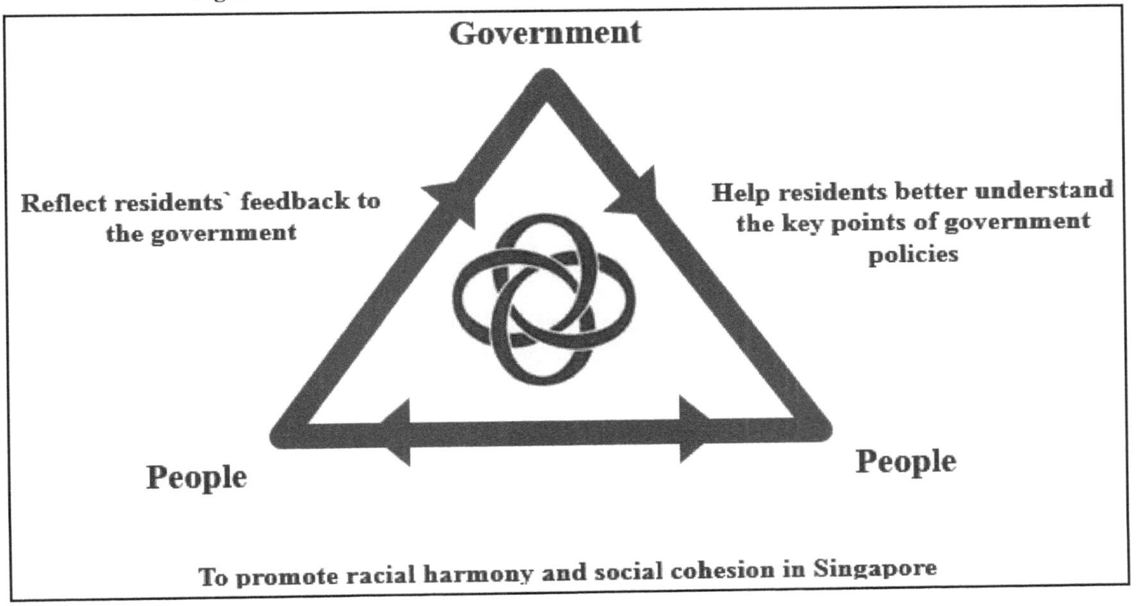

Source: The PA

Figure 3.16: Bridge between the Government and the People

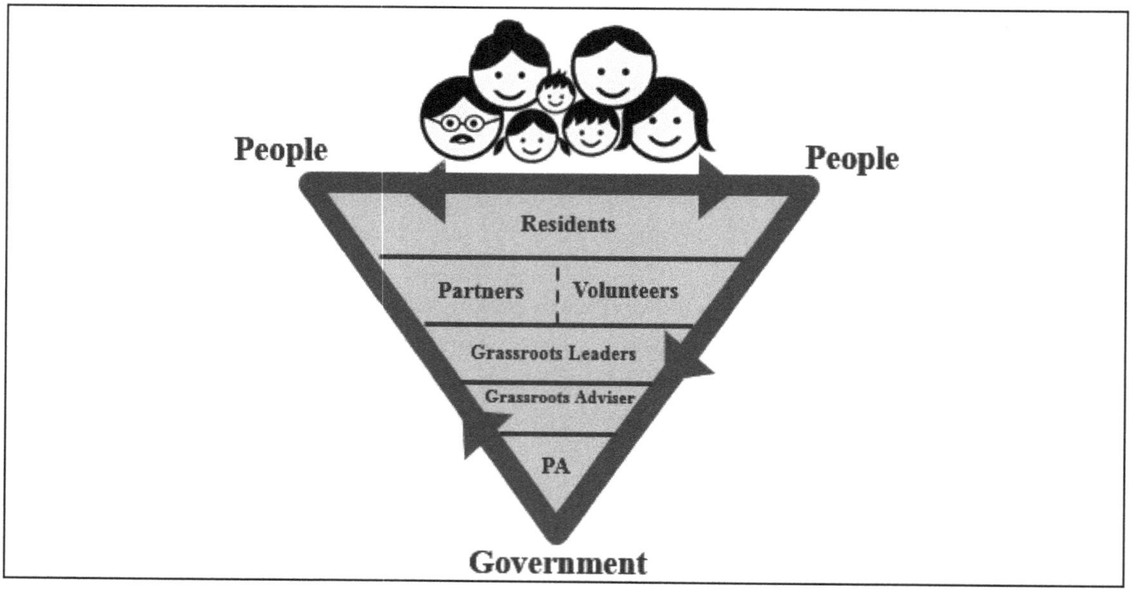

Source: The PA

partners, the PA will observe and try to appoint the best as leaders. These leaders will be expected to implement social programmes and explain the government's policies while leading their respective communities and providing structure to these volunteers and partners. Grassroots advisors from the PA will also be on hand to help leaders on how to best lead their communities and build trust and understanding.

3.8.2 National Pillars of Singapore and the Organisational Structure of the PA

The three main pillars of Singapore are defence, economics and social cohesion. Within the framework of these three main pillars, economics and defence would be unable to be executed without social cohesion, which is the core purpose of the People's Association. A cohesive and united society would be able to more effectively manage and implement economic policy while also working together for defence. If society is not united and cohesive, an effective defence cannot be mounted, and similarly, an effective economic development program will encounter difficulties if the groundwork of social cohesion is not first laid. This is the role of the PA (see Figures 3.17 and 3.18).

Singapore is divided into sections with a community development council dedicated to each section. These development councils are not based on constituency but instead on rough geographical area (see Figure 3.19). The grassroots volunteers in these councils visit residents to encourage community involvement and raise awareness about government issues while also explaining government policy and gathering feedback.

Within individual constituencies, a Citizens Consultative Committee would be the main umbrella organisation, overseeing community and welfare programmes and acting as the main

Figure 3.17: PA's Network between the People and Grassroots Organisations

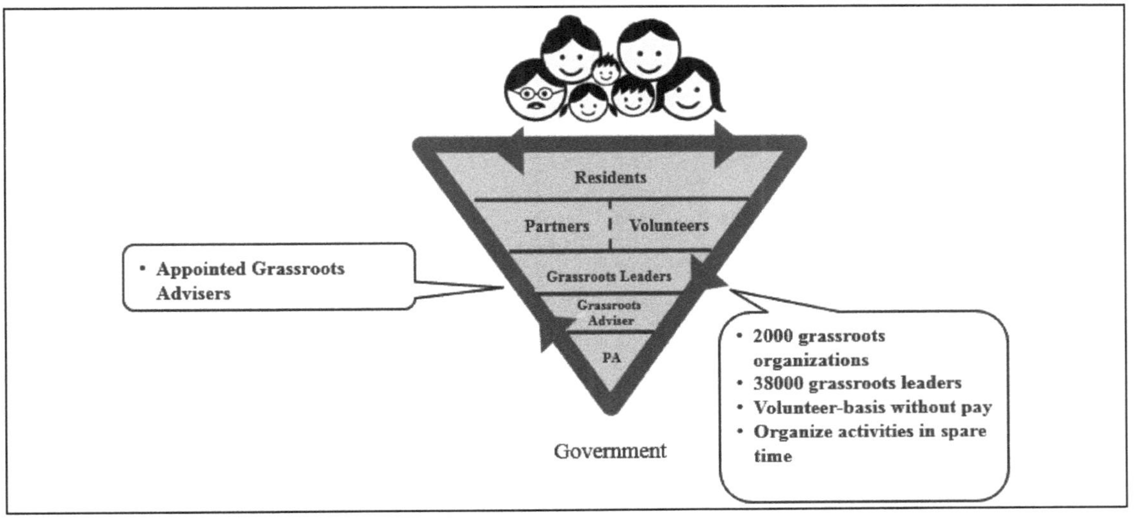

Source: The PA

Figure 3.18: Network between the Government and the People

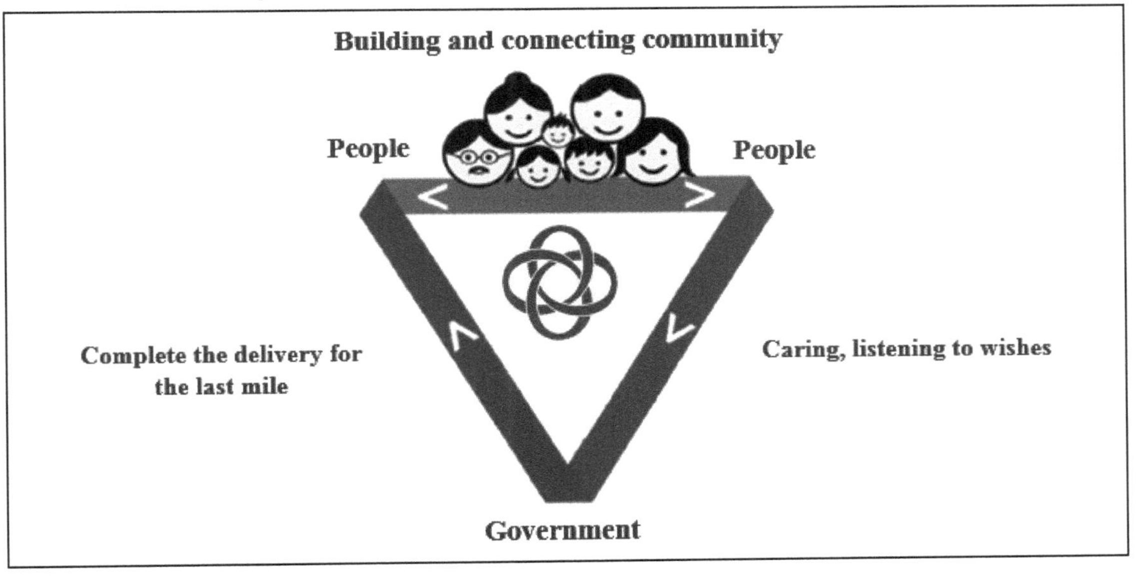

Source: The PA

feedback channel between the government and the people (see Figure 3.20). These committees help organise community forums and administer welfare assistance. Other committees include the Community Club Management Committee which provides recreational activities and learning opportunities, neighbourhood committees, youth committees, resident committees and committees for women and different races. The key goal is to get society as a whole active,

Figure 3.19: Cross-constituency — Community Development Council

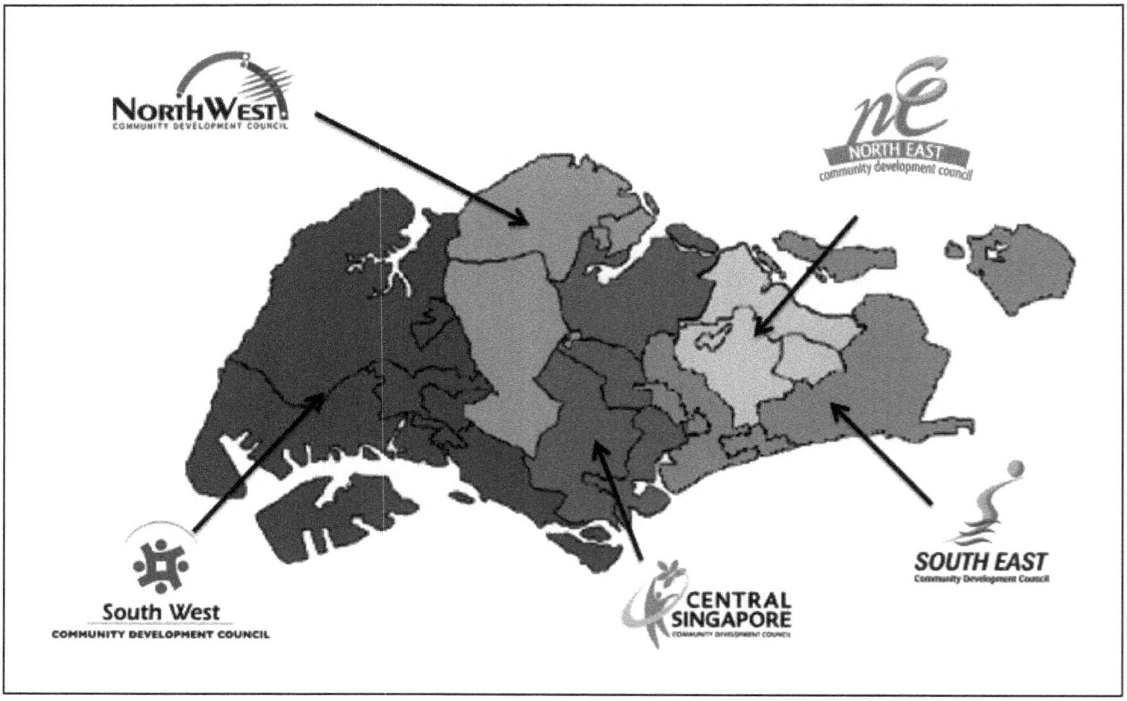

Source: The PA

Figure 3.20: Structure of Grassroots Organisations

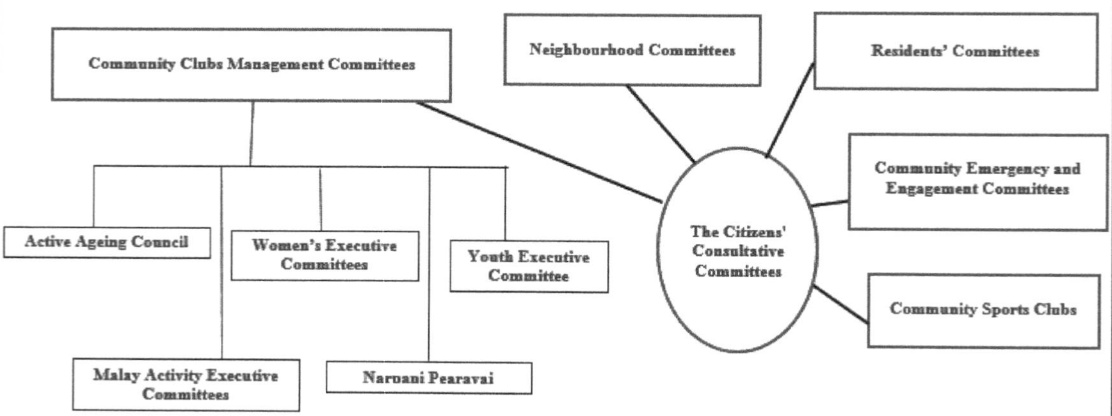

- **Basic networks of every constituency**
- **Targeted at different age groups and needs**
- **A wide range of programmes**

Source: The PA

well-informed, and engaged. Each of these committees handle programmes to engage their respective communities.

3.8.3 The Role of the PA in Bridging the Gap between People and the Government

The bridge between people

To promote racial harmony and social cohesion in Singapore, the PA has organised an array of activities to encourage social cohesion among the people. For instance, the PA has hosted community marathons and health fiestas for residents to exercise and participate in (see Figure 3.21). To engage youth, lantern festival and kayaking activities are held in which children and teenagers from all walks of life participate. This also encourages bonding from an early age. Furthermore, the PA has facilitated in the formation of interest groups such as musical groups and a baking community for like-minded residents (see Figures 3.21 and 3.22).

Apart from contributing to the health and welfare of residents, the interaction between people deepen bonds and relationships between the residents. This is especially crucial in Singapore's multi-racial and multi-religious society as greater tolerance would bring about less disputes and dissatisfaction. Moreover, in an increasingly fragmented world, trust and tolerance between people of different beliefs are of utmost importance. This can likely be achieved by increasing the quantity and quality of time spend by residents together in meaningful activities, regardless of race, language or religion (see Figure 3.23). The PA has also put in place many facilities such as community clubs, residents' committee activity centres, water-venture outlets, and national

Figure 3.21: Showcase of Various Activities and Interest Groups

Health Fiesta | Festivals of different races | Community Marathon | Variety of courses

Source: The PA

Figure 3.22: Interest Groups Community

Source: The PA

Figure 3.23: Participation in Activities by People of Different Races, Languages and Religions

Source: The PA

community leadership institutes (see Figure 3.24), creating an enabling atmosphere for better integration between activities and facilities particularly at community centres (see Figure 3.25).

Through these activities, Singaporeans of different races and religions would develop a deeper understanding towards one another, leading to greater empathy especially when social fault lines in Singapore are constantly emerging. Hence, the PA plays an important role in bridging the gap between people of various background, in a hope to strive towards a stronger and more united community.

Figure 3.24: Facilities of PA

Source: The PA

Figure 3.25: Integration of Activities and Facilities at Community Centres

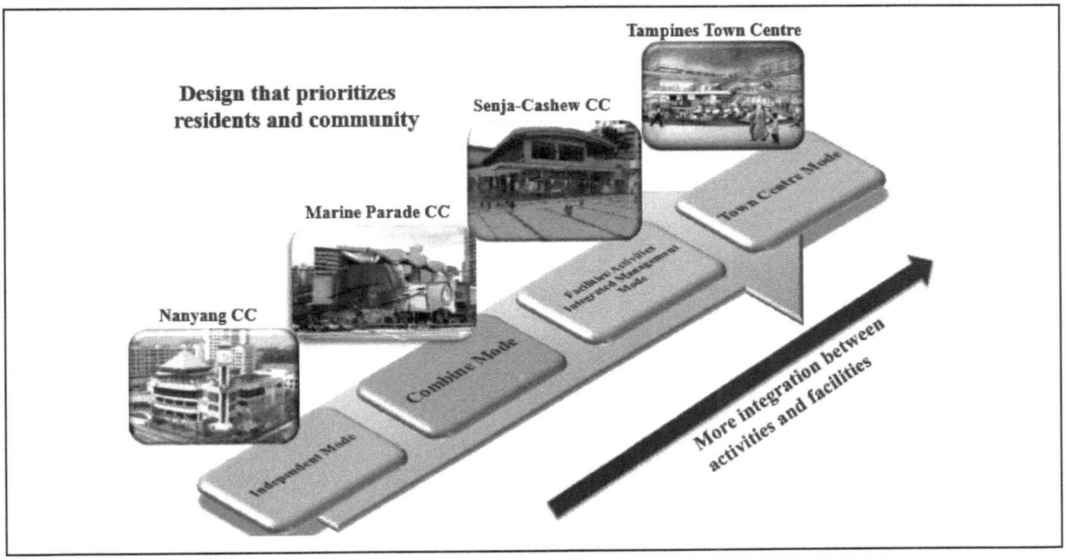

Source: The PA

Bridge between the people and the government

As can be seen in Figure 3.26, the PA has also adopted a bottom-up approach in maintaining an efficient management of the people's views and concerns regarding their welfare and government policies. Residents can share their views through dialogue sessions, house visits and community events like in Figure 3.27. Through these platform, residents can share their feedback to

Figure 3.26: How the PA Can Act as a Bridge from People to Government

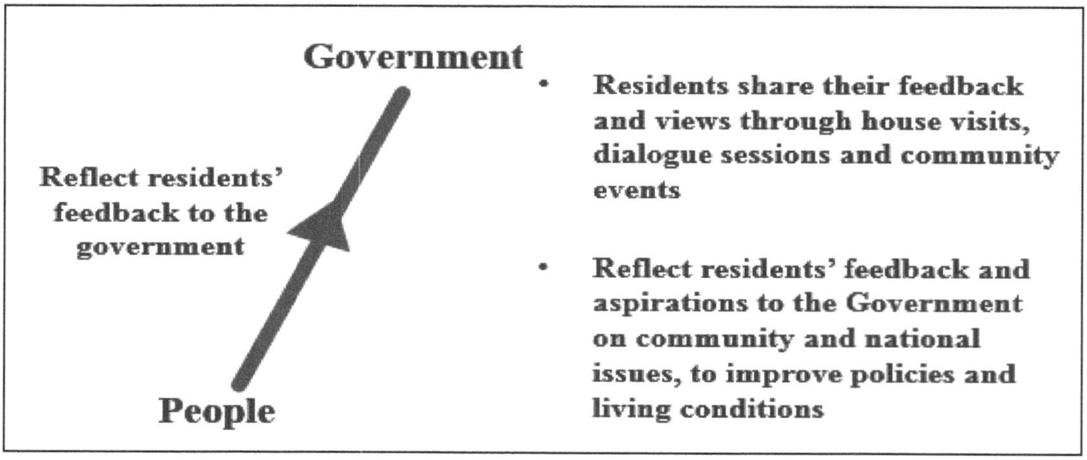

Source: The PA

Figure 3.27: Dialogue and Visit Sessions Conducted by the Government

Source: The PA

grassroots leaders with regard to living conditions, facilities or national policies. PA grassroots leaders would then reflect residents' opinions and feedback through public consultations and dialogue sessions to the government for consideration. Hence, the PA serves as a bridge from the people to the government with the aim of improving the welfare of the general public. Moreover, at the macro level, policies are better shaped to reflect the people's aspirations through efficacious discussions organised by the PA.

Bridge between the government and the people

The PA plays an important role in facilitating the policies implemented by the government as well as leading the residents in contributing to the society. The PA would pass on detailed information to the residents and explain the importance of specific government policies to residents (see Figure 3.28). This would allow residents to have a better understanding of the policies implemented as they can seek clarification during the discussion sessions organised by the PA. As a result, through the PA, there is efficient communication between the government and the people (see Figure 3.29). For instance, the PA had facilitated in the implementation of the mandatory National Service (NS) policy, the establishment of Housing Development Board flats, and the participation of the 'Keep Singapore Clean' Campaign (see Figure 3.30).

Figure 3.28: Proactive Measures by the Government through Active Groundwork

Source: The PA

Figure 3.29: How the PA Can Act as the Bridge from Government to People

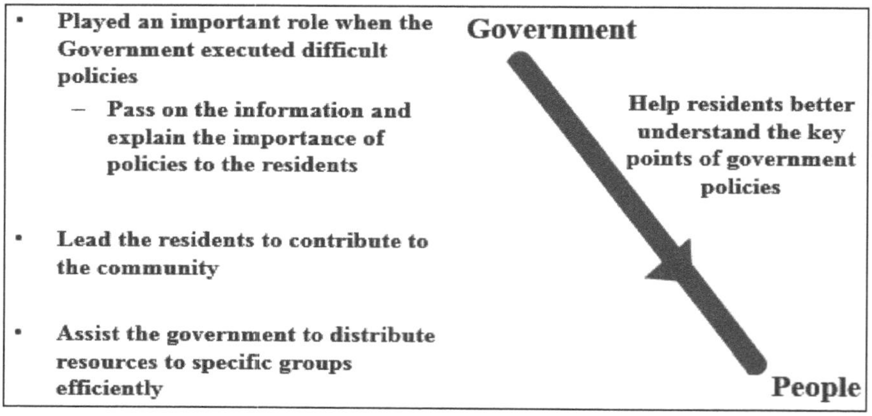

Source: The PA

Figure 3.30: The PA Assisting the Government in Explaining Policy

Explained to the people why the government must expropriate the land to build HDB

When the mandatory NS policy was first introduced, PA assisted the government in explaining to the public its importance and in calming the emotions of the family members

Ministers and the representatives of the Ministry or the organization explained the policy to the grassroots leaders and cleared their doubts

PA lead residents to participate in road building and the "Keep Singapore Clean" campaign

Source: The PA

Figure 3.31: The PA Assisting the Government in Carrying Out Policy

When the haze hit Singapore, grassroots advisers and leaders assisted the government to efficiently distribute masks to low-income households

PA's volunteers teach residents how to prevent the breeding of aedine mosquitos and stop the spread of Dengue Fever through promotional activities

Source: The PA

Moreover, the PA plays a critical role in assisting the government to distribute resources to specific groups when the need arises. For instance, grassroots leaders and volunteers teach residents simple ways to prevent the breeding of aedine mosquitoes through flyers and activities while raising awareness to stop the spread of dengue fever at various communities. When the severe haze affected Singapore back in 2015, grassroots advisors and leaders helped to facilitate in distributing masks to low-income families to better equip residents to combat the haze and manage their healthcare needs (see Figure 3.31).

Furthermore, with the advent of technology, PA's activities and efforts are publicised extensively online on platforms such as Facebook, to raise the people's awareness (see Figure 3.32). The PA has also made offline communications from the government to the people more broad-based and personalised through the setup of booths to engage residents better, in which they discuss topics such as family, career and elderly care. Reader-friendly materials are also made available to residents who require more time to understand specific issues with the help of the PA. With the help of the PA and the various communication platforms, the Singapore government can work together with the people to build stronger communities and a united Singapore.

Figure 3.32: Improving Public Awareness of PA's Activities and Grassroots Works through Various Channels

Source: The PA

3.9 Concluding Notes

Overall, the policy recommendations in this chapter have focused on seven main areas, namely (i) fostering private sector dynamism through further SOE and market reforms; (ii) mitigating regional disparities; (iii) facilitating SMEs' growth as productive, efficient and future-ready enterprises; (iv) promoting labour upgrading for enhanced labour productivity; (v) striving for a balanced economic structure with vibrant and sustainable economic clusters; (vi) ensuring the viability of SEZs and SAEZs as engines of growth as well as laboratories for new policy-making approaches and (vii) bridging the gap between people and the government through the proposed Singapore Institution known as the People's Association for enhancing effective public policy communication, articulation and acceptance. The successful implementation of the proposed policy initiatives will transform the Vietnamese economy, putting it on track to achieve the growth breakthroughs required for it to catch up with the more developed economies in the region.

Improved institutional capacity will be essential for the government to deepen economic reforms. To this end, the public administration should also be reformed with comprehensive training and development of public officials, effective monitoring of their performances, as well as having deployment and promotion practices based on meritocratic principles. In terms of state–people relationship, the government must continuously improve on political communication to build rapport with the people and mobilise their support for development policies. The pioneering PA practiced in Singapore as described in Section 3.8 may provide a useful reference in this respect.

References

ADB. 2009. *Enterprises in Asia: Fostering Dynamism in SMEs — Key Indicators for Asia and the Pacific 2009*. Manila: Asian Development Bank (ADB).

ADB. 2015. *Asia Small and Medium-sized Enterprise (SME) Finance Monitor 2014*. Manila: Asian Development Bank (ADB).

Aggarwal, Aradhna. 2016. "Special Economic Zones in India: Growth Engines or Missed Opportunity?". East Asia Forum.

Altomonte, Carlo, Barba Navaretti, F. di Mauro, and Gianmarco Ottaviano. 2011. "Assessing Competitiveness: How Firm-Level Data Can Help". Mimeo.

Ariffin, Eijas. 2018. "Vietnam to Boost Its Economy with Special Economic Zones". *The ASEAN Post*, 7th March, available at https://theaseanpost.com/article/vietnam-boost-its-economy-special-economic-zones (accessed on 26 March 2018).

Asasen, Choompon, Kanchana Asasen, and Nataya Chuangcham. 2003. *A Proposed ASEAN Policy Blueprint for SME Development 2004–2014*. Regional Economic Policy Support Facility.

Audretsch, David B., and Thurik Roy. 2001. "What's New about the New Economy? Sources of Growth in the Managed and Entrepreneurial Economies". *Industrial and Corporate Change* 10 (1):267–315.

Beck, Thorsten, Asli Demirguc-Kunt, and Ross Levine. 2005. "SMEs, Growth, and Poverty: Cross-Country Evidence". *Journal of Economic Growth* 10 (3):199–229.

De Freitas, Geoff. 2017. "Vietnam Pins Hope for Future Economic Direction on Three New SEZs". HKTD Research.

Enright, M.J., E. Scott, and K. Chung. 2005. *Regional Powerhouse: The Greater Pearl River Delta and the Rise of China*. Singapore: John Wiley & Sons.

ESCAP. 2012. *Policy Guidebook for SME Development*. Bangkok: Economic and Social Commission for Asia and the Pacific (ESCAP).

Farole, Thomas and Gokhan Akinci. 2011. *Special Economic Zones: Progress, Emerging Challenges and Future Directions*. Washington DC: World Bank.

FIAS. 2008. *Special Economic Zones: Performance, Lessons Learned, and Implications for Zone Development*. Washington DC: World Bank.

Fritsch, Michael, and Pamela Mueller. 2005. "The Persistence of Regional New Business Formation Activity over Time — Assessing the Potential of Policy Promotion Programs". *Papers on Entrepreneurship, Growth and Public Policy 0205*.

Garikai, Bonga Wellington. 2011. "Exportation Challenges by Small and Medium Enterprises and Possible Exportation Strategies". *Journal of Finance* 95 (18):105–126.

Harris, Jeanne. 2012. "Data Is Useless Without the Skills to Analyze It". *Harvard Business Review*, available at https://hbr.org/2012/09/data-is-useless-without-the-skills (accessed on 20 October 2017).

Harvie, Charles, and Boon-Chye Lee. 2005. *Sustaining Growth and Performance in East Asia: The Role of Small and Medium Sized Enterprises*, Vol. 3. Cheltenham: Edward Elgar Publishing.

Hilbert, Martin, and Priscila López. 2011. "The World's Technological Capacity to Store, Communicate, and Compute Information". *Science* 332 (6025):60–65.

ILO. 2015. *Small and Medium-Sized Enterprises and Decent and Productive Employment Creation*. Geneva: International Labour Organisation (ILO).

Intal, Ponciano S., Jr., Sothea Oum, and Mercy J.O. Simorangkir, eds. 2011. *Agricultural Development, Trade & Regional Cooperation in Developing East Asia*. Jakarta: Economic Research Institute for ASEAN and East Asia (ERIA).

Katua, Ngui Thomas. 2014. "The Role of SMEs in Employment Creation and Economic Growth in Selected Countries". *International Journal of Education and Research* 2 (12):461–472.

Kwek, Henry, and Khee Giap Tan. 2017. "Three Ways to Transform SMEs". *The Straits Times*, 23rd November, available at http://www.straitstimes.com/opinion/three-ways-to-transform-smes (accessed on 20 December 2017).

Le, Hung. 2016. "Credit guarantee funds operate inefficiently". *The Saigon Times*, 14th March, available at http://english.thesaigontimes.vn/46224/Credit-guarantee-funds-operate-inefficiently.html (accessed on 20 October 2017).

Lefur, Babeth. 2017. "Vietnam inequality challenges — next generation of Doi Moi?" *Tuoi Tre News*, 12th January, available at http://tuoitrenews.vn/society/38983/vietnam-inequality-challenges-next-generation-of-doi-moi (accessed on 23 March 2017).

Ministry of Commerce and Industry of India. 2018. *Fact Sheet on Special Economic Zones*.

Ministry of Planning and Investment. 2014. *White Paper: Small and Medium Enterprises in Vietnam 2014*. Hanoi: Statistical Publishing House.

Nguyen, Truong, and Barry Weisblatt. 2017. "Vietnam Macro — SOE Reform". Viet Capital Securities.

OECD. 2017. "*Financing SMEs and Entrepreneurs 2017 — An OECD Scoreboard*". Paris: OECD Publishing.

Ohno, Kenichi. 2009. "Avoiding the Middle-Income Trap: Renovating Industrial Policy Formulation in Vietnam". *ASEAN Economic Bulletin* 26 (1):25–43.

Palit, Amitendu. 2016. "Getting the basics right on India's SEZs". East Asia Forum.

Parks, Ed. 2011. "Vietnam demands English language teaching 'miracle'", 8th November, available at https://www.theguardian.com/education/2011/nov/08/vietnam-unrealistic-english-teaching-goals (accessed on 20 October 2017).

Porter, Michael. 1980. *Competitive Strategy*. New York: The Free Press.

Rajan, Ramkishen S., Khee Giap Tan, and Kong Yam Tan. 2014. *Fiscal Sustainability and Competitiveness in Europe and Asia.* United Kingdom: Palgrave Macmillan.

Schwab, Klaus. 2016. "The Fourth Industrial Revolution: What it Means, How to Respond", World Economic Forum, available at https://www.weforum.org/agenda/2016/01/the-fourth-industrial-revolution-what-it-means-and-how-to-respond/ (accessed on 20 October 2017).

Shafeeq, Syarafana. 2017. "Better Tech Adoption by SMEs Urged to Help Their Businesses". *The Business Times*, 19th May, available at http://www.businesstimes.com.sg/companies-markets/better-tech-adoption-by-smes-urged-to-help-their-businesses (accessed on 20 October 2017).

Shen, Xiaofang, and Songmin Xu. 2011. "Shenzhen Special Economic Zone: A Policy Reform Incubator for Land Market Development in China". In *Untying the Land Knot*, edited by Xiaofang Shen and Xiaolun Sun. Washington DC: World Bank.

Stel, André van, and Kashifa Suddle. 2005. "The Impact of New Firm Formation on Regional Development in the Netherlands". *ERIM Report Series ERS-2005-075-ORG.*

Tan, Khee Giap, and Kong Yam Tan. 2014. "Foreign Direct Investment (FDI), Productivity Spillovers and the Role of Small and Medium Enterprises (SMEs) Financing: An Overview". *Journal of International Commerce, Economics and Policy* 5 (3):1–5.

Tan, Khee Giap, and Yan Yi Tan. 2014. "Promoting SMEs and Enhancing Labor Productivity in Singapore: A Policy Analysis". *Journal of International Commerce, Economics and Policy*, 5 (3):1–5.

Tan, Khee Giap, and Rui Han Ng. 2017. 'Business Lobby Groups Need to Look beyond Cost-Cutting'. *The Straits Times*, 17th March, available at http://www.straitstimes.com/opinion/business-lobby-groups-need-to-look-beyond-cost-cutting (accessed on 20 October 2017).

Tan, Khee Giap, Sasidaran Gopalan, Jigyasa Sharma, and Kong Yam Tan. 2017a. *Inaugural 2016 Ease of Doing Business Index on Attractiveness to Investors, Business Friendliness and Competitiveness Policies (EDB Index ABC) for 21 Sub-National Economies of India*. Singapore: World Scientific.

Tan, Khee Giap, Mulya Amri, Nursyahida Ahmad, and Kong Yam Tan. 2017b. *2016 Growth Slowdown Analysis, Ease of Doing Business Index, and Annual Competitiveness Studies of Indonesia's Sub-National Economies*. Singapore: World Scientific.

Tan, Khee Giap, Mulya Amri, Sasidaran Gopalan, Nursyahida Ahmad, Duy Nguyen, Shida Zhou, Jigyasa Sharma, Hui Yin Chuah, and Tao Oei Lim. 2017c. *Productivity Tracking and Efficiency Monitoring of Singapore's Small and Medium Enterprises*. Singapore: Asia Competitiveness Institute.

Tan, Khee Giap, Le Phuong Anh Nguyen, Sasidaran Gopalan, and Nguyen Trieu Duong Luu. 2017d. *2015 Annual Competitiveness Analysis, Agricultural Productivity and Development Vision for ASEAN-10.* Singapore: World Scientific.

Thanh Nien News. 2014. "Too Many Vietnam Seaports Spoiling Terminal Business", 21st March, available at http://www.thanhniennews.com/business/too-many-vietnam-seaports-spoiling-terminal-business-24780.html (accessed on 20 October 2017).

The Business Times. 2017. "Making Sense of Future Economy, Now", 8th June, available at http://www.businesstimes.com.sg/government-economy/making-sense-of-future-economy-now (accessed on 20 October 2017).

Times of India. 2014. "SEZs Fail to Have Any Major Impact on Growth", 29th November, available at https://timesofindia.indiatimes.com/business/india-business/SEZs-fail-to-have-any-major-impact-on-growth/articleshow/45314291.cms (accessed on 26 October 2017).

Tuoi Tre News. 2017. "Vietnam Youth Swap University for Vocational Schools for 'Better Future'", 20th September, available at https://tuoitrenews.vn/news/education/20170920/vietnam-youth-swap-university-for-vocational-schools-for-better-future/41656.html (accessed on 20 October 2017).

VCCI and USAID. 2017. *Chỉ Số Năng Lực Cạnh Tranh Cấp Tỉnh Của Việt Nam Năm 2016: Hồ Sơ 63 Tỉnh, Thành Phố Việt Nam* [The 2016 Vietnam Provincial Competitiveness Index: Profiles of 63 Vietnamese Provinces and Municipalities]. Hanoi: Vietnam Chamber of Commerce and Industry (VCCI).

Vietnam Economic Times. 2017. "Vietnam Keen on 'Smart Cities' Development", 28th September, available at http://vneconomictimes.com/article/vietnam-today/vietnam-keen-on-smart-cities-development (accessed on 20 October 2017).

Viet Nam News. 2016a. "Credit Guarantees Should Be Sped up to Help SMEs", 24th March, available at http://vietnamnews.vn/economy/talking-shop/294202/credit-guarantees-should-be-sped-up-to-help-smes.html#rZFCZMrcmZrzHk1y.97 (accessed on 20 October 2017).

Viet Nam News. 2016b. "Foreign Language Project Falling Short of "unrealistic" goals", 3rd November, available at http://vietnamnews.vn/society/345524/foreign-language-project-falling-short-of-unrealistic-goals.html#Sq8L32D3PFs9sOM3.97 (accessed on 17 January 2018).

Viet Nam News. 2018. "HCMC Vocational Schools Struggle to Enrol Students", 4th January, available at http://vietnamnews.vn/society/420552/hcmc-vocational-schools-struggle-to-enroll-students.html#r3iB5AtZXoUXAJxk.99 (accessed on 17 January 2018).

Vietnamnet. 2017a. "Vietnam Slightly Drops in EF English Proficiency Index", 19th November, available at http://english.vietnamnet.vn/fms/education/190557/vietnam-slightly-drops-in-ef-english-proficiency-index.html (accessed on 17 January 2018).

Vietnamnet. 2017b. "Young Vietnamese Opt for Vocational Training". 11th December, available at http://english.vietnamnet.vn/fms/education/191893/young-vietnamese-opt-for-vocational-training.html (accessed on 20 December 2017).

Vietnamnet. 2017c. "Three SEZs Expected to Attract More Investors", 15th June, available at http://english.vietnamnet.vn/fms/business/180012/three-sezs-expected-to-attract-more-investors.html (accessed on 20 December 2017).

Vietnamnet. 2017d. *Đặc khu kinh tế: Chọn sai vị trí, dễ thất bại* [Special Administrative-Economic Zones: Wrong Choice of Locations Will Lead to Failure], 21st November, available at http://vietnamnet.vn/vn/tuanvietnam/dac-khu-kinh-te-chon-sai-vi-tri-de-that-bai-412026.html (accessed on 20 December 2017).

VN Express. 2017. *Ba đặc khu kinh tế đều xác định ưu tiên dịch vụ casino* [Three Special Administrative-Economic Zones Prioritise Casino Services], 10th November, available at https://vnexpress.net/tin-tuc/thoi-su/ba-dac-khu-kinh-te-deu-xac-dinh-uu-tien-dich-vu-casino-3668134.html (accessed on 20 December 2017).

World Bank. 2011. *Vietnam Urbanization Review*. Washington DC: World Bank.

World Bank and Ministry of Planning and Investment. 2016. *Vietnam 2035: Toward Prosperity, Creativity, Equity, and Democracy*. Washington DC: World Bank.

Zeng, Douglas Zhihua. 2012. "China's Special Economic Zones and Industrial Clusters: The Engines for Growth". *Journal of International Commerce, Economics and Policy* 3(3).

Zeng, Douglas Zhihua. 2015. "Global Experiences with Special Economic Zones — With a Focus on China and Africa". World Bank's Policy Research Working Paper No. 7240. World Bank, Washington DC.

Chapter 4

Concluding Remarks and Future Research Agenda

4.1 Summary of Research Findings and Evidence-based Policy Recommendations for Vietnam

Three decades have passed since Vietnam promulgated the *Doi Moi* reform which has proven to be a watershed legislation in the country's economic history. By dismantling the central planning system in pursuit of a market economy and mobilising factors of production from agriculture to manufacturing and services, *Doi Moi* has unleashed the economic potential of Vietnam. Pursuing an export-led industrialisation strategy, Vietnam has experienced robust economic growth over the past 30 years which led to the virtual elimination of extreme poverty and general improvement in the living standards of its people.

However, while the progress that resulted from the *Doi Moi* reform is indisputable, the sustainability of Vietnam's economic growth remains questionable. On the one hand, Vietnam stands to become the next manufacturing hub in Asia, riding on the southward shift of foreign direct investment (FDI) from China and the advantages of having a large, young, literate and relatively low-cost workforce. Moreover, natural endowments in terms of scenic landscapes and fertile lands conducive to the cultivation of rice, tropical fruits and cash crops also bless Vietnam with tremendous potential to become a top tourist destination and a major agriculture producer in the world.

On the other hand, as the analysis in Chapter 2 has pointed out, Vietnam's current growth model may prove to be inadequate to propel the country forward in the next phase of its development. The basic strategy of export-led industrialisation must be augmented by a renewed focus on improving productivity as Vietnam's labour cost advantage is expected to be eroded by an ageing population and rapid technological disruptions. Against this backdrop, it is worrying to observe that labour productivity growth in Vietnam has slowed. This is driven in part by sluggish agricultural productivity growth, worsened by inefficiencies among state-owned enterprises (SOEs) and the lack of synergies between the FDI sector and the local sector. In addition, institutional reforms have not caught up with economic reforms. Gaps in institutional quality including lack of coordination between government bodies, poor state effectiveness and corruption have hampered the implementation of policies aimed at addressing Vietnam's many economic malaises.

Our analysis of economic competitiveness among the 10 members of the Association of Southeast Asian Nations (ASEAN) shows that Vietnam only compares favourably with Cambodia, Laos and Myanmar. However, it lags behind the regional average in terms of productivity performance, competition and regulatory standards, human capital development and physical infrastructure quality. Furthermore, our analysis reveals that Vietnam is gradually losing its cost competitiveness and attractiveness to investors *vis-à-vis* its ASEAN neighbours. This underscores the urgency of economic restructuring under a new growth model.

Meanwhile, imbalanced regional development is another important challenge facing Vietnam. As shown in Chapter 2, greater FDI inflows to the Southern provinces have allowed them to consistently surpass their Northern and Central counterparts in terms of average individual's monthly incomes as well as progress in poverty reduction and healthcare quality. Regional disparities are also reflected in our comparison of Hanoi and Ho Chi Minh City, the two largest cities in Northern and Southern Vietnam, respectively. Despite both being top-tier cities in Vietnam, Ho Chi Minh City has outperformed Hanoi in terms of liveability and economic vibrancy where the gap in GDP per capita between the two cities has widened significantly over time. Worsening regional disparities may lead Vietnam to become one country with two economies where the more developed South pulls ahead of the North and the Central regions which are increasingly being left far behind. This may put Vietnam at risk of becoming over-reliant on the South for economic development, contribute to rising inequalities, and reduce national cohesion.

Thus, we contend that Vietnam is at a critical juncture in its development where "renovation" of the economy is no longer enough. Instead, policy-makers must seek to "revitalise" the Vietnamese economy through a new wave of comprehensive reforms. The Asia Competitiveness Institute (ACI) has prepared a policy roadmap to foster balanced and sustainable development for competitiveness enhancement. We envisage a dynamic growth path for Vietnam whereby the real growth rate of GDP per capita reaches seven percent p.a., which will require the national GDP to grow by 7.8 percent p.a. in real terms on average given current population projections. If this can be achieved, Vietnam's GDP per capita will surpass that of the Philippines and catch up to Thailand and Indonesia by 2040.[1] Furthermore, at US$9,900 (constant 2011 prices), Vietnam's aspirational GDP per capita level in 2040 will be close to that of Malaysia in 2010.[2]

ACI's development vision for Vietnam is underpinned by six policy proposals which are outlined in great detail in Chapter 3. **The first proposal identifies the need to quicken the pace of SOE reforms and strengthen market mechanisms to facilitate private sector development as an urgent policy priority for Vietnam.** It calls on the government to push forward with the equitisation and divestment of SOEs; rationalise and centralise the system to manage state assets; eliminate market distortions in favour of SOEs to level the playing field and encourage the adoption of good corporate governance practices in both the state the private sectors for a healthy market economy.

The second proposal highlights the importance of enhancing intracountry connectivity to mitigate regional disparities. More importantly, it pushes for the upgraded development of Hanoi as the catalyst for the broader development of Northern Vietnam. In particular, we envisage that Hanoi will become the following:

(i) A business and financing hub where all MNCs operating in Vietnam will set up representative offices to benefit from business consultation and administrative service supports with the relevant authorities;

[1] Assuming these economies follow their current growth trajectories and their future growth rates may be projected by three-year moving averages.

[2] See Chapter 1 for the GDP per capita projections for Vietnam under different growth paths.

(ii) A gateway connecting Northern provinces to the global economy, boasting modern airport facilities, first-class urban transport system and seamless infrastructural linkages with Northern industrial centres;
(iii) A tourism hub with improved connectivity and transport services to other tourist hotspots in the North;
(iv) A vibrant city with a creative, innovative, and entrepreneurial young population;
(v) A liveable city with efficient and affordable public services and robust growth of wages backed by improved productivity for ordinary residents.

Successful completion of the above-mentioned agenda will directly improve the livelihoods of more than seven million people currently living in Hanoi. Moreover, Hanoi's development as a business and financing hub will encourage the establishment of more industrial parks in the North to exploit logistic and administrative advantages from being closely linked with the capital. At the same time, tourism in the North will also be boosted thanks to improved international connectivity via Hanoi. These developments will create greater economic opportunities for residents living in Northern provinces, help to narrow the gaps in living standards and quality of life between the North and the South, and thus prevent the emergence of "One Country-Two Economies".

The third proposal relates to nurturing small and medium enterprises (SMEs). While we applaud the government's commitment to support SMEs as exemplified by the passage of the 2017 SME Law, we contend that Vietnam's strategy to support SMEs requires a paradigm shift. Direct interventions through handouts and tax breaks can no longer be the sole *modus operandi* of the government, though they remain important policy tools. Instead, the government should look to play a facilitative role and rely on market-oriented policies to foster SMEs. Such policy initiatives are more sustainable than fiscal interventions in the long run, especially given Vietnam's mounting public debt. In addition, market-based measures are more effective as they are geared towards helping SMEs develop their internal capacity instead of only alleviating their immediate constraints.

Specifically, we propose the establishment of the Enterprise Future Initiative for Vietnam, with the primary focus on evidence-based research which will guide the formulation of actionable plans to enhance the efficiency, productivity and internationalisation potential of Vietnamese SMEs. ACI shall work with Vietnamese partners to extend the Productivity Tracking and Efficiency Monitoring Index (PTEM) to Vietnam. This shall be complemented by the construction of another index to measure ease of doing business at the sub-national level. Examining both the regulatory environment and factors determining an economy's attractiveness to investors, tracking ease of doing business (EDB) at sub-national level, which is based on ACI's EDB Index, will serve as a useful tool to identify province-specific hindrances to ease of doing business for policy interventions.

In addition, we emphasise the importance of building digital capacity as a necessary condition for SMEs to thrive in the upcoming Fourth Industrial Revolution. In this respect, the government has a key role to play in upgrading the telecommunication and Internet infrastructure. Furthermore, it is important to foster a supportive ecosystem in which the government, industry experts and financial institutions work together to help SMEs adapt suitable digital solutions based on their business needs. The government's effort must receive active support from trade associations and business chambers which are well-placed to explain to its member companies the benefits of digitalisation and the potential adverse consequences if they fail to adapt to the digital age.

The fourth policy proposal outlines the strategy for the holistic development of the Vietnamese workforce. We identify widespread skill mismatch and potential obsolescence of skills due to technological disruptions as the two key challenges for workers in the next phase of Vietnam's development. Thus, we propose the launch of the Skills Future Initiative as a national movement with actionable plans to (i) encourage individuals to make well-informed decisions regarding their education and training; (ii) align education and technical training with industry needs; (iii) promote skill-based career development; and (iv) foster a culture of lifelong learning among the workforce.

Among the policies to realise the objectives of the Skills Future Initiative, the Targeted Industrial Internship Model with Placed-Trained-Employed (IIM-PTE) Scheme is an important measure. It is a targeted industry internship programme with a clear pathway to employment upon graduation primarily for students with vocational qualifications or lower. Driven by tripartite participation of the government, employers and employees, the IIM-PTE will serve to facilitate labour productivity enhancement through on-the-job training, increase the attractiveness of vocational schools as a viable pathway to secure good jobs and thus contributing the alleviation of the acute shortage of skilled workers in the Vietnamese economy.

With respect to skill development, the advent of big data and the future pervasiveness of data analytics in all sectors means that the workforce must be trained in critical thinking, numerical skills and data literacy. Moreover, English proficiency and interpersonal skills will be increasingly important for Vietnamese professionals to gain a competitive edge in the increasingly integrated regional labour market and participate in the service economy. At the same time, we emphasise the need for the government to encourage innovation and lay the foundation for an innovation-driven knowledge economy. This is because the capacity to innovate will become the primary determinant of economic growth in the long run.

The fifth policy proposal highlights the importance of a balanced, well-diversified economic structure where manufacturing and services are developed in tandem and backed by a highly productive agriculture sector. It articulates the vision for Vietnam to become the next manufacturing hub in Asia, an excellent centre for service-based industries, and a major agriculture producer in the world. In the quest to achieve these objectives, the government has to play a vital role in resolving the bottlenecks to development and promoting catch-up industrialisation through a proactive industrial policy.

With regard to fostering agricultural productivity growth, Vietnam can draw on the experience of Malaysia, especially in terms of fostering a competitive agribusiness industry; developing close partnership between government agencies, agribusiness firms and research institutes as well as integrating smallholders into agro-based value chains and efficient provision of infrastructure, credit and extension services.

Finally, the sixth policy proposal calls for a comprehensive strategy to develop special economic zones (SEZs) into robust growth areas and test-beds for deeper administrative and economic reforms. In particular, we note that for the newly-proposed special administrative-economic zones (SAEZs) in Van Don, Bac Van Phong and Phu Quoc to succeed, infrastructure investment is key, especially since service sectors are expected to spearhead the development of these zones. Modern international airports to enhance air connectivity are particularly crucial. Moreover, in light of the attempt to establish business services and high-tech industries as major drivers of growth in the new SAEZs, there must be concerted efforts to foster and exploit synergies between SAEZs, Hanoi and Ho Chi Minh City which remain Vietnam's pre-eminent business, financing, and innovation centres with a high concentration of skilled and high-knowledge workers. The long-term sustainability of the SAEZs will also be predicated on their ability to deliver not only benefits in terms of GDP growth, investment and export, but also tangible improvements in living standards and quality of life for workers living in these zones, as well as preserving the environment.

As the experiences of China and India with SEZs reviewed in Chapter 3 have illustrated, the government's commitment to the SEZ model is critical for the zones to succeed. We propose the creation of an SEZ index which will aid the Vietnamese government in tracking the viability, operations and outcomes of the proposed SEZs as well as future zones to be set up in the country. Such an index may be used for detailed analyses to formulate development strategies for SEZs; map and inform foreign investors of potentials and opportunities in these zones; and when the research framework is extended to other Asian developing economies provide an international benchmark for Vietnamese SEZs, thus promoting cross-country learning and adoption of best practices in planning, managing and attracting investors to SEZs.

The implementation of these six policy proposals through the specific recommendations set out in Chapter 3 represent a fundamental overhaul of Vietnam's growth model. Such a colossal task can only be achieved if the government is committed to deepening economic reforms and, more importantly, takes concrete steps to strengthen institutional capacity to ensure the state apparatus can cope with the demands of reforms. To this end, a modern, professional and clean public administration must be developed where there is comprehensive training and development of public officials, effective outcome-based monitoring of their performances and deployment and promotion based on meritocracy. It is also crucial for the government to continuously improve on political communication to build rapport with the people and mobilise their support for development policies. The People's Association model practiced in Singapore, as described in Section 3.8 of Chapter 3, may provide useful insights in this respect.

4.2 Synergies between Domestic Reforms and Deepened International Integration

The government may look to leverage on its international integration strategy to achieve the reform agenda. Indeed, Vietnam's achievements during the *Doi Moi* era were due in large part to its participation in the global economy. Going forward, deepening integration will continue to be vital in invigorating reforms in Vietnam for economic development, in the following ways.

First, by linking up with its regional neighbours in ASEAN to form a single market and production base, Vietnam will be able to exploit the advantages of economies of scale and demographic dividends and at the same time, to mask the weaknesses of development gaps by leveraging on complementarities with its partners in an intraregional economic network. Furthermore, the benefits of larger market access and cost competitiveness offered by a regional bloc will also provide more incentives for the investors and hence increase Vietnam's attractiveness as an FDI destination. The increased inflows of foreign capital can therefore be mobilised to complement the shortfall of domestic capital. In addition, the shortage of skilled workforce faced by Vietnam can be partially relieved through cross-border talents and knowledge sharing, which ultimately will contribute to industrial upgrading from low-end manufacturing to more sophisticated and knowledge-based activities.

Second, FDI inflows will also directly fuel investment in infrastructure development in Vietnam. As discussed in Chapters 2 and 3, Vietnam tends to fall into the deadlock of infrastructure constraints and financial shortfalls which FDI can help to alleviate. Strengthened economic integration in parallel with the incorporation of an inclusivity agenda will ensure a mutually beneficial regional partnership to all economies. Having a stable Vietnamese Dong as a currency and establishing a trade-weighted basket managed float exchange rate regime will be critical to attracting a steady flow of FDI to Vietnam.

Third, deepening economic integration will reduce the cross-border barriers among Vietnam and its partners, which in turn may intensify competition for investment, trade opportunities and international talents. While there may be some diversion effects, the resultant competitive pressure will not only make salient the weaknesses within the economy but may also act as an enabling factor for Vietnam to overcome internal inertia and push forward with the reform agenda. Besides competitive pressure, international obligations from Vietnam's participation in multilateral integration initiatives also serve to create the impetus for speedy implementation of reform measures.

Overall, economic integration will enable Vietnam to revitalise the reform progress. At this critical juncture in Vietnam's development, integration initiatives including the ASEAN Economic Community, the Regional Comprehensive Partnership, the Comprehensive and Progressive Agreement for Trans-Pacific Partnership and the Belt & Road Initiative come timely to propel Vietnam forward. The opportunities offered by these initiatives must be harnessed to bring about the successful implementation of the policy roadmap set out in Section 4.1.

4.3 Future Research Agenda

Vietnam has always been an important feature of the research done at ACI. Aside from the studies cited in this book, Vietnam has also been included as part of ASEAN in ACI's analysis of growth slowdown by income thresholds, study of the effects of exchange rate and exchange rate volatility on FDI and the research on the trade effects of exchange rate in the global value chain context.

Going forward, ACI looks to extend the frameworks for the Productivity Tracking and Efficiency Monitoring (PTEM) Index and the Ease of Doing Business Index to Vietnam. As mentioned in Chapter 3 and Section 4.1, the policy insights derived from these indices will go a long way in helping the government to fulfil its goal of fostering SMEs. ACI looks forward to working with its partners in Vietnam, namely the Vietnam Chamber of Commerce and Industry as well as the Central Institute for Economic Management, in adapting these indices to the Vietnam context. We also look forward to conducting other policy-relevant topical studies which will tangibly contribute to Vietnam's economic development.

Discussant Note

Dr Nguyen Dinh Cung

President, Central Institute for Economic Management (CIEM)

Good afternoon, everyone.

What Is the Nature of Economic Growth in Vietnam?

I think it's a very interesting case study and critical evaluation developed on Vietnam on its development potential. For Vietnam, 30 years with economic liberalisation and quick innovation, we take two wings. Domestically, there was market liberalisation, and internationally there is income integration. And I say that, it was similar to two wings of a bird. If they are strong, the economic growth will be achieved, as the report says.

But recently I think, economic growth slows down very fast. We have only 10 years, with 8 years with 8% growth, but in China they had 22 years. I think in Malaysia, they had 10 or 12 years.

And currently, we try to maintain only 6.5% growth. I told the Prime Minister that we should have at least 8% growth rather than 6/6.5% growth. So I say there is many ways to stimulate growth in Vietnam. And I showed him only two things. The first one is we can improve the efficiency of the state assets. In value, that is about US$200 billion. In market price, I think it is much higher. If we improved for one percentage point of the efficiency so have annually at least US$3 million. It means 1.5% percentage point growth in GDP.

Similarly, for the private sector assets we can improve the efficiency of private sector. Currently in each of these examples, the value of the state sector and the domestic private sector is much lower than the foreign-investing enterprises; and if we improve efficiency, we get, much higher growth than we currently achieve. It means we have huge potential for improving the growth. And we can achieve much higher growth rate than we are currently achieving.

How Big Is the Gap in Productivity between Urban and Rural Areas?

I want to make a comment on our country economics. I don't think that our political system can allow to achieve the one country to accomplish because political voting power in Vietnam lies in the local leaders in the provincial — that is people communities and parties at local level. Therefore, the distribution of resources is required to be equal to the different provinces regardless of the efficiency. And I think that and in the cities; Ho Cho Min, Hanoi account only 35% of GDP. And this share is quite stable for more almost more than 10 years. Meanwhile, the population of the cities increased by around 90%. This means that average income and productivity of the city is lower than the average national average.

Where Should the Vietnamese Economy Go from Here?

And therefore, we thrive to improve the efficiency- to make allocation somehow to concentrate more to the cities, and to improve their infrastructure and to improve the efficiency so that they become a driving force to growth, rather than that- they are not playing the role of driving force now in the country.

For Vietnam, I think, there is low level of market development of economy. It has a rating 147, that is lower than Laos and Cambodia. And in terms of public governance, Vietnam's score also low. And the rankings here, I think Vietnam is below the average, much below the international average. I think if we only introduce the restructuring programs with these tools and these priorities: institutional reforms, development of Human Resources, infrastructure development, restructuring of the SOEs, investment and restructuring of financial institutions. But somehow, I think that we have not achieved as we have planned. One thing is in institutional quality. I agree that it is fundamental challenge to Vietnam development. But you know, analysing what is the policy gap is the key shortcoming of the institution in Vietnam in recent. That is administrative mechanisms in place for in allocation of resources, especially in land public investments in no competition, where there are no big bonuses to the production access.

I think the resolution should be focused on the development of the capital market, so that the capital market can play a major role in allocation of resources so that it can improve and we can make a market even more competitive, so there is improvement in technical, allocative efficiency, and dynamic efficiency so that we can increase the prosperity.

Thank you very much.

Appendix 1

List of Indicators for the Competitiveness Analysis of ASEAN-10 Economies, 2000–2014

No.	Indicator	Unit	Reversed Indicator*
1	**Macroeconomic Stability**		
1.1	**Economic Vibrancy**		
1.1.01	Gross Domestic Product	US Dollars, Constant 2000 Prices	
1.1.02	Real GDP Growth	Percentage Change Per Annum	
1.1.03	GDP Per Capita	US Dollars, Constant 2000 Prices	
1.1.04	Output Agriculture (Value Added)	US Dollars, Constant 2005 Prices	
1.1.05	Output Industry (Value Added)	US Dollars, Constant 2005 Prices	
1.1.06	Output Services (Value Added)	US Dollars, Constant 2005 Prices	
1.1.07	Gross Domestic Savings	Percentage of GDP	
1.1.08	Gross Fixed Capital Formation	Percentage of GDP	
1.1.09	Inflation	Percentage Change Per Annum	R
1.1.10	Money Supply Growth (M2)	Percentage Change Per Annum	R
1.2	**Openness to Trade and Services**		
1.2.01	Current Account Balance	Percentage of GDP	
1.2.02	Exports of Goods and Services	US Dollars, Current Market Prices	
1.2.03	Imports of Goods and Services	US Dollars, Current Market Prices	
1.2.04	Openness to Trade	Ratio	
1.2.05	International Tourism Receipts	US Dollars, Current Market Prices	
1.3	**Attractiveness to Foreign Investors**		
1.3.01	Foreign Direct Investment Inflows	US Dollars, Current Market Prices	
1.3.02	Foreign Owned Companies	Survey Data	
1.3.03	Corporate Income Tax	Percentage of Profit	R
1.3.04	Lack of Discrimination Against Investors	Survey Data	
1.3.05	Levelness of Playing Field	Survey Data	
1.3.06	Transparency of Processes for Investors	Survey Data	
1.3.07	Business Impact of Rules on FDI	Survey Data	

(Continued)

(Continued)

No.	Indicator	Unit	Reversed Indicator*
2	**Government and Institutional Setting**		
2.1	**Government Policies and Fiscal Sustainability**		
2.1.01	Government Revenue (Including Grants)	US Dollars, 2000 Constant Prices	
2.1.02	Tax Revenue	US Dollars, 2000 Constant Prices	
2.1.03	Tax Revenue/Government Revenue	Percentage	
2.1.04	Government Consumption Expenditure	Percentage of GDP	
2.1.05	External Debt	US Dollars, Current Market Prices	R
2.1.06	International Reserves	US Dollars, Current Market Prices	
2.1.07	Net Foreign Assets	US Dollars, Current Market Prices	
2.1.08	International Monetary Fund Credit	US Dollars, Current Market Prices	R
2.1.09	Budget Balance	Percentage of GDP	
2.1.10	Tax Burden	Percentage of GDP	R
2.1.11	Money Supply (M2)	Percentage of GDP	
2.1.12	Deposit Interest Rate	Percentage	
2.1.13	Lending Rate	Percentage	R
2.1.14	Interest Rate Spread	Percentage	R
2.1.15	Exchange Rate Appreciation	Annual Average Percentage Change (Local Currency Unit per US Dollar)	R
2.2	**Institutions, Governance and Leadership**		
2.2.01	Quality of Government Policies	Survey Data	
2.2.02	Government Effectiveness	Survey Data	
2.2.03	Government Environmental Protection Policies	Percentage of Total Territorial Area	
2.2.04	Quality of Central Bank/Monetary Authority	Survey Data	
2.2.05	Government Stability	Survey Data	
2.2.06	Government Responsiveness	Survey Data	
2.2.07	Quality of Political Leadership	Survey Data	R
2.2.08	Political System Risk	Survey Data	R
2.2.09	Legislature/Parliament (Functioning of Government System)	Survey Data	
2.2.10	Strength of Auditing and Reporting Standards	Survey Data	
2.2.11	Institutional Sophistication	Survey Data	
2.2.12	Bureaucracy/Red Tape	Survey Data	
2.2.13	Lack of Corruption	Survey Data	
2.2.14	Lack of Cronyism	Survey Data	
2.2.15	Lack of Market Distortion due to State-Ownership	Survey Data	

(Continued)

(Continued)

No.	Indicator	Unit	Reversed Indicator*
2.3	**Competition, Regulatory Standards and Rule of Law**		
2.3.01	Corporate Governance	Survey Data	
2.3.02	Quality of Regulatory Environment	Survey Data	
2.3.03	Transparency of Government	Survey Data	
2.3.04	Monopolies and Cartel	Survey Data	
2.3.05	Policy Towards Private Enterprise Rating	Survey Data	
2.3.06	Ease of Starting Business	Number	R
2.3.07	Barriers to Trade	Survey Data	
2.3.08	Intellectual Property Rights Protection	Survey Data	
2.3.09	Regional Competitiveness	Survey Data	
2.3.10	Quality of Judiciary	Survey Data	
2.3.11	Effectiveness of Legal System	Survey Data	
2.3.12	Integrity of Legal System	Survey Data	
2.3.13	Quality of Police	Survey Data	
2.3.14	Political Change	Survey Data	
3	**Financial, Businesses and Manpower Conditions**		
3.1	**Financial Deepening and Business Efficiency**		
3.1.01	Claims on Private Sector	Annual Growth as Percentage of Broad Money	
3.1.02	Domestic Credit to Private Sector	Percentage of GDP	
3.1.03	Quality of Banking and Financial System	Survey Data	
3.1.04	Domestic Credit Provided by the Financial Sector	Percentage of GDP	
3.1.05	Listed Domestic Companies	Number	
3.1.06	Market Capitalisation	US Dollars, Current Market Prices	
3.1.07	Total Value of Stocks Traded	Percentage of GDP	
3.1.08	Sovereign Debt Risk	Number	R
3.1.09	Quality of Stock Market Regulatory Authority	Survey Data	
3.2	**Labour Market Flexibility**		
3.2.01	Labour Force	Number	
3.2.02	Unemployment Rate	Percentage	R
3.2.03	Cost of Production Labour	US Dollars, Current Market Prices	R
3.2.04	Availability of Scientists and Engineers	Survey Data	
3.2.05	Cost of Management Staff	US Dollars, Current Market Prices	R
3.2.06	High-quality Management Staff	Survey Data	

(Continued)

(Continued)

No.	Indicator	Unit	Reversed Indicator*
3.2.07	Extent of Staff Training	Survey Data	
3.2.08	Labour Market Rating	Survey Data	
3.3	**Productivity Performance**		
3.3.01	Agriculture, Value Added Per Worker	US Dollars, 2005 Constant Prices	
3.3.02	Industry, Value Added Per Worker	US Dollars, 2005 Constant Prices	
3.3.03	Services, Value Added Per Worker	US Dollars, 2005 Constant Prices	
4	**Quality of Life and Infrastructure Development**		
4.1	**Physical Infrastructure**		
4.1.01	Population	Number	
4.1.02	Local Road System	Survey Data	
4.1.03	Rail Facilities	Survey Data	
4.1.04	Airport Facilities	Survey Data	
4.1.05	Port Facilities	Survey Data	
4.1.06	Electric Power	Survey Data	
4.1.07	Access to Water	Percentage of Population	
4.1.08	Access to Sanitation	Percentage of Population	
4.2	**Technological Infrastructure**		
4.2.01	Telecommunications System	Percentage of GDP	
4.2.02	Telephone Main Lines	Number Per 100 Persons	
4.2.03	Internet Subscribers	Number Per 100 Persons	
4.2.04	Cellular Mobile Telephone Subscribers	Number Per 100 Persons	
4.2.05	Networked Readiness Index	Survey Data	
4.2.06	Personal Computers	Number Per 100 Persons	
4.2.07	Information and Communication Technology (ICT) Expenditure	Percentage of GDP	
4.3	**Standard of Living, Education and Social Stability**		
4.3.01	Literacy Rate	Percentage	
4.3.02	Primary Schooling	Percentage	
4.3.03	Secondary Schooling	Percentage	
4.3.04	University and Post-Graduate Education	Percentage	
4.3.05	Human Development Index	Composite Statistic	
4.3.06	Health Expenditure	Percentage of GDP	
4.3.07	Urban Population	Percentage of Total Population	
4.3.08	Urban Population Growth	Percentage Per Annum	

(Continued)

(*Continued*)

No.	Indicator	Unit	Reversed Indicator*
4.3.09	Public Security and Safety	Survey Data	
4.3.10	Freedom of Press	Survey Data	R
4.3.11	Freedom of Speech	Survey Data	
4.3.12	Access to Print Media	Number	
4.3.13	Freedom of Religion	Survey Data	
4.3.14	Religious Unrest	Survey Data	
4.3.15	Labour Unrest	Survey Data	
4.3.16	Social Unrest	Survey Data	
4.3.17	Labour Activism	Survey Data	R
4.3.18	Daily Organic Water Pollutant Emissions	Kilogram Per 100 Persons	R
4.3.19	Air Quality	Micrograms Per Cubic Metre	R
4.3.20	Traffic Congestion	Number of Vehicles Per Kilometre of Road	R

Note: *R indicates that the indicator is a reversed indicator

Source: Asia Competitiveness Institute

Appendix 2

The Algorithm for ACI's Competitiveness Index

A step-by-step description of the ranking process is described below for N economies, M practical indicators and C environments, with each environment comprising S sub-environments.

(1) Compute the mean value of practical indicator j ($j = 1, \ldots, M$),

$$\bar{X}_j = \frac{1}{N}\sum_{i=1}^{N} X_{ij}$$

where X_{ij} represents the value that economy i ($i = 1, \ldots, N$) takes for practical indicator j.

(2) For each practical indicator j ($j = 1, \ldots, M$), calculate its standard deviation (SD),

$$SD_j = \sqrt{\frac{1}{N}\sum_{i=1}^{N}\left(X_{ij} - \bar{X}_j\right)^2}$$

(3) Compute the standardised value of indicator (SVI) that each economy i ($i = 1, \ldots, N$) takes under each of the practical indicators j ($j = 1, \ldots, M$),

$$SVI_{ij} = \frac{X_{ij} - \bar{X}_j}{SD_j}$$

(4) Compute the 'ranked' standardised value of indicator (RSVI) that each economy i ($i = 1, \ldots, N$) takes under each of the practical indicators j ($j = 1, \ldots, M$):

$$RSVI_{ij} = \begin{cases} SVI_{ij}, & \text{if a higher value is better} \\ -SVI_{ij}, & \text{if a lower value is better} \end{cases}$$

(5) For each of the practical indicators j ($j = 1, \ldots, M$), a ranking can be obtained for economies: economies with a higher value of RSVI for indicator j are ranked ahead of those with a lower value.

(6) For each economy i ($i = 1, \ldots, N$), calculate the RSVI for each sub-environment k ($k = 1, \ldots, S$) belonging to environment l ($l = 1, \ldots, C$),

$$Raw\_RSVI_{i,lk} = \frac{1}{y_{lk}} \sum_{p=1}^{y_{lk}} RSVI_{i,j_{lk,p}}$$

$$Mean\_RSVI_{lk} = \frac{1}{N} \sum_{i=1}^{N} Raw\_RSVI_{i,lk}$$

$$SD\_RSVI_{lk} = \sqrt{\frac{1}{N} \sum_{i=1}^{N} \left(Raw\_RSVI_{i,lk} - Mean\_RSVI_{lk}\right)^2}$$

$$RSVI_{i,lk} = \frac{Raw\_RSVI_{i,lk} - Mean\_RSVI_{lk}}{SD\_RSVI_{lk}}$$

where y_{ik} is the total number of practical indicators under sub-environment k of environment l and $(RSVI_{i,j_{lk,1}}, \ldots, RSVI_{i,j_{lk,y_{lk}}})$ are the RSVIs for economy i that make up sub-environment k of environment l.

(7) For each economy i ($i = 1, \ldots, N$), calculate the RSVI for each environment l ($l = 1, \ldots, C$),

$$Raw\_RSVI_{i,l} = \frac{1}{S_l} \sum_{k=1}^{S_l} RSVI_{i,lk}$$

$$Mean\_RSVI_{l} = \frac{1}{N} \sum_{i=1}^{N} Raw\_RSVI_{i,l}$$

$$SD\_RSVI_{l} = \sqrt{\frac{1}{N} \sum_{i=1}^{N} \left(Raw\_RSVI_{i,l} - Mean\_RSVI_{l}\right)^2}$$

$$RSVI_{i,l} = \frac{Raw\_RSVI_{i,l} - Mean\_RSVI_{l}}{SD\_RSVI_{l}}$$

where (*RSVIi,l*1, . . . , *RSVIi,lS*) are the RSVIs for the S sub-environments under each environment l.

(8) Overall score of economy i ($i = 1, \ldots, N$),

$$Raw\_R_i = \frac{1}{C} \sum_{l=1}^{C} RSVI_{i,l}$$

$$Mean\_R = \frac{1}{N} \sum_{i=1}^{N} Raw\_R_i$$

$$SD\_R = \sqrt{\frac{1}{N}\sum_{i=1}^{N}\left(Raw\_R_i - Mean\_R\right)^2}$$

$$R_i = \frac{Raw\_R_i - Mean\_R}{SD\_R}$$

Economies with a higher R_i are ranked ahead of those with lower value of R_i, and the economy with the highest R_i is the most competitive economy.

Step (5) provides the ranking of each economy for each individual practical indicator. To achieve this ranking, Step (4) adjusts the value of the SVIs so that a higher value will lead to a better ranking in terms of 'competitiveness'. Depending on the nature of the indicator in question, a higher or lower value may reflect a more 'competitive' economy. Take, for instance, the practical sub-indicators 'Gross Domestic Product (GDP)' and 'Unemployment Rate'. A higher GDP but a lower 'unemployment rate' suggest better economic performance which makes an economy more 'competitive'. In most cases where a higher value is better (e.g. GDP), the SVIs of regions are considered, and those with a higher SVI value will have a better ranking. However, for indicators where the inverse is true (e.g. Unemployment Rate), the 'negative SVI' values are compared between economies and a lower SVI value will lead to a better ranking. Step (4) thus seeks to make all standardised values of all practical indicators consistent for ranking purposes.

Step (6) determines the sub-environment rankings of each economy. The average RSVI of all the indicators in the sub-environment are calculated, re-standardised across all the economies and compared to other economies. Economies with a higher average RSVI rank better in the sub-environment.

To arrive at the ranking for each environment, the RSVIs of the sub-environments are averaged and re-standardised across all economies as detailed in Step (7). Finally, Step (8) requires the RSVI values of each environment to be averaged and re-standardised across all economies to determine the overall ranking of the economy. Economies with a higher RSVI are ranked ahead of those with a lower RSVI.

Although the number of sub-environments and indicators may vary for each environment, the aggregate score for each environment is given an equal weight, which is 25 percent of the ASEAN-10 Overall Competitiveness Index. This method is repeated and applied consistently across all economies to ensure precision of the ranking. Mathematically, this can be illustrated as follows:

$$\begin{aligned}&\text{ASEAN-10 Overall Competitiveness Index}\\&\quad = 0.25 \times (\text{Macroeconomic Stability})\\&\qquad + 0.25 \times (\text{Government and Institutional Setting})\\&\qquad + 0.25 \times (\text{Financial, Businesses and Manpower Conditions})\\&\qquad + 0.25 \times (\text{Quality of Life and Infrastructure Development})\end{aligned}$$

Appendix 3

ACI's Competitiveness Framework by the Shapley Weightage Methodology

Shapley value is widely applied in cooperative game theory, which measures the marginal contribution of an agent. In our context, the agent could be indicators, sub-environments and environments. The formula for Shapley value is

$$\Phi(v) = \sum_{S \subseteq N \setminus \{i\}} \frac{|S|!(N - |S| - 1)!}{N!}(v)(S \cup i) - v(S))$$

With different marginal contribution to the overall competitiveness ranking, different weights can be assigned to indicators, sub-environments and environments. We propose an objective weighting method based on Shapley value — the "bottom-up" approach as a robustness check to the equal weightage methodology of the competitiveness framework by the Asia Competitiveness Institute (ACI).

Formally, let v^I be the characteristic function of the indicators, where $v^I{:}2^I \to \mathbb{R}$. Then for each indicator $i \in I$, $v^I(i)$: $\mathbb{R}^E \to \mathbb{R}$, which reflects that the value of indicator i is derived from X_{ei} for all $e \in E$. As we involve large number of indicators in our case studies, for the ease of numerical computation, we simply define that

$$v^I(i) = \sum_{e=1}^{E} |SV_{ei}|.$$

We further assume the Additivity of the characteristic function, v^I, i.e. $v^I(i \cup j) = v^I(i) + v^I(j)$ for any indicator $i, j \in I$

With all these defined, we are able to proceed with the computation of the Shapley value Φ_i^I of indicator $i \in I$:

$$\Phi_i^I = \sum_{\mathbb{I} \subseteq I \setminus \{i\}} \frac{|\mathbb{I}|!(I - |\mathbb{I}| - 1)!}{I!}\left(v^I(\mathbb{I} \cup i) - v^I(\mathbb{I})\right) \quad \text{for all } i \in I$$

$$= \sum_{\mathbb{I} \subseteq I \setminus \{i\}} \frac{|\mathbb{I}|!(I - |\mathbb{I}| - 1)!}{I!}\left(v^I(\mathbb{I} \cup i) - v^I(\mathbb{I})\right)$$

$$= \sum_{\mathbb{I} \subseteq I \setminus \{i\}} \frac{|\mathbb{I}|!(I - |\mathbb{I}| - 1)!}{I!} v^I(i) = v^I(i)$$

Then the indicator weight w_i^I based on Shapley value is simply

$$w_i^I = \frac{\Phi_i^I}{\sum_{j=1}^{I} \Phi_j^I} = \frac{v^I(i)}{\sum_{j=1}^{I} v^I(j)}$$

To operationalise this framework, we pursue the following "bottom-up" approach to calculate ACI's competitiveness index based on Shapley weights. First, we start from the lowest level of analysis (indicators) and identify the inequality of the units being measured (economies and sub-national economies). This is called the "Shapley Value", which is computed from the standardised score of each indicator. Subsequently, the Shapley Value is used to calculate Shapley Weight, where more weights are assigned to those indicators with higher Shapley Values. Next, the weights of Sub-environments are computed in "bottom-up" manner according to both **standardised scores** and **Shapley Weights** of indicators under the respective sub-environments. Finally, the weights of Environments and Overall Index are computed in a similar way.

Asia Competitiveness Institute - World Scientific Series

(Continued from page vi)

2016 Growth Slowdown Analysis by Income Thresholds and Annual Update of Competitiveness Analysis for 34 Greater China Economies
by Tan Khee Giap, Wang Peng & Xie Teleixi (Lee Kuan Yew School of Public Policy, NUS, Singapore)

Inaugural 2016 Ease of Doing Business Index on Attractiveness to Investors, Business Friendliness and Competitive Policies (EDB Index ABC) for 21 Sub-National Economies of India
by Tan Khee Giap, Sasidaran Gopalan, Jigyasa Sharma & Tan Kong Yam (Lee Kuan Yew School of Public Policy, NUS, Singapore)

2016 Annual Competitiveness and Growth Slowdown Analysis for Sub-National Economies of India
by Tan Khee Giap, Sasidaran Gopalan, Anuja Tandon & Tan Kong Yam (Lee Kuan Yew School of Public Policy, NUS, Singapore)

2016 Growth Slowdown Analysis, Ease of Doing Business Index, and Annual Competitiveness Studies of Indonesia's Sub-National Economies
by Tan Khee Giap, Mulya Amri, Nursyahida Ahmad & Tan Kong Yam (Lee Kuan Yew School of Public Policy, NUS, Singapore)

2016 Annual Competitiveness Analysis and Development Strategies for Indonesian Provinces
by Tan Khee Giap, Mulya Amri & Nursyahida Ahmad (Lee Kuan Yew School of Public Policy, NUS, Singapore)

2015

2015 Annual Competitiveness Analysis, Agricultural Productivity and Development Vision for ASEAN-10
by Tan Khee Giap, Nguyen Le Phuong Anh, Sasidaran Gopalan & Luu Nguyen Trieu Duong (Lee Kuan Yew School of Public Policy, NUS, Singapore)

2015 Estimation of Agricultural Productivity and Annual Update of Competitiveness Analysis for Greater China: Optimising Agricultural Productivity and Promoting Innovation Driven Growth
by Tan Khee Giap, Yuan Randong & Xie Teleixi (Lee Kuan Yew School of Public Policy, NUS, Singapore)

2015 Agricultural Total Factor Productivity and Competitiveness Analysis for States and Federal Territories and Five Regions of India: Annual Competitiveness Update and Evidence on the Agricultural Development Models for Selected Indian States
by Tan Khee Giap, Sasidaran Gopalan & Anuja Tandon (Lee Kuan Yew School of Public Policy, NUS, Singapore)

2015 Agricultural Productivity, Decentralisation, and Competitiveness Analysis for Provinces and Regions of Indonesia
by Tan Khee Giap, Nurina Merdikawati, Mulya Amri & Tan Kong Yam (Lee Kuan Yew School of Public Policy, NUS, Singapore)

2015 Annual Competitiveness Analysis and Development Strategies for Indonesian Provinces
by Tan Khee Giap, Mulya Amri, Nurina Merdikawati & Nursyahida Ahmad (Lee Kuan Yew School of Public Policy, NUS, Singapore)

2014

2014 Annual Competitiveness Ranking and Simulation Study for ASEAN-10 and Development Strategies to Enhance Asia Economic Connectivity
by Tan Khee Giap, Sangiita Yoong Wei Cher, Sasidaran Gopalan & Nguyen Le Phuong Anh (Lee Kuan Yew School of Public Policy, NUS, Singapore)

2014 Annual Provincial and Regional Competitiveness Analysis for Greater China Economies: Development Strategies under the New Normal
by Tan Khee Giap, Yuan Randong & Sangiita Yoong Wei Cher (Lee Kuan Yew School of Public Policy, NUS, Singapore)

2014 Regional Competitiveness Analysis and a Master Plan on Regional Development Strategies for India: Annual Competitiveness Update and Evidence on Economic Development Model for Selected States of India
by Tan Khee Giap, Linda Low, Kartik Rao & Tan Kong Yam (Lee Kuan Yew School of Public Policy, NUS, Singapore)

2014 Provincial and Inaugural Regional Competitiveness Analysis: Safeguarding Indonesia's Growth Momentum
by Tan Khee Giap, Nurina Merdikawati, Mulya Amri & Tan Kong Yam (Lee Kuan Yew School of Public Policy, NUS, Singapore)

2014 Annual Competitiveness Analysis and Development Strategies for Indonesian Provinces
by Tan Khee Giap, Nurina Merdikawati, Mulya Amri & Blake Harley Berger (Lee Kuan Yew School of Public Policy, NUS, Singapore)

2013

Annual Analysis of Competitiveness, Simulation Studies and Development Perspective for 34 Greater China Economies: 2000–2010
by Tan Khee Giap, Yuan Randong, Sangiita Yoong Wei Cher & Yang Mu (Lee Kuan Yew School of Public Policy, NUS, Singapore)

Annual Analysis of Competitiveness, Simulation Studies and Development Perspective for 35 States and Federal Territories of India: 2000–2010
by Tan Khee Giap, Linda Low, Tan Kong Yam & Kartik Rao (Lee Kuan Yew School of Public Policy, NUS, Singapore)

Competitiveness Analysis and Development Strategies for 33 Indonesian Provinces
by Tan Khee Giap, Mulya Amri, Linda Low & Tan Kong Yam (Lee Kuan Yew School of Public Policy, NUS, Singapore)

www.ingramcontent.com/pod-product-compliance
Lightning Source LLC
LaVergne TN
LVHW071412210926
848486LV00004B/251

* 9 7 8 9 8 1 3 2 7 3 0 2 3 *